THE NATURE FAKERS

Ah, Love! could you and I with Fate conspire
To grasp this sorry Scheme of Things entire,
    Would not we shatter it to bits—and then
Re-mould it nearer to the Heart's Desire!

Rubáiyát of Omar Khayyám

The Nature Fakers

WILDLIFE, SCIENCE & SENTIMENT

Ralph H. Lutts

FULCRUM PUBLISHING

Book Design by Richard Firmage

Art credits: for jacket, pages 37, 69, 139, 177, 205, 209 and colophon, from
William J. Long, *A Little Brother to the Bear*, Ginn and Company, Boston,
1903; for pages vii, ix and 1, from William J. Long, *School of the Woods*,
Ginn and Company, Boston, 1902; for pages 101, 189 and 209, from
William J. Long, *Northern Trails*, Ginn and Company, 1905; for page iii,
from Gordon Ross, *New York Times Magazine*, 2 June 1907.

Library of Congress Cataloging-in-Publication Data

Lutts, Ralph H.
    Nature fakers : wildlife, science & sentiment / Ralph H. Lutts.
        p.   cm.
    Includes bibliographical references.
    ISBN 1-55591-054-8
    1. Natural history literature--United States--Public opinion-
-History--20th century. 2. Public opinion--United States-
-History--20th century. 3. Nature in literature. 4. American
literature--20th century--History and criticism. 5. Nature--Social
aspects--United States--History--20th century. 6. Roosevelt,
Theodore, 1858–1919--Views on nature. I. Title.
QH104.L88   1990
508.73--dc20   89-29521
                                                                   CIP

Printed in the United States of America

10   9   8   7   6   5   4   3   2   1

Fulcrum Publishing
350 Indiana Street, #510
Golden, Colorado 80401

For Brad—

With the hope that you will grow to love all the earth's creatures and the wonderful, tangled web of life of which they and we are a part.

CONTENTS

PREFACE

More than a century ago, Bradford Torrey found a snake up in a linden tree with a young bird in its jaws. Torrey was a nature writer who loved birds, and, understandably, he wanted to save the poor creature. He shook the serpent out of the tree and tried to crush it with his foot. It escaped, though, leaving behind a dead bundle of feathers. Later, as he thought about the incident, Torrey realized that it had another side. "Who shall say what were the emotions of the snake, as he wriggled painfully homeward after such an assault?" he wrote. "Myself no vegetarian, by what right had I belabored him for liking the taste of chicken?" This new perspective on the little tragedy seemed to make him uncomfortable. "It were well, perhaps, not to pry too curiously into questions of this kind," he continued. "Most likely it would not flatter our human self-esteem to know what some of our 'poor relations' think of us."

Torrey was not the only person asking such questions. A growing number of late nineteenth-century nature lovers were empathizing with their "poor relations," rethinking their ethical and ecological relationships with the natural world, and acting to protect wildlife. By the beginning of the century the public's appetite for nature was enormous. Nature study became a part of the school curriculum. Eager readers made some nature writers wealthy. City dwellers tramped off into the woods. Before long, social critics began to wring their hands over the "cult of nature." This was part of a public environmental awakening equaled only by the great reawakening late in the twentieth century.

Bradford Torrey, though, recognized a problem in the love of nature. Nature does not fit within our traditional notions of love and morality. It certainly does not fit within the cozy framework of Victorian sentimentalism. Should we not love and protect the snake, as well as the bird? How do we deal with a world in which success is measured by survival and the unfit are weeded out mercilessly? "The import of this apparent wastefulness and cruelty of Nature, her seeming indifference to the welfare of the individual," wrote Torrey, "is a question on which it is not pleasant, and, as I think, not profitable, to dwell."[1]

It is, though, a question that cannot be avoided. People had to deal with it in Torrey's time and we have to deal with it now. There is often a conflict between the scientific understanding of wildlife populations, which tends to view individuals as grain for the evolutionary mill, and the caring, empathetic approach to wildlife that is often directed toward individual animals. This frequent and often unfortunate conflict between science and sentiment underlies many present debates about hunting and wildlife management.

The nature fakers controversy was, on its surface, a humorous debate over whether or not foxes ride on the backs of sheep, woodcocks set their own broken legs and then wrap them in mud casts, and hawks take their young to school. In short, it was concerned with whether or not some of the most prominent nature writers of the time were really fraud naturalists. On a deeper level, though, the people mired in the controversy were arguing over the value of science and sentiment in our efforts to understand, appreciate, and protect wild animals. Although the nature fakers controversy took place at the beginning of the century, many of its themes have a familiar ring today.

This "War of the Naturalists," as the *New York Times* called it, was fought on the printed page. It was largely a literary debate argued in magazine articles and book prefaces. The weapons of this war were words, and its action lay in the excitement of competing ideas and points of view. I have tried to let the participants speak for themselves, because it is important to savor their words and gain a sense of their personalities.

The first chapter reviews the events of the nineteenth century that paved the way to the nature fakers controversy, emphasizing the growing popular love of nature. The next three chapters explore the controversy, from John Burroughs's first attack in 1903 to Theodore Roosevelt's killing blows in 1907. Chapter three, in particular, examines the sometimes astonishing claims of the "fakers." My emphasis is not so much on determining whether their stories were true or false, but on revealing how they arrived at and supported their conclusions. In the fifth chapter I try to tease out the issues that underlie the controversy. Chapter six follows the later lives of the key figures. Finally, the afterword explores current events that reflect similar issues.

William J. Long figures prominently in this book. Little is known about him, despite the fact that he was the principal object of attack. Biographies of Theodore Roosevelt, John Burroughs, Ernest Thompson Seton, and Charles G. D. Roberts, as well as many other key players in the controversy, are readily available, but this is not true of Long. Too little information is now available to permit a detailed biography of Long, nor would such be appropriate here. I do, though, explore Long's life in more detail than the lives of the others, and I hope this book will help to shed new light on the life of a man who, although often misguided and obstinate, should not be remembered as a fraud. Indeed, his views of animal behavior were sometimes more accurate than those of his critics.

ACKNOWLEDGMENTS

Although I have long been interested in environmental studies, my early emphasis was on the natural sciences. Many years ago, my friend Steve Maskel first showed me that literature can be analyzed to discover underlying values and attitudes toward nature. Professor David Smith of Hampshire College later demonstrated that literature can also can be used as a tool for the study of environmental history. My study of nature literature was stimulated by our collaborations in Smith's course, "American Landscapes." My study of the nature fakers grew out of an initial interest in John Burroughs that had been stimulated by another friend, Peter Westover. The research began in earnest after I was invited to present a paper at the Earthday X Colloquium, organized by Robert C. Schultz and J. Donald Hughes and conducted at the University of Denver in April 1980. The paper appeared in the proceedings of the colloquium, *Ecological Consciousness* (Washington, DC: University Press of America, 1981), which Schultz and Hughes edited.

I planned to write a book about the controversy, but the project languished for several years. Finally, Anne Blackburn of Fulcrum Publishing prodded me into motion. Patricia Frederick's editorial advice was invaluable, as were the design work of Betsy R. Armstrong, the assistance of Carmel Huestis, and the encouragement of the publisher, Robert C. Baron.

Many people helped me along the way. This is especially true concerning my research into the life of William J. Long, about whom there is relatively little biographical information. I especially want to thank Frances Long Woodbridge (St. Louis, Mo.), Long's "little daughter of the revolution," for sharing her memories and admiration of her father. My trip to St. Louis to interview her was partially funded by a travel grant from Hampshire College. Lawrence J. Sweet, Sr. (New Brunswick, Canada), Long's fishing guide in his later years, and Glenn W. Moon (Stamford, Conn.), co-author of one of Long's anonymous books, generously shared their memories of their friend. Dr. Booker Bush of Harvard Medical School provided diagnostic advice regarding Long's blindness. Dr. Mark A. Pokras and associates at the Tufts University School of Veterinary Medicine conducted a detailed examination of the "cast" on a sandpiper's leg, which shed light on an important incident in the controversy. Elizabeth Burroughs Kelley gave me a tour of Riverby and Slabside and copies of her grandfather's correspondence.

Caryl Simon-Katler, assistant director of the Blue Hills Trailside Museum, made it possible for me to write the first draft of this book by accepting the role of acting director while I was on a leave of absence. Sharon Young of the Orenda Wildlife Trust (Mass.) and Christopher Leahy, Massachusetts Audubon Society, provided advice and critical comments on selected chapters. I also profited from discussions of wildlife rehabilitation issues with Sharon Young, Dr. Mark A. Pokras, and Norman Smith of the Massachusetts Audubon Society. Sharon Young and Patty Finch, National Association for the Advancement of Humane Education, also shared their perspectives on present animal rights issues. Although their assistance was of great value to me, I fear they may not agree with some of my views expressed in chapter five.

Much of my research was done in libraries at the University of Massachusetts (Amherst), Mt. Holyoke College, and Hampshire College. I am indebted to their staffs for their valuable assistance and to Jonathan Stoke, my student assistant during part of the research. I also benefited from discussions with another student, Andrew Campbell. Mt. Holyoke's microfilm set of the Theodore Roosevelt Presidential Papers was of special value. As well, the extraordinary resources of Harvard University were quite valuable. The university's Houghton Library is the home of the outstanding Theodore Roosevelt Collection, as well as of historical correspondence from the files of Houghton Mifflin Company and the _Atlantic Monthly_. Wallace Finley Daily, curator of the Roosevelt Collection, and Rodney G. Dennis, curator of manuscripts, were very helpful. So, too, were the staff of the university's Widener Library and Ann Blum and Mary Keeler of the Museum of Comparative Zoology Library. Dr. Raymond A.

Paynter, Jr., gave me access to the museum's bird collection and catalogs. I was also assisted by Margaret E. Law, the university's registrar, and Sarah A. Polirer of the Harvard University Archives.

Ruth M. Blair of the Connecticut Historical Society and Robert Claus of the Connecticut State Library assisted in my search for information about William J. Long, as did a number of people in Stamford, Conn. These include Thomas Kemp and Robert J. Belletzkie of the Ferguson Library; Elizabeth Haggerty of Long's First Congregational Church; Mrs. Alfred W. Dater, Jr., of the Stamford Historical Society; as well as Josephine K. Deming and Henri McDowell. I also received important assistance from Elizabeth Tyrer, Nantucket Historical Association, Mass.; Natalie Patel, Saint John (New Brunswick) Regional Library; Ruth Quattlebaum, Phillips Academy Archives, Andover, Mass.; Diana Yount, Franklin Trask Library, Andover Newton Theological School, Newton Center, Mass.; Mrs. Philip S. Haring, Nantucket Historical Association; Helen Mahoney and Janet D. McCarthy of Ginn & Company, now Silver Burdett & Ginn; S. Mabell Bates, Clement C. Maxwell Library, Bridgewater State College, Bridgewater, Mass.; Harold F. Worthley, Congregational Library, Boston, Mass.; Pauline Baldwin and Irene Neuvelt, Harcourt Brace Jovanovich; Mildred Bobrovich and Sylvia Diaz, Library of the American Museum of Natural History; and Waitstill H. Sharp, Greenfield, Mass., who shared his memories of his father, Dallas Lore Sharp.

Thanks also to John A. Gable, executive director, Theodore Roosevelt Association, for permission to quote from Roosevelt's correspondence; David Wigdor, Manuscript Division, Library of Congress; Bernard F. Pasqualini, Free Library of Philadelphia; the staff of the Vatican Library and Daniel G. Lutts for translating their reply; Maureen Taylor, *Boston Globe*; Shirley Katzander, Reading Is Fundamental; Gretchen Lagana, University Libraries, University of Wisconsin–Madison; Stephen Zimmer and Bonnie Tooley of the Philmont Scout Ranch, Cimarron, N.M.; Dee Seton Barber, Santa Fe, N.M.; Richard H. G. Cunningham, Auburn, Mass.; Farida A. Wiley, John Burroughs Memorial Association, New York City; Lisa Browar, Beinecke Rare Book and Manuscript Library, Yale University; Charles Niles, Mugar Memorial Library, Boston University; Minneapolis Public Library; Thomas Crane Public Library, Quincy, Mass.; Francis E. Wylie, Hingham, Mass.; Paul Brooks, Lincoln Center, Mass.; Hans Nussbaum, American Association for the Advancement of Science, Washington, D.C.; Ned Pierce, Roman Romach, and William Kochanczyk, Museum of Science, Boston; and the many others who helped make this book possible.

1.
THE RISE OF THE NATURE LOVERS

At the sight of the mouse the president of the United States leaped out of his sleigh and bounded across the snow. A new species! Using his hat and his hand he scooped up the frightened creature and returned to show it off to his party, delighted with his catch. One can picture him shouting with joy and flashing his famous wide, toothy grin—and can also imagine the puzzled grins of his military escorts.

This discovery capped a morning's fruitless search for bear tracks in the spring snow surrounding the Yellowstone geysers. In the afternoon, while the rest of his party was fishing, Theodore Roosevelt, Jr., carefully measured the specimen, expertly skinned it, and prepared it for shipment to C. Hart Merriam, chief of the United States Biological Survey, back in Washington, D. C. Merriam later reported that, although it was the first time the animal had been collected in Yellowstone National Park, it did not, alas, prove to be a new species.[1]

This mouse was the only creature the president killed during two months of traveling through the West in the spring of 1903. His reputation as a big game hunter did not always endear him to a public that was growing increasingly fond of wildlife and the beauties of nature. A political cartoon that appeared before he left on the trip, for example, showed a note to Roosevelt from the western animals ("Delighted to read that you are coming west . . .") informing him that they were heading east. Sensitive to public opinion in this year before his re-election, Roosevelt made sure the press knew he was making the trip without a gun, although he regretted that he was unable to "keep the camp in meat." He traveled in the company of John Burroughs, the elderly naturalist and author known around the world as an apostle of nature and its wonders. Roosevelt genuinely admired Burroughs, but also knew it was good politics to be associated with the venerable naturalist, who seemed more impressed by the buttercups he found blooming near the geysers than by the president's search for bear. As one magazine editor wrote, "There is perhaps no nature lover in this land of ours who did not envy the President of the United States his good luck in the prospect of a few weeks' companionship with rare old John Burroughs."[2]

They seemed a strange pair. One was an outgoing and extraordinarily vigorous forty-four-year-old man from a wealthy family, a former New York Assemblyman, U.S. Civil Service Commissioner, New York City Police Commissioner, assistant secretary of the navy, war hero, governor of New York, and now president of the United States. The other was a quiet and somewhat retiring sixty-six-year-old essayist, natural historian, farmer, and advocate of the simple life. Nevertheless, they shared mutual admiration and a love of nature. Ten years earlier, in his book *The Wilderness Hunter*, Theodore Roosevelt had written, "Foremost of all American writers on outdoor life is John Burroughs; and I can scarcely suppose that any man who cares for existence outside the cities would willingly be without anything that he has ever written. . . . his pages so thrill with the sights and sounds of outdoor life that nothing by any writer who is a mere professional scientist or a mere professional hunter can take their place, or do more than supplement them." Roosevelt went on with even greater praise: "As a woodland writer, Thoreau comes second only to Burroughs." For his part, Burroughs would later write:

> Why, I cannot now recall that I have ever met a man with a keener and more comprehensive interest in the wild life about us—an interest that is at once scientific and thoroughly human. . . . When I accompanied him on his trip to the Yellowstone Park in April, 1903, I got a fresh impression of the extent of his natural history knowledge and of his trained powers of observation. Nothing escaped him, from bears to mice, from wild geese to chickadees, from elk to red squirrels; he took it all in, and he took it in as only an alert, vigorous mind can take it in. On that occasion I was able to help him identify only one new bird. . . . All the other birds he recognized as quickly as I did.[3]

Roosevelt and Burroughs were brought together amidst the geysers of Yellowstone by the first salvo (blasted in ink from the old man's pen) of a controversy that was to shake the limbs of the nation's nature lovers. In February, Burroughs had attacked several prominent nature writers, accusing them of writing fraudulent nature stories—overdramatized and inaccurate stories designed solely to extract money from gullible readers. An editorial in the *New York Times* found some humor in the event:

> the lovers of Nature are in the thick of as pretty a quarrel as ever raged around a ballroom belle on the lower east side. Not the first, perhaps, but the most conspicuous entry into the lists was made by the venerable John Burroughs, who is the dean of Nature lovers in this country and was at one time apparently the high priest of the cult. In a recent article in *The Atlantic Monthly* he took— seized we might say—the opportunity to criticize with great plainness and some acerbity the qualifications of Mr. Seton-Thompson and the Rev. William J. Long to officiate in the temple of Nature and to bring to her altars the tributes of truthful and accurate praise.[4]

Burroughs's criticism sparked national attention as nature writers and their readers rallied to join the attack or to defend the authors whose stories they enjoyed. The president wrote to tell Burroughs that he had read the essay and approved and to invite the naturalist on the trip to Yellowstone. Little did Roosevelt know that the debate over the "sham naturalists" would continue for nearly five more years or that he would become a central figure in the controversy.

The nature fakers controversy that Burroughs began in 1903 and Roosevelt ended in 1907 revealed a good deal about public attitudes toward nature at that time. A conflict between science and sentiment as methods of understanding and appreciating the lives of the creatures of field, forest, and our own backyard, it set a new standard of accuracy for the responsible nature writer and nature lover. To better understand the controversy, we must explore the landscape of public attitudes toward nature in the United States at the turn of the century and the events that shaped it.

The United States of 1903 was in the midst of a major environmental awakening on a scale, perhaps, equaled only by the reawakening marked by Earth Day 1970. The public was alive with interest in wildlife and nature and seemed as thrilled to see John Burroughs as the president on their western holiday journey. Schoolchildren met the president's westward train in St. Paul with the banner, "The John Burroughs Society." Pushing their way through the crowd and tossing flowers into the lap of the white-haired naturalist, they were part of an extraordinary social phenomenon.[5] Nature study was taught in public schools around the nation; nature books were immensely popular (and lucrative in some cases); national efforts were under way to protect threatened species and natural resources; and thousands of people were eagerly camping, hiking, butterfly collecting, bird watching, and pursuing a host of other outdoor activities. A growing number of businesses, as well as civic and governmental organizations, were happily supporting and being supported by these endeavors. Burroughs and Roosevelt had, each in his own way, helped to birth and nurture this new social phenomenon—an environmental movement that was the culmination of more than a half-century of American history.

John of the Birds

Born in 1837, John Burroughs grew up a farm boy in the hills of New York's Catskills. Shortly before turning seventeen he left the farm to support himself as a schoolteacher, fitfully pursue his own education, and try to puzzle out his future. He would not realize until years later the enduring influence of his youthful experiences in the fields, woods, and rolling terrain of the Catskills. He married at twenty-one (a lasting but troubled alliance). He had a difficult time making an adequate income to support himself and his wife, Ursula; nevertheless, he found time to write. At the time, he was so influenced by Emerson that one of Burroughs's unsigned essays was mistakenly attributed to the great Transcendentalist. He also began to study natural history, first wildflowers and then, after stumbling upon John James Audubon's bird illustrations in the West Point Library, birds. Birds were his special love, and over the years the two became inextricably linked in the public's image of Burroughs as "John o' Birds."[6]

In 1863, motivated by the pressures of economic necessity and a dissatisfied wife, the excitement of the Civil War, and his admiration for Walt Whitman, Burroughs sought employment in Washington, D.C. He eventually took a job with the Currency Bureau of the U.S. Treasury Department. He disliked the work and the iron-vault wall facing his desk, but he worked nearly ten years for the Treasury and wrote some of his finest early nature essays in the shadow of that despised iron wall.

The fields and woods surrounding the capital provided some release from his unrewarding job and home life. Washington was a much smaller city then; open spaces and wildlife were not far away. "The National Capital is a great place for buzzards," he wrote, "and I make the remark in no double or allegorical sense either, for the buzzards I mean are black and harmless as doves, though perhaps hardly dovelike in their tastes." He especially appreciated the city's clear sky and dazzling autumn and winter light.

> It seemed as if I had never seen but a second-rate article of sunlight or moonlight until I had taken up my abode in the National Capital.... I sally out in the morning with the ostensible purpose

John Burroughs and Animal Friend. From John Burroughs, *Locust and Wild Honey*, Riverby Ed. (Boston: Houghton Mifflin, 1904).

5

of gathering chestnuts, or autumn leaves, or persimmons, or exploring some run or branch. It is, say, the last of October or the first of November. The air is not balmy, but tart and pungent, like the flavor of the red-cheeked apples by the roadside. In the sky not a cloud, not a speck; a vast dome of blue ether lightly suspended above the world.[7]

He also found solace in his friendship with Walt Whitman. They met frequently (sometimes daily) while Burroughs lived in Washington and remained friends until the poet's death. The young naturalist may have had difficulty in keeping up with the poet's lofty concepts, but he emerged with an expanded vision of what his own writing might accomplish in both ideas and technique. Burroughs, in turn, was Whitman's guide to natural history and suggested the thrush song for "When Lilacs Last in the Dooryard Bloomed."[8] Burroughs was a lifelong proponent of Walt Whitman and his work. He wrote, with a good deal of help from his subject, *Notes on Walt Whitman as Poet and Person*. Released in 1867, it was both Burroughs's first book and the first book ever published about the poet.

His next book was a collection of nature essays, *Wake Robin* (a title selected by Whitman), published in 1871. Praise came from both literary and scientific circles. One reviewer described it as "a book about the birds by one who knows and loves them—not a dry catalogue, but an exhibition of live birds on the wing, and in the nest; birds in love, and birds in song; birds at work, and birds at play." Another wrote, "Mr. Burroughs adds a strain of genuine poetry which makes his papers unusually delightful, while he has more humor than generally falls to the ornithological tribe. . . . It is in every way an uncommon book that he has given us; fresh, wholesome, sweet, and full of a gentle and thoughtful spirit." A few years later the prominent ornithologist Eliott Coues wrote to tell Burroughs that the book was faithful in its ornithology and so vivid in its descriptions that it gave him a new appreciation of the birds that had been the object of his lifelong study.[9]

His second nature book, *Winter Sunshine*, came in 1875. In a review, Henry James described Burroughs as "a sort of reduced, but also more humorous, more available, and more social Thoreau," and continued, "We heartily commend his little volume for its honesty, its individuality, and, in places, its really blooming freshness." *Birds and Poets with Other Papers* came out in 1877 and *Locusts and Wild Honey* in 1879. He followed these with a steady stream of essays and books, publishing more than two dozen volumes before his death in 1921.[10]

In 1873, after ten years in Washington, John Burroughs returned to his native New York, supporting himself as a National Bank examiner, farmer, and writer. For his wife he eventually built a fine house, Riverby. It stood on the edge of the Hudson River and sported all of the traditional comforts. Over the years he also established two rustic retreats for himself—Slabsides, located a short distance away, and, later, Woodchuck Lodge, in his home town of Roxbury, New York. Both were designed in the simpler style he preferred and provided an escape from the visitors, both famous and unknown, who increasingly made pilgrimages to his door.

By the turn of the century he had established a worldwide reputation and was one of the most renowned and respected figures in the United States. His advocacy of nature and the simple life and his grandfatherly image, fostered by his long white hair and beard, added to his appeal. In 1901, an admirer described Burroughs this way:

> That old Silver-Top out there in the celery has done more than any other living man to inaugurate the love of Out-of-Doors that is now manifesting itself as a Nature Renaissance. Within twenty years a silent revolution has been working out in favor of country life; and this new sympathy with our mute brothers, the animals, has come along as a natural result. A man down near Poughkeepsie said to me, "I believe John Burroughs has influenced everybody for twenty miles around here in favor of not killing birds and things."
>
> And I answered, "Sir, John Burroughs has influenced the entire civilized world against killing things."[11]

Burroughs was more comfortable with the familiar than the exotic. Whitman once said, "John goes . . . for usual, accepted, respectable things." Even the Yellowstone geysers failed to impress. "The novelty of the geyser region soon wears off," he wrote of his visit there with Roosevelt. "Steam and hot water are steam and hot water the world over, and the exhibition of them here did not differ, except in volume, from what one sees by his own fireside."[12]

Part of Burroughs's attraction for his readers was that his landscapes were accessible and familiar and that he helped them to better see and appreciate what was near at hand. He wrote of the fields and woods, the birds and wildlife of people's own farms and yards. This contact with the pastoral landscape was valued by an increasingly urbanized populace that was coming to regret its loss. Reading a Burroughs essay was much like going for a walk in a field, now and then stopping to observe and contemplate a wildflower or bird. Although his style may seem a bit old-fashioned to a late twentieth-century reader, it was fresh and lively in the nineteenth.

Burroughs was hardly the first American to write about nature—a subject with a long history in this country, from narratives of the discovery, exploration, and cataloging of a new continent to overtly literary reflections on the aesthetic and spiritual values of the human encounter with nature. With the growing influence of eighteenth-century Romanticism and nineteenth-century Transcendentalism, people began to find emotional and spiritual values in nature. Before this, nature was valued primarily as a resource and wilderness was seen as a frightening chaos ordained to be conquered for cultivation. As the nineteenth century progressed, the public's view of nature changed. For example, in the early decades of the century, the Leatherstocking tales of novelist James Fenimore Cooper, which extolled the beauties of the wilderness, found a very appreciative readership. Cooper's daughter, Susan Fenimore Cooper, was one of the first American literary naturalists. Her *Rural Hours*, probably the most popular pre–Civil War nature book, appeared in 1850 and saw six printings in the four years before Thoreau's *Walden* was published.[13]

One of the first "modern" nature writers, Henry David Thoreau, planted his beans, nailed his shack together, and set up housekeeping beside Walden Pond when Burroughs was a mere boy of eight years doing chores on his father's farm. Thoreau's great contributions, however, received only limited popular acclaim in his lifetime. Before he died in 1862, no more than two thousand copies of *Walden* had been sold. The new appreciation of nature began as a luxury largely of the urban, financially secure, and well educated, but wider public appreciation would come as the nineteenth century progressed.[14]

Burroughs had the advantage of contributing to and riding the same wave of popular interest that led to the "rediscovery" of Thoreau later in the century. Burroughs's literary abilities, knowledge of natural history, prolific pen, and longevity created a special place for him in the profession of literary natural history. He was both predecessor and contemporary of the others who were writing about nature at the time he explored Yellowstone with President Theodore Roosevelt; most had, like the president, grown up with Burroughs's books and were following in his footsteps. He helped to establish nature study as a popular pursuit, set many of the standards for nature writing, and gave the natural history essay its definitive form.[15]

The task of the literary naturalist was twofold in Burroughs's view: to report both the objective facts of nature and also one's subjective feelings. Burroughs felt neither half of the combination was complete in itself: The first might make good science but produced poor literature, while the latter might make good poetry but produced a fancy that had little to do with the bird, flower, or landscape as it existed apart from the poet's sentiment. Instead, the literary naturalist must combine both the facts and the human significance of nature. He used the honeybee as a metaphor to make his point. Nectar does not become honey until it has passed through the chemistry of the bee's body. Similarly, observations of nature must be processed within the writer's mind. The final product, though, still is true to the raw materials. In 1895, Burroughs wrote:

> The literary naturalist does not take liberties with facts; facts are the flora upon which he lives. . . . To interpret Nature is not to improve upon her: it is to draw her out; it is to have an emotional intercourse with her, absorb her, and reproduce her tinged with the colors of the spirit. . . . if I relate the bird in some way to human life, to my own life,—show what it is to me and what it is in the landscape and the season,—then do I give my reader a live bird and not a labeled specimen.[16]

The requirement that the writer combine and be faithful to both the scientist's and the poet's visions of nature provided an important part of the creative challenge for a literary naturalist. The inherent tension in this dichotomy is what lay at the heart of the controversy faced by Burroughs and Roosevelt in 1903.

The Naturalist President

Theodore Roosevelt's own outdoors writing was faithful to Burroughs's definition. He was a superb naturalist, acknowledged as one of the world's authorities on the large mammals (which is to say, big game animals) of North America. His hunting books were remarkable examples of both fine writing and careful natural history. They established a new standard for the genre, and some of his extended descriptions of the natural history and behavior of specific species outclassed any previous attempts.[17] He had an extraordinary ability to express almost simultaneously his admiration of an animal's beauty, the details of its natural history, his efforts to turn that animal into a trophy, and his outrage at the depredations of greedy and unsporting "game hogs" who were destroying wildlife.

Theodore Roosevelt was born in 1858 into a wealthy New York City family of merchants and businessmen. A sickly and asthmatic child, at the age of twelve he began to build up his body with the bulldog discipline that would characterize him throughout his life. From early childhood he had a deep interest in natural history, a subject he studied with enormous seriousness and enthusiasm. He began hunting to provide himself with specimens for his taxidermy work. His interests broadened to sport hunting, and over his lifetime he managed to kill an extraordinary number of animals. Roosevelt entered Harvard College in 1876 determined to become a research naturalist. Only later, while courting his future wife, did Roosevelt change his plans and turn to a career in politics, but he never gave up his study of natural history. A man of enormous vigor and wide-ranging interests, he was able to work on a professional level as a historian (writing books on the War of 1812 and the history of the American West) and as a scientist while pursuing his principal career in politics. He read the scientific literature and published scientific papers of his own, maintained contacts with some of the prominent scientists of his day, was a keen observer of nature, and participated in lively technical discussions with professionals.[18]

In 1884, after suffering a political defeat and the overwhelming tragedy of both his mother and his wife dying on the same day, Theodore Roosevelt left New York and traveled to the Dakota Badlands to become a cattle rancher on the Little Missouri River. Along with the writing of Owen Wister and the art of Frederic Remington, Roosevelt's widely read accounts of ranch life played an important role in creating the mythic image of the American cowboy.[19] His books were rooted in the western landscapes and wildlife at his doorstep, which formed the bedrock of invigorating days spent both at hard work close to nature and on wilderness trips, hunting game to feed his ranchmen and for sport. In _The Wilderness Hunter_, for example, he wrote:

> The nights in summer are cool and pleasant, and there are plenty of bear-skins and buffalo robes, trophies of our own skill, with which to bid defiance to the bitter cold of winter. The summer time we are not much within doors, for we rise before dawn and work hard enough to be willing to go to bed soon after nightfall. . . . In the still fall nights, if we lie awake we can listen to the clanging cries of the water-fowl, as their flocks speed southward; and in cold weather the coyotes occasionally come near enough for us to hear their uncanny wailing. The larger wolves, too, now and then join in, with a kind of deep, dismal howling; but this melancholy sound is more often heard when out camping than from the ranch house.[20]

Roosevelt knew coyotes better than most, well enough to believe that there was only a single coyote species. Other students of the coyote

Theodore Roosevelt "On the Trail" in his Western Garb. From Theodore Roosevelt, *Hunting the Grizzly and Other Sketches*, Homeward Bound Ed. (New York: Review of Reviews, 1910).

believed there were several distinct species. The issue was not one of finding all the species, but one of how to go about placing names to the wealth of specimens preserved in museum collections. Should they be divided into many separate species or lumped together within just a few? In 1897, long after he had returned to political life, Roosevelt debated coyote taxonomy with C. Hart Merriam, the eminent mammalogist and chief of the U.S. Biological Survey. Merriam, a "splitter," had named eleven species. Roosevelt, a "lumper," believed there was only one. He and Merriam exchanged views via articles published in the journal _Science_. In May, a month after Roosevelt became assistant secretary of the navy, he and Merriam argued their positions at a meeting of the Biological Society of Washington, held at the Cosmos Club. Roosevelt's view has prevailed.[21]

Although an enthusiastic hunter, Roosevelt was appalled by the slaughter of wildlife by "game butchers." He proposed establishing rigid game laws to protect wildlife and national forest reserves to provide breeding grounds for game.[22] His personal hunting ethic, although distressing to many present-day readers, was advanced for his time:

> I never sought to make large bags, for a hunter should not be a game butcher. It is always lawful to kill dangerous or noxious animals, like the bear, cougar, and wolf; but other game should only be shot when there is need of the meat, or for the sake of an unusually fine trophy. Killing a reasonable number of bulls, bucks, or rams does no harm whatever to the species; to slay half the males of any kind of game would not stop the natural increase, and they yield the best sport, and are the legitimate objects of the chase. Cows, does, and ewes, on the contrary, should only be killed (unless barren) in case of necessity; during my last five years' hunting I have killed but five—one by a mischance, and the other four for the table.[23]

In 1888 Roosevelt helped to found the Boone and Crockett Club, an elite organization of hunters dedicated to the protection of wildlife, especially large game animals. The first of its kind, the club was established by Roosevelt, George Bird Grinnell (editor of _Forest and Stream_ magazine), and a select group of prominent citizens who were deeply concerned about the rapid disappearance of large game animals. With Roosevelt as its first president, the club worked to protect and enlarge Yellowstone National Park, support passage of the Forest Reserve Act in 1891, establish zoos in Washington and New York, and protect many valuable and threatened natural areas.[24]

Roosevelt maintained a broad interest in natural history throughout his career as a politician. He wrote and spoke, both publicly and privately, in support of nature writers, scientists, outdoor life, and a variety of conservation issues. He continued hunting throughout his presidency, providing easy copy for an eager press. Just five months before his Yellowstone trip with John Burroughs, Roosevelt had refused to shoot a tethered bear during a hunt in Louisiana. Newspapers picked up the story, and a short time later an enterprising toy store commemorated the event by inventing a doll named after the president: the Teddy Bear. The soft and cuddly toy swept the nation, giving countless children a kindly impression of bears.[25]

Americans Outdoors

More than good hunting was at stake as the nineteenth century came to a close. The frontier was gone, the wilderness was being converted to commercial grazing and agriculture, and the new railroads were promoting western tourism as a means to increase business. A profound change was happening in the public's attitudes toward wilderness. Where the very sight of wilderness would have distressed the cultured person of the seventeenth century, in the nineteenth century there was a growing public

On the Way to the Yosemite Valley. From a sketch by Paul Frenzeny. *Harper's Weekly*, 30 Nov. 1878.

interest in protecting wild lands and their beauty. Yosemite had first been designated "for public use, resort and recreation" by Congress in 1869, and the first national park, Yellowstone, was established in 1872. By the turn of the century, wilderness protection had mushroomed into a movement.

After their 1903 stay in Yellowstone, Burroughs turned homeward and Roosevelt continued on to California to visit in Yosemite with one of the founders of the wilderness preservation movement, John Muir. Muir was an original, a nature mystic who delighted in the wilderness and was able, through the extraordinary power of his personality and gift of language, to make others share in that delight. "When I was a boy . . . ," he wrote, "I was fond of everything that was wild, and all my life I've been growing fonder and fonder of wild places and wild creatures."

During the Civil War, Muir went to Canada to escape the draft and began supporting himself as a mechanic (he was a self-taught mechanical genius) while studying botany in the surrounding countryside. He continued working as a mechanic after returning to the United States, but after temporarily losing his sight in an accident he realized that he should devote his life to what was most precious. Thus began a lifetime of mountain exploration and studies in botany and glacial geology. Now, years later, he was the apostle of the American wilderness and at the center of a new movement to preserve it. Muir wanted to preserve wilderness not for its timber resources or game but for its very wildness, beauty, and spiritual significance.[26]

California's Yosemite Valley and the Sierras became his special loves, and he their voice and protector. Muir had the time and resources to devote himself to the new politics of wilderness. He had married in 1880 and spent the next several years making his fortune as a fruit farmer. In 1892, he became the first president of the newly founded Sierra Club. (It was modeled after the Appalachian Mountain Club of the East, founded in 1876.) The club gave Muir and his friends a vehicle to continue his campaign to protect Yosemite National Park, which had been created in 1890. He gained broad public support as he spread his vision of wilderness and the importance of wilderness preservation through articles in national magazines and books about his experiences in mountains, forests, and glaciers.

Roosevelt told Muir that he wanted "to drop politics absolutely for four days and just be out in the open" with Muir in the wilds of Yosemite. To the consternation of local politicians and the presidential escort, he did just that. Much of their time together they traveled alone (not counting the cook and two packers) on horseback and slept under the stars and, one night, under four inches of snow. Roosevelt was not able to entirely escape politics, however, because Muir used the opportunity to argue his cause, and he did it skillfully. The day after they parted, the president gave an order to enlarge the Sierra reserve.[27]

Although Yosemite was relatively close to San Francisco, most wilderness reserves were beyond the reach of the vast majority of the nation's people. Many simply could not afford the trip, especially before the Civil War. Nevertheless, natural areas were important tourist destinations early in the nineteenth century. Europe could boast cities and monuments that symbolized its long history and succession of civilizations. America's history and grandeur, on the other hand, lay in its vast wilderness, monumental natural features, and prodigious untapped natural resources. A tour up the Hudson River or a visit to Niagara Falls was something of a pilgrimage to landscapes symbolic of the nation's destiny. The importance of the pilgrimage was underscored by the fact that it could be made only by a select few—those who had the wealth necessary to afford the trip.[28]

When transportation costs dropped after the Civil War, tourism became more accessible to the middle class. However, even people who could not afford to travel across country found opportunities to enjoy nature closer to home. Local parks and long stretches of countryside abounded in the nineteenth century, as did numerous forms of outdoor recreation. Ocean bathing was acceptable even early in the century, and city dwellers found escape in visits to neighboring beaches, forests, and lakes. They traveled by foot, bicycle, carriage, train, and, later, trolley. The bicycle, in particular, was a liberating device. As safe and efficient bicycle designs became available late in the century, the machine provided travelers, especially women, a new independence and opportunity to explore the countryside. The increasing popularity of photography and moderately priced cameras (including a "bicycle Kodak" designed to mount on the handlebars) allowed people to preserve memories of their own excursions and to vicariously enjoy other landscapes, captured on film, that they might never see in person.[29]

There were also many possibilities for vacations at woodland or mountain resorts. Investors took advantage of the opportunity to sell unusual outdoor experiences. As one example, in 1856 a New Hampshire corporation, the Carriage Road Company, began constructing a toll road for tourists to the summit of New England's highest and most dangerous peak, Mount Washington. The road, completed in 1861, became a popular tourist attraction. The next year an adventurous Mr. Thorn drove a sleigh up the mountain. "A winter visit to the top of Mt. Washington would hardly come within the purposes or desires of the pleasure tourist," reported an 1873 guide book. "Yet at present it can be safely and even agreeably made in the early part of the season. A sleighing party to the Summit is by no means without its pleasures, to those adventurous enough to engage in it." Such adventures, though, were for people of means. With mountain hotel rooms priced at $4.50 a day, people with a modest income stayed closer to home or, if they were adventurous, went hiking or camping.[30]

There were also more opportunities to enjoy nature and outdoor recreation in cities, first in scenic cemeteries and later in landscaped parks. The arguments in favor of city parks were built on much more than aesthetic and romantic fancy, especially as the century progressed. People began to realize that the ability to enjoy the outdoors—whether in an urban park, in the countryside, or in the mountains, with open space, clean air and water, vegetation and wildlife, and opportunities for healthy exercise and recreation—was also a matter of good physical and mental health. Simple living and the outdoors were regarded as good therapy for increasing common problems of nervous tension. Others added that this was also important to one's moral and spiritual development. The conditions of urban overcrowding, poor sanitation, and polluted air were overwhelming, especially for the tenement poor. Parks, it was argued, provided relief from the filth and stress of the city and an opportunity to restore physical, mental, and spiritual health amidst open space and greenery. (A more worldly rationale, but perhaps no less important to their funding, was that parks also enhanced the value of adjoining property.) Efforts to establish New York's Central Park began in the 1850s; Frederick Law Olmsted completed its design in 1858. Other city parks and park systems followed. In addition to lush vegetation, winding paths, and picturesque ponds, park plans often included opportunities for physical exercise and recreation. Gymnastic exercise became popular, and around 1890 the nation's first free, public, outdoor gymnasiums, including the nation's first sandboxes, were provided by the Boston park system. There was also a growing movement to establish public swimming pools and baths as a means of improving the health and hygiene of the urban poor.[31]

Organized camping provided a way to get children into a more healthful environment. In 1871, Frederick William Gunn founded what is generally recognized as the first organized camp to provide summer activities for students at his private school. The Fresh Air Camps for urban poor children had their beginning two years later and in 1887 began receiving financial support through public contributions to funds established by newspapers and magazines. Initially taking slum children on outdoor excursions and arranging stays in country homes, Fresh Air groups served 545,273 children in 1895. In 1874 the Young Women's Christian Association established a "'vacation retreat' for industrial working girls," becoming the first national organization to support camping.

Most camps of the period, though, were for boys. A physician in Pennsylvania organized a camp for "weakly" boys in 1876, and Camp Chocorua was established in 1881 on an island in Lake Asquam, New Hampshire, as an alternative to, its founder wrote, "[t]he miserable conditions of boys belonging to well-to-do families in summer hotels." The Young Men's Christian Association's first camp, now known as Camp Dudley, began in 1884. Whether for rich or poor, boys or girls, the camps emphasized recreation and proper moral and physical development in an outdoor environment. By the turn of the century, more than twenty other private summer camps had been established, most of them located in the Northeast. Although it got off to a slow start, the camping movement grew rapidly in the twentieth century; more than twenty more camps were founded in the four years before the end of 1903.[32]

Women also showed an increased interest in camping, be it organized summer camps or summering in the wilds with friends. At least five girls' camps were founded in the years 1900 through 1903; nineteen more were organized by the end of the decade. "The establishment of summer camps for girls seems to have settled conclusively that girls are quite able to look out for themselves in the most unconventional way of living, and that they can manage to have just as 'good a time' in camp life as do the boys and young men," proclaimed a writer for a Boston newspaper. He continued in words that rang with the spirit of the growing women's suffrage movement:

> The happy day has come at last in the "emancipation" of femi-
> ninity, when athletic young American womanhood stands on a
> plane of equal freedom with young American manhood; when
> girls can own jack-knives and hatchets, drive nails and whittle
> with entire respectability; when they can even catch their own
> fish and "clean 'em, too," and roast them over camp fires built by
> their own well trained hands; when they can tramp into the deeps
> of wildwood quite unprotected by brothers or fathers or any other
> species of man; when they can "rough it" for weeks at a time, living
> close to the heart of nature, and not even run the risk of being
> dubbed "tom-boys."[33]

Other women who ventured into the nineteenth-century wilds did so from the comfort of resort hotels. This was most likely the case with Miss Diana, a New York society lady featured on the cover of an 1883 *Harper's*

Weekly, rifle in hand, staring across a lake at the buck she had just shot. The article spoke respectfully of her hunting skill and sporting unwillingness to shoot the animal while it was in the water, unlike "the cowardly deer butchers from the city who frequent the Adirondacks." It also told of a "Michigan school-teacher" who exclaimed after a successful shot, "There! I've killed a deer. Now if I can only shoot a bear I shall be ready to die and go to heaven."[34] By the turn of the century, though, more and more women were turning their backs on the resorts in favor of a tent in the wilderness.

Miss Diana in the Adirondacks—A Shot Across the Lake. By W. A. Rogers. From *Harper's Weekly*, 25 Aug. 1883.

Such women found plenty of advice.

A Woman Tenderfoot (1900), feminist Grace Gallatin Seton-Thompson's account of her travels in the Rocky Mountains with her husband, Ernest, was full of tips for fellow tenderfoots. "There is no reason why a woman should make a freak of herself even if she is going to rough it," she wrote. "As a matter of fact I do not rough it, I go for enjoyment and leave out all possible discomforts," and went on to tell women how she brought all the comforts along with her. Another author, in an article peppered with the advice of a practical outdoorswoman, cautioned against allowing cooking duties to be assigned to "one of the feminine members of the party." "Don't attempt to do the cooking yourself," she warned. "You'll regret it if you do." She advised women to bring a cook with them or be sure that one of their guides cooked.[35]

Ever alert for an opportunity to turn a profit, the clothing industry was quick to meet the real and imagined needs of the female camper. One fashion writer made a skilled play upon the ambivalence between women's aspirations for emancipation in the outdoors and their traditional role expectations by describing the new woman who

> paddles like an Indian through the chain of lakes. She sends a bullet into the heart of a deer without a touch of "buck fever." She can construct a lean-to, and build and light a smudge in front of it with the best of the men; and withal, she is still so charmingly feminine that the best men flock around her as devoted slaves. . . . Of course to be so masculine in action and yet so true to her womanly self in mind and appearance, this camping-out girl of the day needs clothes and plenty of them. Clothes which enable her to do what her brothers do, and yet continue to look like their dearest and sweetest of sisters.

But a more realistic outdoorswoman warned against the "enticing little silver adornments designed specially for the woman camper" and urged sensible, practical clothing, including knickers and matching short skirts, "which she puts on when convention demands. . . . For, after all is said and written, the true art of camping out is living simply and naturally with a mind and heart ready for the benediction of the woods."[36]

Protecting Nature

By the end of the nineteenth century, some people were beginning to realize that more than the fashion, tourism, and recreation industries depended on nature. Nature, in the form of rangeland, forests, minerals, soils, and water, was also the material foundation of agriculture, industry, and daily life. So long as there was a frontier, there seemed to be an endless supply of these natural resources, but now the nation had to face the growing realization that even nature had its limits and the United States was in danger of killing its golden goose. One of the earliest and most articulate of warnings was voiced in 1864 by George Perkins Marsh in his influential book *Man and Nature*. A scholar and diplomat, Marsh had seen the Old World and the enormous damage that older civilizations had done to their environments and, thus, to themselves. "Wherever [man] places his foot," he wrote, "the harmonies of nature are turned to discords." He warned that the New World was in danger of repeating this folly. He described the earth as our home and warned that we were bringing our house down upon ourselves. Marsh feared that restoring the existing damage around the world would require a new moral, economic, political, and technological foundation.[37]

There were, though, methods for preventing further destruction. European foresters, for example, had long known the importance of managing forests to insure a sustained yield by cutting no more trees than were replaced by new growth. This assured a continuous supply of wood for generation after generation by protecting both timber and forested watersheds. These techniques were little known or practiced in the United States of the nineteenth century, but the ideas spread as the years

The Setons Roughing it in the West. By S. N. Abbott. From Grace Gallatin Seton-Thompson, *A Woman Tenderfoot* (New York: Doubleday, Page, 1900).

passed. As early as 1871 the need to protect the Hudson River watershed was used as an argument for setting aside New York's Adirondack Mountains as a park. In the 1890s Gifford Pinchot, one of the first American foresters to undergo European training, became an outspoken advocate of scientific forest management. In 1899 he became chief forester, heading the U. S. Department of Agriculture's Division of Forestry. Pinchot was one of the president's closest advisors on natural resource matters during Roosevelt's administration. Roosevelt, who already understood the philosophy of conservation, became its staunch advocate. The term *conservation* as we now know it would not be coined until 1907, but its root idea, the scientific management of natural resources to insure a sustained economic yield, was gaining support.

The battle lines, though, were also already being drawn between the conservationists and the preservationists—those who wanted to protect "God's creation" for its own sake rather than as just another economic resource. Forest lovers John Muir and Harvard's Charles S. Sargent rejected Pinchot's scientific methods as inappropriate for wilderness forest reserves after serving on the National Forest Commission with him and touring western timberlands in 1896. The conflict between utilitarian and non-utilitarian views of nature would become a major theme within the environmental movement of the twentieth century. This was not simply economic conflict; it was also religious and philosophical. Nor was it limited to natural resource issues, but also included animal welfare.

A new view of the relationship between people and nature was emerging in Western culture, although this view was traditionally held by native peoples and many Far Eastern cultures. Some were beginning to argue that perhaps plants, animals, and the rest of the natural world did not exist solely to satisfy the needs and whims of humans; perhaps these lives were of value in and of themselves.[38]

Sympathy for animals was nurtured throughout the nineteenth century in part by the growing acceptance of theories of organic evolution and of our common bond with other creatures. In his journal of 1837 Charles Darwin wrote, "If we choose to let conjecture run wild, then animals, our fellow brethren in pain, disease, death, suffering and famine—our slaves in the most laborious works, our companions in our amusements—they may partake of our origin in one common ancestor—we may be all melted together." Before the end of the century this "wild conjecture" was shaping the beliefs and behavior of many people, although some might be shocked if they became aware of it. Sympathy for and empathetic sharing in animal suffering had become widespread. Albert Schweitzer would not coin the phrase "Reverence for Life" until 1915, but its foundation had already been laid.[39]

This view had its widest expression in efforts to prevent cruelty to animals. The idea that animals suffer pain and that humans should not contribute to this suffering became popular in the nineteenth century. Establishing a toehold first among the upper classes, this notion eventually became widespread. Societies for the prevention of cruelty to animals and anti-vivisection organizations grew in Victorian England and spread to the United States, working to both forge and enforce a new morality toward animals.

It is difficult to appreciate the extent of cruelty to animals before animal welfare laws and humane values became an accepted part of our culture. Dogs, cocks, and other animals were set to fighting each other for sport. Petty abuse, torture, and mutilation of dogs, cats, and other domestic animals were common among both children and adults. People lived much more closely with a greater variety of animals than is now the case for urban, suburban, and even most rural people. This was so even in cities, where cows and other "farm animals" were common—New York City boasted an estimated ten thousand hogs on its streets in 1842. In these days before the automobile, people relied on animals for hauling and transportation; even dogs were used to pull carts. Horses, used commercially to pull wagons and cabs, were often overworked mercilessly to wring every possible penny from their efforts.[40]

In 1890, the American Humane Education Society published an American edition of Anna Sewell's *Black Beauty*. Originally published in 1877, the book had already sold more than ninety thousand copies in England. Proclaiming it the *Uncle Tom's Cabin* of the horse, the society sold the book at the low price of twelve cents in hope that it would reach a wide audience, including schoolchildren and horse drivers. The book, the life story of the horse Black Beauty as told in his own voice, described in heart-rending detail the kindness and terrible cruelty that he and his animal friends experienced. It included an alphabetical index of these acts, from overdriving cab horses to docking tails to whipping. George T. Angell, founder of the society and a prominent figure in the animal welfare movement, used the first pages of the book to provide the reader with information essential to the humane treatment of animals. The nature of this information reveals a good deal about the status of animal welfare in 1890 and the need to establish even the most basic of humane treatment. The first pages of *Black Beauty* provided illustrated instructions for humanely killing horses (a pistol shot or blow "with a heavy axe or hammer"), dogs (pistol shot), and cats (potassium cyanide, force fed).[41]

The movement to promote the welfare of individual domestic animals helped establish a climate for wide public support of wildlife conservation. This was especially evident in the effort to protect wild birds. By the late nineteenth century, many species of birds had been driven to the edge of extinction by market hunting. Passenger pigeons, whose flocks once totaled millions of birds each, were becoming scarce. Waterfowl were hunted for sale by the barrel in urban markets. The fashion of using bird feathers in women's clothing, especially in hats, was decimating many of the world's most attractively plumed species. Professional hunters had devised imaginative and very efficient methods of slaughtering birds, including enormous nets and guns capable of mass destruction.[42]

In 1886 George Bird Grinnell, editor of *Forest and Stream* magazine and soon to be a founder of the Boone and Crockett Club, decided to use his magazine to help stem the tide of feathered fashions. He invited all interested parties to join his Audubon Society. Membership was free to anyone pledging not to kill birds, except for food; not to destroy eggs or nests; and not to wear feathered garments. He struck a responsive chord in thousands of people who cherished the beautiful, harmless, and "care free" creatures outside their windows. Wrote one Audubon supporter in her essay "Woman's Heartlessness":

> To-day I saw a mat woven of warblers' heads, spiked all over its surface with sharp beaks, set up on a bonnet and borne aloft by its possessor in pride! Twenty murders in one! and the face beneath bland and satisfied, for are not [in the words of the fashion news] "Birds to be worn more than ever?" . . . Year after year you come back to make your nest in the place you know and love, but you shall not live your humble, blissful, dutiful life, you shall not guard your treasured home, nor rejoice when your little ones break the silence with their first cry to you for food. You shall not shelter and protect and care for them with the same divine instinct you share with human mothers. No, some woman wants your corpse to carry on her head.[43]

Women may have been the enemy of birds, as ornithologist Frank Chapman maintained, because they wore decorative feathers, but women were also their salvation. Women were the strength and, often, the leaders of the Audubon societies. Most of those who taught and wrote about birds were also women.[44]

Within a year more than twenty thousand members had signed their pledges and received their membership certificates sporting portraits of the society's namesake, John James Audubon, and a pair of cedar waxwings. There were nearly fifty thousand members by the end of 1888. *Forest and Stream* could not handle the flood of work and the expense that came with such success, and the Audubon Society was discontinued in 1889. The idea was revived seven years later when a group of society women organized the Massachusetts Audubon Society, the first of the state Audubon societies, and selected the dean of American ornithology, William Brewster, as its president. By 1898 fifteen more states had Audubon societies, and the Audubon movement continued to grow. The societies worked to protect birds through public education and by collaborating with the American Ornithological Union on legislation. Most eventually affiliated and metamorphosed into the National Audubon Society, but several continued to maintain their independence, including the original Massachusetts group.[45]

The effort to save birds from destruction generated widespread public interest. "A great crusade against bird slaughter is sweeping over the country," wrote G. O. Shields, president of the League of American Sportsmen, editor of *Recreation,* and outspoken defender of wildlife. "Thousands of progressive educators have inaugurated courses of nature study in the schools, which include object lessons in bird life. Bird protective associations are being formed everywhere."[46]

One might wonder why George Bird Grinnell placed such emphasis in his Audubon pledge against the destruction of eggs and nests. At that time, many people collected bird eggs and nests. The author of a field guide to eggs wrote about the practice, expressing regret that "At some time during youth, the desire to collect something is paramount; it has very frequently culminated in the indiscriminate collecting of birds' eggs, merely to gratify a passing whim or to see how large a number could be gotten together, without regard to classification." He warned that this contributed to "the great decrease in numbers of certain birds." Another author of a guide to bird eggs and nests couched his warning in the language of the animal welfare movement. "Don't add a new terror to the many that already beset anxious little bird-mothers," he wrote, "by disturbing them during the breeding season or taking their eggs for a so-called 'collection.' "[47]

Still, in the late nineteenth century collections of this sort were so well accepted that the first issue of *Audubon Magazine* promoted, as a part of its list of "useful and entertaining books" sold by the publisher, a guide to egg and nest collecting and five taxidermy manuals. Not all bird lovers viewed collecting eggs and skins as an evil. For example, Florence Merriam Bailey (C. Hart Merriam's sister) argued that "Naturalist collectors are far from being the ruthless destroyers of life they are often supposed to be. It is, indeed, those who collect the birds, study them most deeply, and know them best, who are doing the most for their protection."[48] Many, perhaps most, of those infected with the urge to collect eggs and nests, however, were not serious naturalists.

Similar collecting fervor was directed at butterflies, moths, and other insects. "One of the commonest pursuits of boyhood is the formation of a collection of insects," proclaimed one butterfly guidebook. The same was true of plants, rocks, and a variety of other objects of nature. There was even a significant market for specimens by trade or sale, which became an important element, perhaps exaggerated, in Gene Stratton Porter's 1909 novel, *A Girl of the Limberlost*.[49] Even bird watching was often done with a shotgun. The poor quality of the field glasses and bird guidebooks of the day often required that the nature lover blast the bird out of the sky in order to identify it and, perhaps, to preserve it as a study skin or taxidermy mount. For countless children and adults such hobbies held the same attraction as stamp collecting: the thrill of the search, the beauty and variety of forms, the ease of preservation (if not storage), the ready accessibility, and the known rarities that lent excitement to the hunt. Collecting also had the advantage of being done outdoors, close to nature. These were also educational pastimes linked in one way or another to the new educational movement of nature study.

Nature Study

The study of nature in schools and as a hobby was not new. In their youth, both John Burroughs and Theodore Roosevelt had themselves been students of natural history and collectors of specimens. Although their interest was scientific, the most popular motivations at that time were theological and aesthetic. Natural theology, which attempted to fuse religion and science, proposed that by studying the intricate and complex details and design of nature one confirmed the existence and creative genius of the Maker. It was as if one was examining the marvelous mechanism of a watch and thus appreciating and wondering at the skill of the watchmaker. In 1691, the naturalist John Ray argued that the study of God's creation in nature was a form of worshipful praise. "And therefore," he wrote, "those who have Leisure, Opportunity, and Abilities, to contemplate and consider any of these Creatures, if they do it not, do as it were rob God of some Part of his Glory, in neglecting or slighting so eminent a Subject of it, and wherein they might have discovered so much Art, Wisdom, and Contrivance." This unification of science and theology turned out to be quite productive, because its emphasis on studying design in nature and the ways that organisms were adapted to their environment gave rise to the fields of ecology and evolutionary biology. Ray's book *The*

Wisdom of God Manifested in the Works of the Creation has been called "one of the earliest works of ecology."[50]

During the first half of the nineteenth century, the idea that natural history and religion were united was a commonplace notion taught in homes and schools, remaining a part of popular culture long after it had been shed by scientists. For example, an 1831 book on insects intended for family study concluded that honeybees "and their instincts loudly proclaim the power, wisdom, and goodness of the GREAT FATHER of the universe, and prove, beyond all cavil and doubt, the existence of a superintending Providence, which watches with incessant care over the welfare of the meanest of his creatures." Another series of books, approved for use in public schools in 1839, began, "We are about to commence a course of study, which will lay before us, in detail, abundant proofs of beneficent design," and did so via a detailed examination of the natural history of winter, spring, summer, and fall.[51]

Natural theology also provided a religious justification for the Victorian taste for collecting objects of natural history, many of which were transformed into home decorations. Stylish homes sported a mummified menagerie of birds, butterflies, and assorted beautiful fragments of the natural world. Living objects of nature in the form of house plants, some quite exotic, were also in vogue, as were the new interests in decorative flowers and flower gardening. The Victorian fern craze, which peaked mid-century, was made possible by the invention of the Wardian case, the sometimes extraordinarily ornate precursor to the modern terrarium that graced many a parlor. The market for decorative and exotic ferns prompted new discoveries regarding their biology and propagation. The expensive case had an added snob appeal. "Hanging [plants] were in fashion in 1860," noted one writer a decade later, "but after a year or two they were as common in the tenement of the mechanic as in the palaces on Fifth Avenue. They gave way to the more expensive rustic stand or Wardian case, which being less readily imitated by people of limited means, is likely to continue longer in fashion."[52]

Although natural theology declined as the century progressed, the pastimes of nature study and collecting remained popular. The widespread fascination with science at the end of the century only strengthened these interests, as did the growing enjoyment of outdoor recreation and concern about protecting wildlife and natural resources. These were all brought to focus by a major educational reform movement called nature study.

The new nature study movement was interested in much more than collecting dead fragments of nature or pedagogical reform as an end in itself. As one of the first of the great nature study textbooks, *Nature Study and Life*, put it: "Humanity, like the giant Antaeus, renews its strength when it touches Mother Earth. Sociological studies suggest that city life wears itself out or goes to decay after three or four generations, unless rejuvenated by the fresh blood from the country. Thus these deeper relations to nature are not only ancient and fundamental but are also immanent and persistent." This text was published in 1902, at the beginning of the movement's Golden Age decade and just a year before Roosevelt and Burroughs journeyed together to Yellowstone. Its author, Clifton F. Hodge, argued that this educational approach had many advantages: Students would gain an understanding of the economic impacts of beneficial and harmful plants and animals, develop aesthetic appreciation of the world around them, and learn the ethical and social lessons of not harming the earth's creatures and respecting laws that protected nature. Nature study promised to be an amazingly effective vehicle for the entire school curriculum, especially science.[53]

Teachers found that schoolchildren loved nature and that lessons that began with this interest provided an avenue for teaching many subjects. Nature provided a means to integrate or correlate the entire school curriculum. "For example," explained one textbook, "coal may be studied in the nature lesson as to formation and composition. If the State of Pennsylvania were studied at the same time, it would greatly enhance the nature lesson if the coal mines and the coal industry of the state were also studied." Another writer argued:

> The correlation of nature study with language lessons is almost inevitable. The child sees certain living creatures and is interested in their life and habits and almost involuntarily he tells what he sees; if the teacher is in sympathy with him, he likes quite as well to write about his observations as to tell about them. And since he is trying to express only what he knows and has experienced, his English is simple and straight-forward; and, even when it is faulty, it may be corrected better by good example than by that ogre of school work in English, the blue pencil.[54]

Nature study also contained a vestige of natural theology, which was often revealed in its claims of moral and spiritual value. One textbook writer noted, "The study of the wonderful things of the world, their beautiful fitness for their existence and functions, the remarkable progressive tendency of all organic life, and the unity that prevails in it create admiration in the beholder and tend to his spiritual uplifting." Hodge wrote that "no one can love nature and not love its Author, and if we can find a nature study that shall insure a sincere love, we shall be laying the surest possible foundation for religious character." These were grand expectations indeed, and they were held by many educators concerning the study of birds and bugs.[55]

The movement originated in educational theories emphasizing the importance of each child's full sensory participation in his or her learning, stretching beyond books to learning through experience. Nature study employed the direct observation of nature and, through this, the development of observation and reasoning skills. Object teaching, which became popular in the United States in the latter part of the nineteenth century, was an important precursor. Teachers used objects to focus their students' attention on the lesson. If, for example, the lesson was about rocks, students would actually handle and examine rocks. This might seem passé now, but in its day object teaching was an innovative alternative to rote learning.

The eminent scientist and educator Louis Agassiz provided early inspiration for nature study. His summer natural history school for teachers was especially important. In 1873, Agassiz brought more than fifty teachers and scientists together on Penikese Island, one of the Elizabeth Islands off the south coast of Massachusetts, for an intensive workshop in natural history. The venture was made possible by John Anderson, a New York merchant who donated the island, its buildings, and fifty thousand dollars.

The poet John Greenleaf Whittier memorialized the school's opening ceremony. "On the isle of Penikese /," he wrote, "Ringed about by sapphire seas, / Fanned by breezes salt and cool, / Stood the Master with his school." Agassiz, the Master, emphasized and modeled the importance of involving students in the direct observation of nature. "Take your text from the brooks," he told them, "not from the booksellers."[56] It was an extraordinary summer, one that had a lasting impact upon Agassiz's students. The school did not continue beyond that season, because its founder died before the year ended. It was, though, an important event in the development of nature study because a number of Agassiz's students became leaders in the field. One, David Starr Jordan, became president of Indiana University and, later, the first president of Stanford University. His voice in support of nature study gave the movement credibility and prestige.

By the beginning of the twentieth century, nature study was well established in classrooms throughout the nation, especially in elementary schools. After-school nature clubs that often featured outdoor activities and field trips had also become popular. One of the first, the Agassiz Association, was established by a high school principal in 1875. It was modeled after similar school science societies in Switzerland (Europe was ahead of the United States in nature appreciation) and named for the great naturalist. By 1887 the association was composed of 986 local societies with a total membership of more than ten thousand.[57] At the turn of the century, John Burroughs societies could also be found in schools throughout the country. Nurtured by Burroughs's publisher, they both motivated students to study nature and fostered a new generation of readers. The children who tossed flowers at John Burroughs on his way to Yellowstone represented a legion.

Burroughs's books were introduced into the schools in the 1880s by Mary Burt, a Chicago schoolteacher who believed that "When the child's mind is aglow with ideas the words come as a secondary matter." She set out to use the ideas in nature literature as a vehicle for teaching reading and asked the board of education for thirty-six copies of Burroughs's *Pepacton* for her sixth-grade class. This was an unusual step because schools did not use contemporary authors in those days, but it was an educational success. After investigating what she was doing in Chicago, Houghton Mifflin Company invited Burt to edit a special collection of Burroughs's essays for the classroom. The result, *Burroughs's Birds and Bees,* was published in 1887. It was used in sixth-, seventh-, and eighth-grade classrooms throughout the nation. Other school-reader collections of his essays, *Sharp Eyes and Other Papers* and *A Bunch of Herbs and Other Papers,* followed. They were well received, with three hundred thousand copies sold between 1889 and 1906.

In addition, Ginn & Company published *Little Nature Studies,* a pair of readers also based on Burroughs's work and edited by Burt. "The intention of the books," announced one advertisement, "is to introduce the child and the teacher to out-of-door studies, to a love for the woods, fields, skies, plants, and other real things in life, and to the acquisition of the habits of the naturalist." More than simply a collection of Burroughs's essays, this was a carefully designed reader for young learners. It included extensive illustrations integrated into a text that carried students through progressive levels of skill. Other publishers recognized a good thing, and by the turn of the century school readers rooted in nature study were a publishing staple. People who predicted that "text-books, as a main means to an education, are doomed" by the superior methods of studying "the open book of Nature" were sadly mistaken.[58]

The nature study movement had a wide-ranging impact on the public's understanding and appreciation of the natural world as a result of both the numbers of people reached and the depth of their involvement. Nature study entered into millions of American households as parents became involved with their children's schoolwork. In many states, nature study became a mandatory part of the school curriculum. It grew into a major educational reform movement, the first to combine educational theory with an interest in the natural environment. Although the movement declined in the 1920s, it gave rise to modern science education. At the turn of the century, though, it was a mixture of science, aesthetic appreciation, resource conservation, animal welfare, and more traditional pedagogic perspectives. Its focus was not entirely or even primarily on science. According to the author of a text for young ornithologists, for example, "what is needed at first is not the science of ornithology,—however diluted,—but some account of the life and habits, to arouse sympathy and interest in the living bird, neither as a target nor as a producer of eggs, but as a fellow-creature whose acquaintance it would be pleasant to make." Nature study emphasized the child's relationship with the natural world in his or her ability to live in harmony with nature.[59]

Charles W. Eliot, then president of Harvard University, also recognized the cultural importance of nature study. "A brook, a hedgerow, or a garden is an inexhaustible teacher of wonder, reverence, and love," he wrote. For him, though, the sympathetic and scientific appreciation of nature were not at odds with each other: "The idea of culture has always included a quick and wide sympathy with men; it should hereafter include sympathy with nature, and particularly with its living forms, a sympathy based on some accurate observation of nature."[60]

The popular meaning of the term *nature study* was wider than simply school studies of nature. It came to mean the general study of nature, regardless of whether it was studied in the schools or as a hobby, pursued individually or with friends, or engaged in as an educational or a recreational activity. The opportunities to pursue it were many and the public was eager. The nation was full of nature lovers by the end of the nineteenth century, and their numbers were still growing.

Clerks of the Woods

As the new century began, the nation was awash with books about nature. "It is a part of the progress of the day that the Nature study is coming into prominence in our schemes of education, and, beyond these, is entering into our plans for coveted diversion," wrote a book reviewer in 1901, ". . . yet it is a real surprise that so large and increasing a number of each season's publications are devoted to the purpose."[61] The reviewer had reason for surprise. The seeds that Thoreau, Burroughs, and others had planted in the mid-nineteenth century had grown and borne fruit in abundance. Just a year before, one writer had felt compelled to explain why she had "the temerity to offer a surfeited public still another book on wild flowers."[62]

The nation had discovered Henry Thoreau. *Walden*, in print continuously since the mid-1860s, and *A Week on the Concord and Merrimack Rivers* were the only books published in his lifetime, but others were issued posthumously and an eleven-volume collected edition of his works was published by Houghton Mifflin in 1893. Thoreau's extraordinary journals would not be published until 1906 (in fourteen volumes), but beginning in the early 1880s excerpts had been edited into books on seasonal themes. Many a nature lover, including Burroughs and Muir, made pilgrimages to Walden Pond to honor the memory and capture the spirit of Thoreau's vision. (Burroughs, finding "a clean bright pond, not very wild," was disappointed at not finding Thoreau's cabin site. Muir, true to form, wrote to his wife, "No wonder Thoreau lived here two years. I could have enjoyed living here two hundred years or two thousand.")[63] The literary table spread before the nature lover was grand and varied. Burroughs's pastoral essays, Roosevelt's hunting exploits, and Muir's mountain adventures were much-loved staples.

Bird books were plentiful. As a few examples, bird books by Olive Thorne Miller, a contemporary of Burroughs, had appeared regularly since the late 1880s, as had those by the younger, adventurous Florence A. Merriam (C. Hart Merriam's sister). Mable Osgood Wright, a founder of the Connecticut Audubon Society, published *Citizen Bird* and *Birdcraft*. Neltje Blanchan's bird books were published by her husband, Frank Doubleday, and earned a place in the company's Nature Library, along with W. J. Holland's exceptional guides, *The Butterfly Book* and *The Moth Book*. Blanchan's wildflower guide, *Nature's Garden*, was also a part of the series. Gene Stratton Porter's sentimental *The Song of the Cardinal* was published in 1903 and followed by her fantastically successful novels *Freckles* and *A Girl of the Limberlost*. Men, too, were writing about birds. Frank Chapman's books saw many editions, and Bradford Torrey had been publishing books about his ornithological rambles since the 1880s.[64]

The fare was not limited to birds. Charles M. Skinner wrote *Nature in a City Yard*, and Charles C. Abbott reported his experiences of familiar wildlife encountered during a night excursion. Turning his back on his study, Hamilton Wright Mabie put himself "into the hands of my old friend, Nature, for refreshment and society." He found that "Throughout the whole range of her activity one never comes upon any trace of effort, any sign of weariness" and extolled her personified virtues in a text that was, each page, embedded in lavish decorative illustrations of Arcadian landscapes populated by shepherds, satyrs, and Grecian maidens. William

Hamilton Gibson rendered much more practical yet equally intricate and beautiful illustrations for his own volumes of essays about aspects of insects, fungi, plant tendrils, and other things that might otherwise escape the nature lover's eye.[65]

A new kind of nature writing had also appeared—the "realistic" wild animal story. Animals have always appeared in story and fable.[66] The popularity of Rudyard Kipling's *The Jungle Book*, published in 1894, demonstrated the public's appetite for animal fiction, as had *Black Beauty* nearly twenty years before. Close on Kipling's heels, nature writers began to cast the natural history and behavior of wildlife in the form of stories with animal heros. These were immensely popular. Wildlife stories followed the lives, thoughts, and experiences of individual animals, often from the animal's own point of view. They represented a merging of the animal welfare approaches to domestic animals and the traditional wildlife essay—Black Beauty in a wolf's clothing, one might say. The best were written by people who knew the animals and had substantial experience in the outdoors.

Ernest Thompson Seton and Charles G. D. Roberts are generally credited with creating the genre, and they were among its most enduring practitioners. Both began writing realistic wild animal stories in the early

Lobo and Blanca. By Ernest Thompson Seton. From Ernest Thompson Seton, *Wild Animals I Have Known* (New York: Charles Scribner's Sons, 1898).

1890s. Seton was the best known of these writers. The popularity of his first book, *Wild Animals I Have Known*, was akin to that of the novels *Quo Vadis?* and *Trilby*, which were displayed beside it in shop windows. It enjoyed sixteen printings in less than four years. Seton's success motivated Roberts to continue writing his own animal stories and prompted many others to enter this new field. It was an idea whose time had come.[67]

The first story in Seton's book, "Lobo: The King of Currumpaw," based on his own experience hunting wolves in the Southwest, became a classic and set the pattern for many of his others. Lobo, the great wolf with the cunning to avoid all of the hunter's traps and schemes, was invincible until Seton and his assistants killed Lobo's mate, Blanca. Lobo began wailing and searching for her.

> There was an unmistakable note of sorrow in it now. It was no longer the loud, defiant howl, but a long, plaintive wail; "Blanca! Blanca!" he seemed to call. And as night came down, I noticed that he was not far from the place where we had overtaken her. At length he seemed to find the trail, and when he came to the spot where we had killed her, his heart-broken wailing was piteous to hear. It was sadder than I could possibly have believed. Even the stolid cowboys noticed it, and said they had "never heard a wolf carry on like that before."

They used the scent of Blanca's carcass to mark a trail into a field of traps, and Lobo followed. That was the wolf's downfall. "Poor old hero," Seton wrote, "he had never ceased to search for his darling, and when he found the trail her body had made he followed it recklessly, and so fell into the snare prepared for him." It was Lobo's downfall, but his fidelity to his mate also ennobled him. Seton's stories both revealed the natural history of his heroes and confirmed the moral order that he found in nature.[68]

Charles G. D. Roberts played less with traditional morality and more with the Darwinian view of nature. "When Twilight Falls on the Stump Lots," for example, pitted a cow protecting her calf against a bear seeking food for her cubs. "Before all else in life was it important to her that these two tumbling little ones in the den should not go hungry," he wrote. But the cow, too, wanted to protect the life of her own. As fate had it, the cow won and the gored and trampled bear struggled back toward her den and her cubs.

> She hungered to die licking them. But destiny is as implacable as iron to the wilderness people, and even this was denied her. Just

a half score of paces from the lair in the pine root, her hour
descended upon her.... The merry little cubs within the den were
beginning to expect her, and getting restless. As the night wore
on, and no mother came, they ceased to be merry. By morning
they were shivering with hunger and desolate fear.

They were, though, spared days of starvation by a pair of foxes, who made
a meal of the cubs. Meanwhile, the farmer found the cow and calf. The calf
"was tended and fattened, and within a few weeks found its way to the cool
marble slabs of a city market."[69]

Some readers were disturbed by the sad endings of many animal stories. Seton defended his stories by pointing out that "The fact that these
stories are true is the reason why all are tragic. The life of a wild animal
always has a tragic end." There was another facet of these stories that was
even more remarkable, although their readers appear not to have noticed
(which is remarkable in itself): They were sympathetic to predators. Although wolves and bears may threaten livestock and humans may be
pressed to kill them, their ways of life were a part of nature, natural and not
evil. If anything, this underscored the new attitude toward nature that was
growing in the nation. The animal story, wrote Roberts, "leads us back to
the old kinship of earth" and releases us from human selfishness. It allows
people to overcome their own self-centeredness by seeing the world from
the perspective of other animals.[70]

Seton and Roberts were both Canadians, and the animal story they
created has been called a distinctly Canadian form of literature, although
it also attracted writers from other countries. Where the nature literature
of the United States focused on the human experience, this new Canadian
approach focused on the animal's experience. "The animal story at its
highest point of development," wrote Roberts, "is a psychological romance
constructed on a framework of natural science."[71] It was rooted in natural
history fact, constructed within an interpretation of the animals' mental
processes, and held together by a good story. Nature writing had expanded
to include animal psychology.

A number of authors assured readers that their stories were truthful
and accurate. Unfortunately, they rarely made a distinction between the
faithful reporting of events and the soundness of their psychological interpretations. Few were as careful as Olive Thorne Miller, who wisely qualified her claim of accuracy for her bird essays with, "I may have sometimes
misunderstood the motives of the little actors in the drama, but the account of their actions may be implicitly relied upon."[72]

William J. Long was another very popular writer of animal stories. He was born in Massachusetts and, interestingly, spent part of each year in Canada. Although his essays were generally narrated from his own rather than the animal's perspective, he too described the animals' thoughts. Indeed, one reviewer described Long as "our foremost animal psychologist." More anecdotes than animal biographies, his tales rarely ended in tragedy, which probably made them more appealing than those of Charles G. D. Roberts. In a report on the antics of rabbits, for example, Long wrote:

> Had it been one of Nature's own sunny spots, the owl would have swept back and forth across it; for he knows the rabbits' ways as well as they know his. But hawks and owls avoid a spot like this, that men have cleared. If they cross it once in search of prey, they seldom return. Wherever man camps, he leaves something of himself behind; and the fierce birds and beasts of the woods fear it, and shun it. It is only the innocent things, singing birds, and fun-loving rabbits, and harmless little wood-mice—shy defenseless creatures all—that take possession of man's abandoned quarters, and enjoy his protection. Bunny knows this, I think; and so there is no other place in the woods that he loves so well as an old camping ground.[73]

Although Long's stories were more peaceful and reassuring and less tragic than many other animal stories, they were no less committed to the view that we are all kindred of the wild.

One of the best-selling novels of the time, Jack London's *The Call of the Wild,* combined the dog story with the wild animal story and the wilderness adventure novel. The success of London's book was anchored both in the public's appetite for wild animal stories and in its setting in the Alaska gold rush of the late 1890s. Dreams of a wealth of Klondike gold for the taking by anyone who could survive the northern wilderness fit well with the romantic fantasies of nature lovers. Publishers fed this interest with handbooks for gold seekers and books about Alaska. London's stirring account of Buck, the Saint Bernard who became leader of a wolf pack, covered all the bases: Buck's abuse by cruel masters, his experience of human kindness, the stirring of his ancestral memories of the wilderness, and his joyful escape from the bonds of civilization to achieve fulfillment in the wilderness. London revealed the dog's thoughts and emotions with a psychological sophistication and literary skill that convinced the reader he was faithful to Buck's innermost self.[74]

John Muir also entered the field with an Alaskan dog story of his own. He had already written two memorable essays, "The Douglas Squirrel" and

"The Water-Ouzel," but these were more in the tradition of the nature essay than the animal story. His story of Stickeen, the little dog that shared his adventure trying to cross a glacial crevasse in the midst of an Alaskan storm, was extraordinary. John Burroughs judged it "almost equal to 'Rab and his Friends,'" his own favorite dog story. The events happened in 1880, but it was not until 1897 that the story was published. In the interim, though, the story became well known among Muir's acquaintances; a master storyteller, Muir was often asked to repeat it. Although it was not a story of a wild animal, its setting and style appealed to the same audience.[75]

But there was a storm gathering over the forest. The very popularity of nature books meant there was an enormous market for them, which meant there was money to be made in writing and publishing nature books. Many authors rushed to take advantage of this new market. Not all, however, knew what they were writing about, and not all publishers seemed to care, so long as the money rolled in. "A whole lot of goody-goody books of the natural history kind have been getting published lately," wrote a reviewer expressing a growing concern, "and they have been doing a considerable amount of harm by making the impression that the love of animals is not a rational sentiment, but is founded, to a large extent, in silly pretense." The same reviewer went on to praise the animal stories of William J. Long as models of good writing. "Children ought to be taught nothing but the truth. . . . Mr. Long knows wild animals with personal acquaintance, and he writes about them as he personally knows them, not as sentimentalists misrepresent them."[76]

Ironically, it was William J. Long and kindred nature writers who brought Theodore Roosevelt and John Burroughs together in Yellowstone in 1903—drawn together by their shared outrage at the excesses of the animal stories. And it was the bewildered, beleaguered, and pugnacious Long who would face the brunt of their attack.

2.
JOHN BURROUGHS AND WILLIAM J. LONG—THE BATTLE BEGINS

John Burroughs was known as a kindly and gentle man, but when he got riled he could be a literary terror. In March 1903, the *Atlantic Monthly* published his opening salvo against the new animal stories: "I suppose it is the real demand for an article that leads to its counterfeit, otherwise the counterfeit would stand a poor show." He acknowledged that some nature books, "a very small number," were of real value as both natural history and literature. He felt that most, however, were written simply to satisfy a market created by an eager and uncritical public. "The current is setting that way; these writers seem to say to themselves, Let us take advantage of it, and float into public favor and into pecuniary profit with a nature-book." With these words, Burroughs launched into a blistering attack on those whom Roosevelt later dubbed "nature fakers."[1]

Others had criticized the new writers even before Burroughs's article. Certain reviewers had complained about the excessive sentimentalizing and anthropomorphizing of nature. Some books even had the creatures talking with each other. A 1901 review in *Our Dumb Animals* had praised a book by William J. Long for telling the "truth" about animals, rather than covering it "with a mass of mawkish sentimentalism." Another writer, Charles Atwood Kofoid, reported that some naturalists and scientists were so critical of nature stories that they "would even relegate the whole anthropomorphic menagerie to the forests of Wonderland." A year later, in 1902, Kofoid complained:

Naturalists have no quarrel with the romances of animal psychology. They enjoy the stories as much, if not more, than do
other folk. When, however, the romancers claim to be explorers
in animal psychology and assiduous contributors _to natural history_
the startled scientist scans in vain the [scientific journals] for some
revelation of their discoveries. The credulous public as well as the
naturalists will have difficulty in separating the fabric of romance
from the framework of facts in any contribution prepared to meet
the demands and rewards of the popular animal story.

The naturalist Ernest Ingersoll agreed. Later that year, commenting on
Long's School of the Woods, he wrote that the honest reader "revolts on
every page. . . . It would be an epoch-making book in both zoology and
psychology could its statements be established." He also questioned
whether the schoolbooks based on Long's stories were accurate.[2]

These complaints, though, were not enough to stop the abuses.
Burroughs was one of the few people who had the stature, respect, and
credibility necessary to make the world pay attention, and many people
had been waiting, hoping that he would pick up his pen and take a stand.
His _Atlantic_ article, entitled "Real and Sham Natural History," was just
what they had been waiting for.[3]

The article began with praise for Bradford Torrey, Fannie Hardy
Eckstorm, Leander S. Keyser, Florence Merriam, Frank M. Chapman, and
Ernest Ingersoll, whose recent books exemplified good nature writing.
Dallas Lore Sharp received special commendation for _Wild Life Near
Home_, the product of "a deep and abiding love of Nature, and of power to
paint her as she is." Burroughs pointed out that the danger he and Sharp
always faced as writers was that "of making too much of what we see and
describe,—of putting in too much sentiment, too much literature,—in
short, of valuing these things more for the literary effects we can get out of
them than for themselves." The eighteenth-century English parson-
naturalist Gilbert White, author of _The Natural History of Selborne_, was
Burroughs's model of the writer who, without self-consciousness, "remem-
bers only nature. . . . There is never more than a twinkle of humor in his
pages, and never one word of style for its own sake." Burroughs identified
Charles Dudley Warner as the "father" of the contemporary animal story
and praised Warner's _A-Hunting of the Deer_ as a model of the truthful
animal story.

Then he singled out Charles G. D. Roberts, Ernest Thompson Seton,
and Reverend William J. Long as the objects of his displeasure. Roberts
escaped easily, for in his _The Kindred of the Wild_[4] "one finds much to admire

and commend, and but little to take exception to." Burroughs thought Roberts's story "A Treason of Nature," about an amorous moose led to its death by a hunter's moose call, rang true. "Of course," Burroughs cautioned, "it is mainly guess-work how far our psychology applies to the lower animals. That they experience many of our emotions there can be no doubt, but that they have intellectual and reasoning processes like our own, except in a very rudimentary form, admits of grave doubt." He did question Roberts's porcupine that coiled into such a tight protective ball that it rolled downhill when nudged by a panther—an unlikely behavior for an animal that must remain upright for an effective defense. Roberts's other porcupine descriptions, however, met with Burroughs's approval.

Seton and "his awkward imitator," Long, were less fortunate. These men, accused Burroughs, repeatedly crossed "the line between fact and fiction" and deliberately attempted "to induce the reader to cross, too, and to work such a spell upon him that he shall not know that he has crossed and is in the land of make-believe." Seton's *Wild Animals I Have Known*, which begins with the words, "These stories are true," was filled with examples of sham natural history.[5] Claiming that the book was better titled *Wild Animals I Alone Have Known*, Burroughs wrote, "Are we to believe that Mr. Thompson Seton, in his few years of roaming in the West, has penetrated

Old Vix Rides a Sheep to Safety. By Ernest Thompson Seton. From Ernest Thompson Seton, *Wild Animals I Have Known* (New York: Charles Scribner's Sons, 1898).

farther into the secrets of animal life than all the observers who have gone before him?" He pointed, for example, to Seton's extraordinary fox that jumped upon a sheep and rode it for several hundred yards as a way to confuse the dogs that were hot on its scent—the same animal that tried to free her captive young and, unable to do so, fed it poison, knowing that death was better than captivity. There was Silver Spot, the crow that counted to thirty and exercised personal leadership over its flock, which it commanded like a drill sergeant. Burroughs was especially upset with Seton's claim that crows teach their young how to forage for food. The old may teach their young by example, he argued, but is this schooling in the human sense?

To Seton's assertion, "Those who do not know the animals well may think I have humanized them, but those who have lived so near them as to know something of their ways and their minds will not think so," Burroughs responded, "This is the old trick of the romancer: he swears his tale is true, because he knows his reader wants this assurance; it makes the thing taste better." The nature writer, Burroughs argued, must not deceive the reader:

> It is always an artist's privilege to heighten or deepen natural effects. He may paint us a more beautiful woman, or a more beautiful horse, or a more beautiful landscape, than we ever saw; we are not deceived even though he out-do nature. We know where we stand and where he stands; we know that this is the power of art. But when he paints a portrait, or an actual scene, or event, we expect him to be true to the facts of the case.

Then Burroughs turned his attention to William J. Long and Long's claim in the "ridiculous book" *School of the Woods* that animals tutor their young in the skills of survival.[6] "Now the idea was a false one before Mr. Long appropriated it [from Seton], and it has been pushed to such length that it becomes ridiculous. There is not a shadow of truth in it. It is simply one of Mr. Thompson Seton's strokes of fancy." Long had gone so far as to state that animals teach their young just as do humans and that an animal's survival "depends, not upon instinct, but upon the kind of training which the animal receives from its mother." Yet, argued Burroughs, although mother birds do not teach their young how to build a nest, a year later young birds are building them. Long's books were works of "mock natural history," despite his assertions that his stories were truthful. Burroughs jeered:

There is a school of the woods, as I have said, just as much as there is a church of the woods, or a parliament of the woods, or a society of united charities of the woods, and no more; there is nothing in the dealings of animals with their young that in the remotest way suggests human instruction and discipline. The young of all the wild creatures do instinctively what their parents do and did. They do not have to be taught; they are taught by nature from the start. The bird sings at the proper age, and builds its nest, and takes its appropriate food, without any hint at all from its parents.

And their stories! Long wrote of kingfishers and fishhawks that caught fish and released them, injured but not dead, into little pools where their young could practice fishing under the careful instruction of the adults. He also had a story about a porcupine rolling downhill purely for fun. And there was the partridge that held roll call for its young and counted out nine to discover two missing. Long claimed that red squirrels had cheek pockets that could hold six chestnuts, when red squirrels have no cheek pockets at all. Seton wrote of a fox that lured the chasing hounds onto a railroad trestle to have them killed by a passing train. Then there was the fox that played possum when it could not escape, allowing itself to be tossed over the trapper's shoulder and carried home only to run off at the first opportunity. Burroughs even disagreed with Long's views of how animals die— for example, Long's story about an eagle gently dying on the wing high in the air and gliding gracefully to the ground—an amazing aerodynamical feat even if one accepts the idea that a bird can die in flight. There was also Long's story about the fox that coaxed chickens out of a tree by running around and around the tree in circles until the chickens became dizzy and fell. "How the old humorist must have chuckled in his sleeve!" Burroughs jabbed, thinking of the old farmer who probably told the story to Long.

In short, Long did not know what he was writing about. "Mr. Long's book reads like that of a man who has really never been to the woods, but who sits in his study and cooks up these yarns from things he has read in *Forest and Stream*, or in other sporting journals." John Burroughs branded William J. Long a fraud.

Despite all appearances, Burroughs had been reluctant to draw blood. When he sent an early version of the article to his personal assistant, Clara Barrus, for typing, he asked her whether he was "too severe" with his opponents and whether his article showed "bad blood." He also sent a copy to Dallas Lore Sharp for comment. Sharp was obviously honored that the great naturalist sought his advice. Although he shared Burroughs's views, Sharp counseled moderation, fearing that too aggressive an attack might backfire and win sympathy for Long.[7] Burroughs accepted their advice and softened the tone of his article.

At the end of December 1902, Burroughs sent his article to Bliss Perry, editor of _Atlantic Monthly;_ with it he enclosed a cover letter declaring his anger at the sham naturalists, calling Long a fraud, and urging quick publication. Perry found the article somewhat peevish and "ill-natured," and asked Burroughs to moderate it still further. After sending the revision to Perry, Burroughs still had reservations and tried to submit yet another draft, but by then it was too late for changes. "Poor devil!" he later wrote of Long, "I begin to feel sympathy for him. I'm sorry the article is so blunt and savage, but I couldn't deal with [him] in any other way." Although he continued to have reservations, even after the article was published, he was to find that William J. Long was quite capable of taking care of himself.[8]

The Response to Burroughs's Article

The _Atlantic_ article received swift response. There were many laudatory letters and articles, including a statement from the poet and editor of _Century Magazine_ Richard Watson Gilder, who said that Burroughs never did "a more honest or conscientious thing" in his life. The author Hamilton Wright Mabie commended him for a courage that "most of us are lacking." The most winning compliment came from the president of the United States, whom Burroughs had met and begun corresponding with ten years before. "I was delighted with your _Atlantic_ article," Roosevelt wrote to Burroughs. "I have long wished that something of the kind should be written."[9]

Theodore Roosevelt was especially upset, as was Burroughs, with writers who misrepresented their stories as factual. (Rudyard Kipling's jungle stories were acceptable, the president said, because they were not represented as anything other than fiction. He was not happy, though, with Kipling's assumption that all wild animals mate in the spring.) And Roosevelt warned Burroughs not to make too much of animal instinct, but to allow "sufficiently for the extraordinary change made in the habits of the wild animals by experience with man, especially experience continued through generations!" That wild animals learn to avoid humans only after prolonged contact with them, for example, demonstrated that they have greater behavioral flexibility than Burroughs seemed to acknowledge. Roosevelt also cautioned him to temper his praise of Charles Dudley Warner. Although _A-Hunting of the Deer_ is "an excellent little tract" against hunting does in the summer while they are rearing their young, Warner mistakenly wrote of a buck protecting a doe during this period. In the wild, Roosevelt argued, a real buck would not associate with does in that season. Burroughs agreed with the president's criticisms, writing back that he had forgotten some of the details that Roosevelt raised.[10]

Roosevelt ended the letter with a compliment greater than the elder naturalist ever expected—an invitation to travel with him that spring in Yellowstone National Park. He promised to insure that Burroughs "endured neither fatigue nor hardship." Thus began a long and warm friendship,[11] which over the next few years centered upon their joint campaign against the sham naturalists.

On March 7, the same day the president wrote his letter of praise to Burroughs, the *Boston Evening Transcript* entered the fray by featuring a defense—a peculiar defense—of Long. Headlined "Discord in the Forest," Charles Prescott Daniels's article began by accusing Burroughs of prejudice against the clergy because his article continually referred to Long by his title of Reverend:[12]

> The next time he finds an inaccurate nature book, I think that in common fairness he ought to be sure of his man before he slaughters him in the pages of the parlorly *Atlantic* after his brutal fashion. It is not such a very vicious thing in Mr. Long that he is a clergyman, and certainly it would be a very happy thing for this world if all clergymen were as faithful and useful and inspiring in their pulpits as Mr. Long has been. It is unfair for Mr. Burroughs to charge Mr. Long with pecuniary rapacity. He is not that kind of person.

But what did Daniels have to say about the substance of Burroughs's attack? After citing examples of Long's personal integrity, he reported an incident that took place during Long's days as a student at Andover Theological Seminary. In response to a professor's question, Long began by saying, "I always love to think . . . ," which led Daniels to propose that

> What he has loved to think and not what he ought to think has colored whatever has met his eyes in the theological as well as the biological world. . . . Honest, absolutely honest, and yet not quite telling the truth . . . His finished product is art, not science; it is the forest plus Mr. Long, it is the woodland folk introduced, interpreted, beloved—I had almost said at the first, created by Mr. Long.

Burroughs, Daniels argued, had the temperament to write nature books, but Long did not and should seek a collaborator who would act "as a check upon rash, half-formed opinion and excited reasoning."

This was a strange defense indeed. It was a defense of Long the person, not of Long the nature writer. The article went on to confirm the wisdom of Dallas Lore Sharp's advice that Burroughs soften his attack for fear that it might backfire and generate sympathy for his target. Daniels suggested that Burroughs left "the reader with a kinder feeling for Mr. Long than for Mr. Burroughs, and [left] him, too, with a suspicion that, after all, the beasts and birds will forgive Mr. Long for having so amiably misrepresented them."

Daniels seemed to know Long well and seemed to suggest that they had attended the Andover seminary together. Long disputed this a year later, claiming never to have met the man and that the classroom incident mentioned had involved not himself, but another student.[13] Nevertheless, the article rings true and the picture of Long is, as we shall see, compatible with that painted by others who knew him.

* * *

Long did not dispute Daniels's article when, a week later, he rallied to his own defense. He was ready and eager for battle. The thirty-seven-year-old Connecticut minister, who would later write, "I have faced death a few times and danger many times, and so far as I can remember I have never once been fluttered or scared by any man or beast," was not afraid of Burroughs and would prove to be equally intrepid toward the president. A great part of Long's strength came from his abiding conviction about the truthfulness of what he wrote; he presented a substantive defense.

Long's article in the *Boston Evening Transcript* began with a marvelous display of disdain. "There is a storm in the forest," he wrote. "Fortunately in the forest storms never strike the ground. . . . One hears the sound thereof, but scarcely feels a breath of it upon his face." Then, promising a fuller statement in a future issue of the *North American Review*, he went on the attack. After condemning Burroughs's discourtesy, Long pointed out that his critic had skeletons in his own closet. In 1880, Thomas Wentworth Higginson, then editor of the *Atlantic Monthly*, had accused Burroughs of unjustly attacking the botanical accuracy of poets James Russell Lowell and William Cullen Bryant.[14] Burroughs had, for example, accused Lowell of inaccuracy in depicting dandelions and buttercups abloom together, when they actually bloom at different times. This might be true in Burroughs's locality, wrote Higginson, but not in Lowell's Cambridge, Massachusetts, where Higginson had also seen them blooming together. In Long's view, Burroughs made the mistake of assuming that what was true of dandelions and buttercups in his own dooryard was true for dandelions and buttercups everywhere. But nature is much more varied than that.

Similarly, Burroughs overlooked the adaptability of wildlife. This was much the same criticism that Roosevelt had made, but Long carried it farther. "Personally," he wrote, "I do not attempt to describe or study animals in classes any more, for the simple reason that I cannot find any two animals of the same species that are alike." Burroughs's porcupines might not roll downhill, but Long's did—in Long's view, different individuals behaved differently under different circumstances. Defending Seton, Long reported that he too had personal knowledge of foxes that repeatedly led hounds onto railroad tracks, intending that they be run over by a train. He knew of at least three dogs killed that way, including two of his own. He also knew of a wolf that had poisoned its captive pups. Long gave Burroughs a sound thrashing regarding learning in animals, giving examples of animal learning and teaching. In short, his observations "cannot be changed by Mr. Burroughs's dogmatic denial on the sole ground that he has not seen them."

Finally, Long protested that he was not an imitator of Ernest Thompson Seton as Burroughs had claimed. In fact, he asserted, he had not even read Seton's book until recently. This is difficult to believe, however, given Seton's extraordinary success as a nature writer and the popularity of his books and stories among nature lovers by 1903.[15]

Seton Responds

Seton provided an even more effective defense—silence. He had met Burroughs earlier, on "a proud day" when Richard Watson Gilder, editor of *Century Magazine*, introduced them in his home. Seton, who had high regard for the elder naturalist, was stung by the attack but felt it was so outrageous as to require no defense. He was also confident of his natural history, had an enormous public following, secure finances, and enough sense not to fan the flames—a stance advised by many friends, including William T. Hornaday, director of the New York Zoological Park. Many felt that, in Seton, Burroughs had aimed at the wrong target. Ornithologist William Brewster sent Seton a letter expressing his anger at what he considered an unjust attack. Novelist Hamlin Garland wrote to Burroughs in Seton's defense and later spoke with him personally, saying that Seton's "stories are based on careful observation." According to Garland, Burroughs responded that he liked Seton and his work but that Seton should not represent his stories as factual natural history, saying "I didn't mean to include him or [Charles G. D.] Roberts in my diatribe. They are both good men of the woods." Garland carried this report to Seton and, soon after, was present when the two naturalists first discussed their conflict.[16]

Ernest Thompson Seton in his "Camping Outfit" (1906). Courtesy of Seton Memorial Library, Philmont Scout Ranch.

Seton and Burroughs met in New York at the annual literary dinner hosted by Andrew Carnegie at his Fifth Avenue home. It was Saturday, March 28, 1903, only three weeks after Burroughs's article appeared in the *Atlantic*. Reports of the event vary. Carnegie's memory was that Richard Watson Gilder, manager of the affair, had mistakenly arranged to seat Burroughs and Seton together. Catching his error and trying to avoid a confrontation, he rearranged the seating to keep them apart. Carnegie surreptitiously put their seating cards back together, and, to his delight (and Gilder's surprise), the naturalists "both enjoyed the trap I set for them" and reconciled their differences.[17]

In Garland's memory of the event, he and Seton arrived together and saw Burroughs in conversation with Hamilton Wright Mabie. "Seton," he reported, "did the manly thing," walking up to Burroughs and offering his hand. The men shook hands in friendship, Burroughs saying, "I didn't intend to bring you into my indictment, Seton. I was so mad at the fakers that my bile slopped over on some of my friends." The other literary luminaries smiled at the sight and, wrote Garland, "If I am not mistaken, Seton asked to be seated beside Burroughs at the table."[18]

Seton provided a fuller and more dramatic account of the meeting, in keeping with his romantic imagination and sense of self-importance: He bearded the literary lion.[19] Entering the reception room with Garland, Seton spotted Burroughs off in a corner, deep in discussion with Mark Twain and William Dean Howells. He alerted Garland to watch and learn how such things were done. Joining the group, Seton shook hands with Twain and Howells, but Burroughs turned away and stared at a painting hanging on the wall. The timid Howells fled the scene and Twain watched in amusement as Seton cajoled the red-faced old naturalist into conversation. Burroughs apologized, but Seton pretended to be unaware of the *Atlantic* article, at which point Carnegie swept Seton away to another part of the room. Seton used this opportunity to ask where he and Burroughs would be seated for dinner. Carnegie indicated opposite ends of the room, but readily agreed to Seton's request to seat them together and watch the fun.

According to Seton, Burroughs was not comfortable with his dinner partner, but Seton "assumed the mastery" and drew him into a natural history discussion. On Burroughs's admission that he had no personal experience or knowledge of wolves, Seton asked what authority he had to judge Seton's knowledge of wolves. Burroughs blushed and argued that there were fundamental principles that applied to all wildlife. Seton told the naturalist that he was not concerned for himself, but presented a dark picture of poor Long (of whom he later claimed to know nothing), crushed, on the edge of despair, and near suicide, and warned of an imminent tragedy whose blame would rest on Burroughs's shoulders. At this point Burroughs broke into tears.[20]

Carnegie's and Garland's recollections of the evening were written seventeen and eighteen years later; Seton's were published thirty-seven years later. Memories can change over time, and published recollections may tell more about the author's imagination than about the events themselves. What were the key players' actual impressions at the time? There are two clues. Seton's journal shows a one-line entry for the day, indicating only that he and Garland went to the dinner and met Burroughs. Three nights after the dinner, Burroughs arrived at the White House to begin his journey to Yellowstone. Before going to bed he wrote a letter to his son, Julian, reporting that he had met Seton, who had asked to sit with him, "behaved finely," and "won my heart."[21]

Seton and Burroughs were brought together again some time later by the prominent ornithologist and curator at the American Museum of Natural History, Frank Chapman. Chapman was a long-time friend and supporter of Seton, whom he had commissioned to illustrate some of his books. Before the *Atlantic* article was published, Burroughs told Chapman that, in the piece, he had "given your friend Seton the devil." Chapman had tried to assure him that Seton's observations were sound. After Burroughs returned from Yellowstone, Chapman invited the two to his home in an effort to build their friendship.[22]

Seton later invited Burroughs to Wyndygoul, his extraordinary haven in Cos Cob, Connecticut. His books brought him a good income, and he was creating an estate appropriate to his image as a wealthy naturalist. When he had moved in just a year before, the place was an old farm, but it was being transformed into a private wildlife sanctuary. Charles G. D. Roberts described it in idyllic terms:

> In a woodland of two hundred acres, the boundaries do not crowd or obtrude. There is room for the privacies and mysteries of the forest itself. The wild creatures who inhabit there, guarded but unspoiled by a protection which is not thrust upon their notice, find ample space to choose their own most fitting resorts, whether of deep swamp-thicket, or high, rocky brush-tangle, or overhanging bank by the brown water, or grassy glade sun-steeped at noon. There are seclusions within seclusions, so that the shy and various inhabitants of Wyndygoul are not forced into associations of other than their own choosing.

Burroughs was amazed by it all when Seton drove him through the woods to the house, which was built of rough stone and timbers. At the time, it was unfinished and only a third of its planned size. Inside, Seton showed Burroughs his extensive library of books, photographs, and field notes; his museum of study skins; and his collection of his own artwork and field drawings. Burroughs was, by Seton's report, very impressed.[23] And he had reason to be.

Born in 1860, Ernest Thompson Seton's boyhood studies of the Canadian wildlife of farm, forest, and city led him to dream of becoming a naturalist. His family could not afford the university training he needed to become a scientist, so in 1876 he became a local portrait artist's assistant, planning to integrate his artistic abilities and natural history ambitions as a wildlife artist. He eventually undertook studies in Paris, where his painting *Sleeping Wolf* was selected for display at the Grand Salon of Painting in 1891. Before reaching Paris, though, he pursued his own natural history studies in England and while homesteading in Manitoba, where he was appointed official province naturalist, a largely honorary post. He also spent time in New York, where he did the illustrations for the *Century Dictionary* and gained the friendship of a number of prominent scientists, including Frank Chapman, William T. Hornaday, and C. Hart Merriam, who encouraged him in his natural history studies.

At his birth, Seton was given the name Ernest Evan Thompson. In 1877, though, he legally changed his name to Ernest Evan Thompson Seton. He believed that he had a claim to Scottish nobility under the Seton name. Later, though, his mother made him promise to use the Thompson name, so he adopted the *nom de plume* of Seton-Thompson until her death in 1897. Naturally, this led to some confusion among his readers. One journalist referred to him as, "Ernest Thompson, or Ernest Seton-Thompson, or whatever his name happens to be at this particular moment . . ."

Although he achieved artistic recognition and was a better artist than scientist or writer, Seton turned his attention to writing as a better vehicle for expressing his views of nature. His was a vision of nature rooted in science—and, even more strongly, of humans as an integral part of nature rather than as lords of creation. His first book, *Studies in the Art Anatomy of Animals*, published in 1896, was a landmark description of animal anatomy specifically written for artists. It was based on his own detailed observations and dissections. Seton's attention to biological detail in his artwork and journals attests to his skills as a naturalist and observer. His animal stories often incorporated field observations originally recorded in his journals, while the natural history was woven into a narrative based on animal heroes that lived lives of moral significance.[24]

Seton never entered directly into the public debate about nature faking. One reason was that he was confident in his work and chose to let it speak for itself. In addition, he had already learned a bitter lesson from a public battle a decade earlier over whether one of his paintings would be hung in the Canadian exhibit at the World's Columbian Exposition. The painting, originally entitled *The Triumph of the Wolves*, showed a pack of wolves with its kill—a wolf hunter—one wolf gnawing on his skull. (The title was soon changed to the more conservative *Waiting in Vain*, thus shifting the focus to the victim's family, waiting in their cottage on the horizon.) It was a sensational and improbable scene, and its non-judgmental presentation of nature triumphing over humans was offensive to Victorian taste. It certainly presented an unpleasant image of Canada. *Waiting in Vain* was initially rejected, but after a major public controversy that Seton helped to create, it was finally accepted for the exhibit. The painting, however, was hung so high that it went practically unnoticed. Seton had won a hollow victory.[25] Perhaps he had learned his lesson and felt there was little to be gained from a battle with John Burroughs.

Seton valued his new friendship with Burroughs, although he had a much lower opinion of Burroughs's capabilities as a naturalist than of his skills as a writer. Seton brought to his own writing many of the tools of a research naturalist: photographs, sketches, journals, and prepared specimens, including preserved study skins of birds and mammals. Burroughs, he felt, did none of this and functioned only on a literary level.[26]

Burroughs remained on friendly terms with Seton, although he continued to believe that Seton blurred the line between fact and fiction. In 1904, Burroughs wrote in the *Atlantic*, "Mr. Thompson Seton, as an artist and *raconteur*, ranks by far the highest in this field, and to those who can separate the fact from the fiction in his animal stories, he is truly delightful." (Seton quoted this statement in his autobiography, but omitted the qualifying phrase about separating fact from fiction.) Later still, Burroughs wrote to a friend that he had been reading Seton's *Animal Heroes*, which "I am pleased with, so far. He easily throws all other animal story writers in the shade."[27]

Seton was out of the line of fire.

The Storm Continues

On April 1, 1903, Burroughs set off in a carriage with Theodore Roosevelt to meet their train and begin their western tour.[28] "Think of me," he wrote in a journal letter, "the Henpecked, riding down Pennsylvania avenue in a carriage beside the President of the U.S., and treated by him as a friend and equal!" The train stopped at city after city for speeches and receptions. The president kept the naturalist close by his side. In Chicago, Burroughs reported, they sat together at "the finest banquet I ever saw—cost $24 a plate, Secretary [to the President] Loeb says." Burroughs was pleasantly surprised by all the people who were eager to meet him as well as the president.

On April 6, while passing through the Dakota prairies, Burroughs expressed his incredulity at how the natives could enjoy living in a landscape so different from his own:

> The farm-houses look lonesome as a ship at sea. How monotonous life must be on these farms . . . no corner in which to seek shelter; no individuality in the farms, each one like every other; unending sameness. . . . Now we are passing a prairie grave-yard. How lonely it looks out there on the open naked bosom of the world! No tree, no shrub, no fence.[29]

Theodore Roosevelt and John Burroughs in Yellowstone. Courtesy of Theodore Roosevelt Collection, Harvard College Library.

They reached Yellowstone four days later. Burroughs dreaded riding on horseback, but was mortified to discover that he was expected to ride inside a horsedrawn ambulance to their next destination, Fort Yellowstone. It was, though, an exciting journey. The ambulance raced off ahead of the cavalry and cowboys accompanying the president, bumping and swaying its way toward Fort Yellowstone. Not until later did Burroughs discover that his driver had lost control of the team, which had been frightened by the presidential cavalcade.[30]

Roosevelt and Burroughs spent two weeks in the park. First they camped in the northeast section, and then traveled by sleigh to the geyser region in higher country. It was an exhilarating adventure for Burroughs, whose previous experiences of nature had been in the more pastoral and intimate landscapes of the Northeast. Roosevelt was Burroughs's delighted guide to the new landscape and fauna.

By April 25, Burroughs was on his way home, taking a long route through Washington State. (Roosevelt went on to Yosemite.) He wrote to the president from Spokane on May 5, reporting that children in the Webster School had organized a John Burroughs Society and that the State Normal School at Cheney had a John Burroughs Anti-Cigarette Society. He was the object of much attention before he arrived back home.

When Roosevelt and Burroughs emerged from Yellowstone, they discovered that in their absence the nation had continued discussing Burroughs's attack on Seton and Long. Roosevelt was particularly upset by an article written by "Hermit" and published in his friend George Bird Grinnell's magazine, _Forest and Stream_.[31] "I do not care to express an opinion on either side [of the controversy] at present," wrote Hermit, "but do desire to call attention to some of Mr. Burroughs's false natural history." He went on to quote Burroughs's views, followed by his own refutations. In response to Burroughs's assertion that robins do not teach their young how to sing, Hermit argued, "I hear the old males sing, for the purpose of teaching the young, every season. The singing is not in the loud notes of the mating time, but is confined to a minor key. One cannot go blundering through the woods and hear the robin teach its young. It takes hours of patient observation to overcome the fear of man, before the robins will go on with their domestic affairs." The males learn singing from their fathers and the females learn nest building from their mothers, he wrote. To Burroughs's assertion that cats do not teach their young what to do with a mouse, he responded, "That a naturalist should ask such questions is beyond my comprehension. I thought every one knew that cats teach their kittens all the ways of cat life." It was absurd, he claimed, for Burroughs to assert that animals are born with an understanding of their parents' calls—as absurd as believing that a human child is born knowing its parents' language.

From Gardiner, Montana, Roosevelt fired off a six-page, typed letter to Grinnell, the first of a series of similar letters to editors and publishers whose editorial policy appeared to give comfort to sham naturalists. It was a spirited defense of Burroughs and a condemnation of the anonymous Hermit. Asking Grinnell to treat it as a private letter, since as president he could not speak publicly on the matter, he proceeded to thrash both Long and Hermit. He was incredulous over Hermit's bird stories:

> he says that a song sparrow in his dooryard is now teaching "his year-old boy to sing." Seriously, have you ever read such non-sense? His "year-old boy"! This must mean a song sparrow raised the previous year. How in the name of all that is sacred can he know that he is "his year-old boy?" Of course he knows nothing of the kind. He is either guessing at it or else he has made up the whole incident out of his imagination.... Tomorrow I go back to the political world, to fight about trusts and the Monroe Doctrine and the Philippines and the Indians and the Tariff; but today I allow myself the luxury of calling your attention to this attack in the *Forest and Stream* upon one of the Americans to whom all good Americans owe a debt, an attack which I am sure you would not have permitted in the paper if you had been fully aware of what it contained.

Roosevelt was not satisfied with Grinnell's reply, which he promptly for-warded to Burroughs, who was equally dissatisfied. They were not alone. C. Hart Merriam had written to Grinnell with similar complaints about Hermit's article.[32]

However, not everyone shared Roosevelt's views. John R. Spears wrote a letter to the *New York Times* to commend the "sincerity" of Hermit's writing and the way he "conclusively proved" that Burroughs's knowledge of natural history was not infallible. "We owe a great debt to Mr. Burroughs for his books," Spears wrote, "in spite of the errors they contain, but we owe a greater one to Mr. Thompson Seton because, happily, he has turned a still greater host to the observation of nature's beauties. It seems worth adding that the good nature as well as the sincerity of 'Hermit' will commend his article to every reader."[33]

Later in 1903, Hermit published an extraordinarily anthropomorphic collection of essays under his real name, Mason A. Walton ("The Hermit of Gloucester"). He proudly announced his new natural history discover-ies, including the fact that "the wood-thrush conducts a singing-school" for its young, and that "the red squirrel owns a farm or fruit garden, and locates his male children on territory which he preempts for the purpose." The *Dial* reviewer, May Estelle Cook, proclaimed that Walton's stories "have the stamp of truth which only long and sympathetic intimacy can give. Consequently they are the best sort both to enjoy and to make deductions from." She also pointed out, erroneously, that Walton was "merely an observer" and did not leap to conclusions like William J. Long, who was "both observer and interpreter."[34]

An editorial in *Connecticut Magazine* complained about "the hard cold severity of the aging naturalist whose last few weeks have been spent roughing it with President Roosevelt in the great northwest," and leapt to the defense of Connecticut residents Long and Seton. Defending Long's personal integrity, the editorial attested to his wilderness experience and competence, observing that "Sometimes he has lived in the wilderness alone for months at a time; again he follows his animals with Indian hunters, whose whole life has been a study of the natural and animal worlds.... Moreover, as his work shows, he is intensely sympathetic; his knowledge of the animal world has the added force of intuition as well as of long study, and the *Dial* calls him 'our foremost animal psychologist.'" Until his recent trip, it pointed out, Burroughs's life had been spent "largely on the farm," which ill equipped him to criticize reports about wildlife in the wilderness. Of Long's facts, the editor wrote, "I have no doubt whatever; for I know Dr. Long's habit of never publishing an observation till he has verified it, either by a second observation or by the witness of reliable trappers and Indians."[35]

The editorial was followed by William J. Long's own defense. It was similar to his earlier article in the *Boston Evening Transcript*. He made a special effort to rebuke Burroughs for his unwillingness to acknowledge that animals teach their young. "Mr. Burroughs's whole argument in this connection misses the point altogether," Long wrote, arguing that *School of the Woods* did not reject the notion of instinct. "For an animal's knowledge is, like our own, the result of three factors: Instinct, training and experience. Instinct begins the work (for the lower orders this is enough), the mother's training develops and supplements the instinct, and contact with the world finishes the process." He went on to explain his method for verifying his observations and theories: "Not only have I watched these animals myself, but I have taken infinite pains to compare my observations not with the books but with the experience of trappers and Indians who know far more of animal ways than the books have ever provided; and I have heard from old Indians whose lives have been spent in the woods, stories of animal cunning and intelligence beside which my own small observations seem very tame and commonplace."[36]

Book learning, then, was of little value to Long in his effort to understand and appreciate the ways of wildlife. He did not take literary or scientific volumes about nature into the woods with him, because reading them came between him and the direct experience of nature. "It is like trying to read a volume of poems in the presence of a lovely woman, who is infinitely more interesting herself than any of the poems she has inspired ... [T]he only book to read out of doors is the book of Nature herself." He did, though, take other kinds of books on his wilderness travels: *Faust*, works by Shakespeare, Martineau's essays, and the King James Bible.[37]

The Reverend Dr. William J. Long

Burroughs and Roosevelt thought Long was a conscious fraud acting principally for personal enrichment. They misjudged the intellectual sophistication and moral conviction of their opponent.

William J. Long, who until recently was the pastor of the First Congregationalist Church in Stamford, Connecticut, was born in 1866 on a farm in North Attleboro, Massachusetts.[38] He was the youngest of a dozen children born to Irish immigrant parents. At the age of sixteen, he qualified to enter Harvard College but, unable to afford the expense, he enrolled at the Bridgewater Normal School in 1883 and, in only three years, completed its four-year program of teacher preparation. In 1888, Long became principal of the Nantucket High School, on an island off the coast of Massachusetts, where he taught English, French, and Latin. He stayed at his post for three years. The island's relative isolation and natural beauty, with its heathlands and ocean vistas, may well be what held him there, for William J. Long was a nature lover. When free from teaching and academic studies, he spent his spare time walking the island and watching wildlife from bird blinds. He spent summers in the wilds of eastern Canada.[39]

After leaving Nantucket, Long entered the senior year at Harvard, completed five courses and received an A.B. in 1892. He then attended the Andover Theological Seminary to prepare for the Congregational ministry. (He had broken with his family several years earlier when, at the age of eighteen, he left the Roman Catholic church to become a Congregationalist.) He graduated first in his class in 1895. Long received a scholarship and, as a fellow of the seminary, traveled to Europe, where he studied philosophy, theology, and history in Berlin and Heidelberg. The University of Heidelberg awarded Long A.M. and Ph.D. degrees in 1897. Before returning to the United States he did further study in Paris and in the Vatican Library.[40] He returned home in 1898, a scholar with the best of credentials and great prospects before him. The poor Irish farm boy was moving up in the world, but there was a rocky road ahead. He was about to enter a theological controversy that would set the pattern for his defense against John Burroughs a few years later.

In 1898, Long preached a few times at the North Avenue Congregational Church in Cambridge, which was seeking a minister.[41] He must have done a good job, because in early May the congregation voted unanimously to make him pastor. He delivered his first sermon as pastor on June 5. All that remained was ordination by the Cambridge Council, the local church association. The council examined him two weeks later—and rejected him. The pivotal issues were Long's fundamental belief in universal salvation and in his position that each pastor must preach on the basis of his own beliefs. The Cambridge church's creed embraced eternal damnation—a punishment incompatible with Long's belief in a merciful God. Nevertheless, the council wanted Long in the position and restated the question in a form that might be more acceptable but still allow the possibility of eternal punishment. But Long remained steadfast. After his examiners adjourned to make a decision, Long waited in moral turmoil,

William J. Long—Clergyman and Scholar. Courtesy of Frances Long Woodbridge.

pondering the church's creed. Concluding that he could not accept the creed, he marched into the room, interrupted the council in its deliberations, and stated his beliefs in unmistakable terms. He succeeded in making himself clear and was rejected by a thirty-two to twenty vote.

More was at stake, though, than the question of who would become the pastor of the North Avenue Church. Long was taking a principled stand based on freedom of religious belief and a modern, liberal interpretation of the Bible. He was caught in a doctrinal conflict between the creeds of the Cambridge Council and of his seminary (whose representatives voted in his favor), between the conservative theology of the local churches and the more liberal stance of Andover. It was an issue rooted in recent church history that had broad implications for Congregationalism. As one pastor, a Universalist, noted, "it is a glaring sign of the times that twenty out of fifty-two orthodox Congregationalists should vote to ordain and install over an orthodox church a man who fearlessly and without hesitation avowed himself a believer in doctrines which they must have known were thoroughly Universalist and Unitarian. Verily the heresy of twenty-five years ago is fast becoming the orthodoxy of today." The affair became a topic of national discussion within the church and in the press.

Two days later, less than two months after being voted into his first pastorate, Long submitted his resignation. This gave the congregation an opportunity to affirm his position by refusing to accept the resignation. The national magazine, the *Outlook*, shared Long's views and took up his defense. "In our judgment, the effect of this action will be to discredit Councils more than to discredit Mr. Long," it editorialized. "If the Congregational church at North Cambridge is united in desiring Mr. Long for its pastor and leader, and has faith in the principles of Congregationalism, it has a fine opportunity to bear witness to its faith." The church, however, accepted his resignation on July 1. But in doing so the church formally placed "on record its high estimate of the character and ability of Dr. Long, its recognition of his exceptional power as a preacher, its belief in his absolute candor, sincere consecration and fine spirituality, [and] its affectionate appreciation of the quality and purpose of the work which he had begun to do with and for his church." Unwilling to let matters rest there, William J. Long wrote a public letter in response to an editorial in the *Congregationalist*, whose editor had been moderator of the examining committee. It was a spirited defense of himself and freedom of religious thought.[42]

The zeal Long brought to this controversy blossomed again in his defense during the nature fakers controversy that began five years later. He provided an impassioned and articulate defense of his views in professional journals. He also knew how to use the newspapers and the popular press to rally public support for his position. Newspapers eagerly reported the debate.

Although he lost the job, William J. Long earned a great deal of respect for his religious conviction and integrity. At the end of September the Congregationalist association in Andover, Mass., renewed his license to preach, which had expired while he was in Europe. Many considered this an endorsement of his position in the controversy. A year later, in November 1899, he was ordained by a council in Stamford, Conn., and became pastor of its First Congregational Church. Even the conservative *Congregationalist* had praise for Long. "The council was greatly impressed by the splendid personality of the candidate, the profundity and clearness of his statements and, perhaps, most of all by his evident spirituality,

William J. Long in the Field. Courtesy of Frances Long Woodbridge.

loyalty to Christ and vitality of belief and purpose," it reported. "The church is united and enthusiastic in the welcome to its new leader, and no one expressed satisfaction in the abundant evidence of new life more heartily than the former beloved pastor, Rev. Samuel Scoville."

Long was a dynamic and volatile preacher. He was handsome, and his force of presence and six-foot-three stature made him an imposing figure. His congregation grew to respect his "finely phrased English" and spirituality. The new pastor, though, had another iron in the fire. Before arriving in Stamford he had been developing a second career as a writer and now this, too, was bearing fruit as his magazine articles and poetry saw print. He published a historical novel for children in 1898, and his first volume of nature stories, *Ways of Wood Folk*, was published in 1899. An avid outdoorsman, he continued to vacation in the northern woods, where he fished and observed woodland animals, his "wood folk." In 1900 Long married Frances Bancroft, a history teacher at Andover Academy and the principal's daughter. Just before the wedding ceremony he presented his bride with what must have been among his proudest possessions, the first copy of, and the copyright to, his second nature book, *Wilderness Ways*. A daughter was born a year later (two more children were to follow in the next six years). He seemed to have it all: a congregation, scholarly achievements, social standing, publishing success, a family, and a home in a town that would become his lifelong residence.[43]

On January 24, 1903, a month before John Burroughs launched his attack in the *Atlantic Monthly*, William J. Long resigned his post as pastor. "In Dr. Long we have recognized a great intellectual and spiritual leader," read the church's formal acceptance of his resignation. "Few men, indeed, combine in so great measure the component qualities of genius. His sermons have been unique in power and spirituality and have been a constant inspiration to all his hearers."[44] Why did Long resign? The simple reason was that he was in poor health, suffering from a "weakness" of sight in one eye and a nervous breakdown.

Almost nothing is known about Long's health, but, whatever its state, there may have been additional reasons for the resignation. By accounts, he wanted to make his living as a writer. This must have been attractive, given the popularity of his books. Nevertheless, he was deeply committed to the ministry and the desire to write was not reason enough to resign. One author reported that Long found that he was "temperamentally unfit" for the job of church pastor. Another reporter pointed out that "Mr. Long is of Irish extraction—inflammable, poetic and volatile in temperament. ... This has come out in his preaching. Eccentricities and extremely radical outbursts have had a disturbing effect upon his audiences and have limited his success." This must have created some problems with his congregation, despite the high regard that many held for him.

Preaching problems aside, Long may also have alienated influential members of his congregation. Although he got along very well with children and townspeople and was often loved by them, he did not relate well with his social peers. Frank Chapman, for example, told of Long's 1901 encounter with Mabel Osgood Wright at the Connecticut Audubon Society's annual meeting in Stamford. Long, who delivered the welcoming address, was later introduced to Wright, the society's president. "Wright, Wright," he responded, "you're the bird woman, aren't you? It seems to me that I have a letter from you at home, but I haven't read it yet." She replied "with icy clearness, 'Well, it couldn't be from me, for I never heard of you before.' "[45]

Long's reasons for resigning were not simple. When John Burroughs's *Atlantic* article hit the newsstands, the Stamford clergyman was most likely in the midst of medical, ministerial, and personal crises. Although Seton claimed not to have met Long, the picture he painted for Burroughs of a man on the edge of despair may not have been far from the truth. Long's public response to Burroughs's attack, though, was less one of despair than of personal affront and anger, even rage. Five years before, in Cambridge, embroiled in a fateful controversy, he had defended his principles and emerged on top. Now he was prepared to win once more.

Long's Next Move

Long's definitive response to Burroughs's attack appeared in the May issue of the *North American Review*. He began by claiming the philosophical high ground, arguing that

> the study of Nature is a vastly different thing from the study of Science; they are no more alike than Psychology and History. Above and beyond the world of facts and law, with which alone Science concerns itself, is an immense and almost unknown world of suggestion and freedom and inspiration, in which the individual, whether animal or man, must struggle against fact and law to develop or keep his individuality. It is a world of *appreciation*, to express it in terms of the philosophy of Professor Royce, rather than a world of *description*. It is a world that must be interpreted rather than catalogued, for you cannot catalogue or classify the individuality for which all things are struggling. . . .
>
> In a word, the difference between Nature and Science is the difference between a man who loves animals, and so understands

them, and the man who studies Zoology; it is the difference between the woman who cherishes her old-fashioned flower-garden and the professor who lectures on Botany in a college class-room.

Long argued that science cannot deal with unique, individual behavioral variations, which can best be recorded as anecdotes. In his view, the nature writer was better equipped than the scientist to record these truths, which required intimate knowledge of individual animals before one could understand their diversity and significance. "The modern nature-student ... knows that animals of the same class are still individuals," he argued, "... they are not more alike than men and women of the same class, and that they change their habits rapidly—more so, perhaps, than do either governments or churches—when the need arises." To do the job properly, the nature writer "must have not only sight but vision; not simply eyes and ears and note-book; but insight, imagination, and, above all, an intense human sympathy, by which alone the inner life of an animal becomes luminous, and without which the living creatures are little better than stuffed specimens, and their actions the meaningless dance of shadows across the mouth of Plato's cave."

People who watch wild animals very closely and patiently, he wrote, will be rewarded by seeing things that no naturalist or scientist could ever know. The student of nature can also rely on reports from people who have lived close to nature. "In the State of Maine alone I have talked with at least fifty different guides and trappers. They all follow the same classes of animals, yet every guide has a different record of the habits of those animals, and nearly every one of them has at least three or four animal stories that would not be believed if they were printed." It is not because they were liars that they had differing stories, he argued, but because they were each seeing different animal individuals. And how does one know which stories to trust? "[N]o animal story told me as a fact by an honest man will leave me incredulous," Long stated. This was why he trusted Ernest Thompson Seton's stories, even though some of his own theories differed radically from Seton's. "That is either because I have seen less, and less sympathetically, than he has, or because I have watched bears and wolves with different individual habits. But Mr. Thompson-Seton is a gentleman ... to question his veracity, and deny what he has seen because I have not seen it, would be simply to show my own lack of courtesy, and arouse suspicion that I might be jealous of his hard-won and well-deserved success."[46]

The truthfulness and credibility of wildlife observations and of nature writing was, thus, reduced to a matter of gentlemanly conduct. One never

questioned the integrity of another gentleman. Long displayed a gentlemanly pride more typical of the Old World and expected others to live up
to this standard. (He also believed that anyone he looked in the eye while
they were talking could not lie to him.)[47] Little wonder that scientists were
troubled by Long, because if each individual is unique, no observations can
be verified except, perhaps, by again observing the same individual. But,
Long might respond, there is no need to be distressed by this—a report is
true if made by a gentleman.

Long then proceeded to defend, one by one, the stories that Burroughs
branded as frauds and to illustrate his points with more stories of his own.
He defended Seton's story of the fox riding on a sheep's back, saying that
one winter he witnessed the same thing by interpreting tracks in the snow
of a sheep field. Of Burroughs's assertion that fishhawks do not teach their
young to fish, he wrote, "Dr. Philip Cox, the best ichthyologist in Canada,
found a new species of fish that the fishhawks had stored in a [practice] pool
in just this way; and Mr. Mauran Furbish, who probably knows more of the
New Brunswick wilderness than any other man, has told me since my book
was written that he had seen the same thing." Red squirrels, Long
protested, may not have cheek pouches, but they and other rodents do
carry food in their mouths and cheeks. And perhaps partridges do not
count to eleven, but they need not use Arabic numerals to recognize that
one of their young is missing.

Long went on to demonstrate the extraordinary capabilities of individual animals with a new tale about oriole nest building. It merits quoting
entirely, because this marvelous nest resurfaced a year later in discussions
among professional scientists.

> Years ago, when a small boy, I watched two orioles building their
> nest. The twig upon which they hung it forked too widely to suit
> them. They deliberated plainly upon the matter; then they
> brought up a twig from the ground, laid it across the forks, and tied
> it there with strings as a third support to the nest. Moreover, when
> they tied the strings, they took the ends in their beaks and hung
> their weight upon them so as to draw the knots tight. For twenty-
> five successive years I watched other orioles building, to see if this
> astonishing bit of calculation should be repeated. Then, last
> spring, two orioles built in a buttonwood tree, after having been
> driven away from their favorite elm by carpenters. They wanted
> a swinging nest, but the buttonwood's branches were too stiff and
> straight; so they fastened three sticks together on the ground in
> the form of a perfectly measured triangle. At each angle they

fastened one end of a cord, and carried the other end over and made it fast to the middle of the opposite side. Then they gathered up the loops and fastened them by the middle, all together, to a stout bit of marline; and their staging was all ready. They carried up this staging and swung it two feet below the middle of a thick limb, so that some leaves above sheltered them from sun and rain; and upon this swinging stage they built their nest. The marline was tied once around the limb, and, to make it perfectly sure, the end was brought down and fastened to the supporting cord with a reversed double-hitch, the kind that a man uses in cinching his saddle. Moreover, the birds tied a single knot at the extreme end lest the marline should ravel in the wind. The nest hangs above

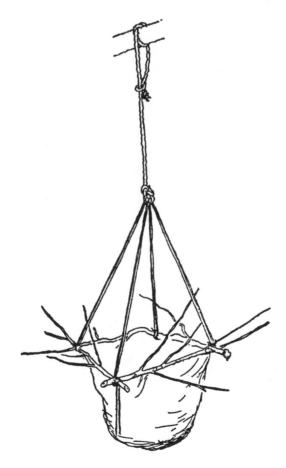

The Orioles' "Mare's Nest." By Clifton Johnson. From *Science* (22 July 1904).

my table now, the reward of twenty-five years' search; but not one in ten of those who see it and wonder can believe that it is the work of birds, until in the mouths of two or three witnesses who saw the matter every word has been established.

How, in Long's view, should Burroughs have approached the task of criticizing such tales? In the accepted manner for criticizing works of art and literature, of course. "Criticism is an art with a continuous historical development," Long wrote in conclusion, "and he who would criticise [sic] must first learn courtesy, and then he must understand the canons of criticism that prevail from Homer to Heine and from Bede to Balzac."

None of Long's critics was satisfied with the oriole story. The drawing of the nest (described as a "mare's nest" by one scientist) that surfaced later did not help. Actually, Long had not seen the birds build the nest in the buttonwood. He first saw this nest in the home of a dying man to whom he had ministered, and the grateful family gave it to him. After investigating, Long found four people ("all of them honest and trustworthy people") who claimed to have witnessed its construction. However, a sworn, notarized statement from one of the witnesses still did not convince the critics. William T. Hornaday, director of the New York Zoological Park, later wrote to the witness for more details. The prompt reply was that the birds tied the knots with their beaks, rather than their feet. It is difficult, though, to tell what in the reply was fact and what was simply the guesswork of an uncritical observer. Hornaday was not impressed and pointed out that the letter was expertly typed, although the signature was that of someone who was barely literate, implying that the "eye witness account" had been written by someone else. One can guess whom he had in mind.[48]

John Burroughs was not impressed by Long's defense either. He pointed out that the male oriole does not assist the female with nest building. To demonstrate that birds had only limited skill with strings, he described three birds that were hanged by strings that were a part of their own nests. He thought Long made such a poor defense that the man was not worth the waste of further effort. However, Long did not let the matter rest. In June the *Dial* published an article by Long that branded most nature writers as superficial and some as cruel. Although Long did not name any names, Burroughs considered it a personal attack, wrote another article about false natural history, and sent it to the *Atlantic Monthly*. The magazine, though, was gun-shy about the controversy. It had refused to print a response from Long and now, after pondering the article a few weeks, it refused Burroughs's rejoinder. *Century Magazine*'s Gilder, however, was interested in the article and printed it in two parts after the turn of the year. Although the article did not criticize Long by name, it took on, to President Roosevelt's delight, the oriole story. Burroughs wrote:

> These orioles built a nest so extraordinary that it can be accounted for only on the theory that there *is* a school of the woods, and that these two birds had been pupils there and had taken a course in strings. . . . After such an example as this, how long will it be before the water-birds will be building little rush cradles for their young or rush boats driven about the ponds and lakes by means of leafy sails, or before Jenny Wren will be living in a log cabin of her own construction.[49]

The line about Jenny Wren had been supplied by Roosevelt in July during a memorable visit. Burroughs was aglow when the presidential yacht cruised up the Hudson for a visit at the naturalist's West Park home. They retreated to his cabin, Slabsides, where they fervently discussed natural history and literature. Roosevelt declared that Long's extraordinary oriole's nest was so fanciful that "He might just as well say that Jenny Wren built herself a log cabin with a bark roof—a miniature Slabsides—as to claim that an oriole did *that*" and branded the errant nature stories "yellow journalism."[50]

Many other people, though, were wondering whether Burroughs had stumbled in his criticism of Long. The minister's defense had an impact, but the response to it was often an attempt to reconcile the two writers, rather than to reject Burroughs. "No one who has not made a saint of Burroughs, and has not been in love with William J. Long, can appreciate the nightmare effect of that *Atlantic* article," confided the *Journal of Education* in a review of Long's latest school reader, *Wood Folk at School* (a shorter version of *School of the Woods*). Judging the book first-rate, the reviewer urged educators to read both naturalists' books: "you will not love either the less, and you will surely appreciate the matchless insight of Mr. Long into the lives of wood folk." A Michigan reviewer took a more partisan stand and advised teachers that the whole controversy was worthwhile if it did no more than introduce the public to Long's two books. Long's publisher, Ginn & Company, added fuel to the fire by printing and widely distributing a pamphlet defending its author.[51]

At this turn-of-the-century pivot point, there was more going on in the United States than the nature fakers controversy. Industrial monopolies were shaping America and labor was organizing. Automobiles were beginning to appear on the streets and would soon reshape the landscape.

Five days after Roosevelt sailed up the Hudson to visit John Burroughs and his family, for example, Henry Ford sold his first Model A automobile. That summer also marked the appearance of the first Ford dealership; there would be four hundred fifty by 1905. Previously, automobiles had been sold on the side by blacksmiths and by bicycle and farm machinery dealers.[52] Roosevelt, for his part, had more than sham naturalists on his mind. He still had the full responsibilities of his presidency, and that autumn he plotted the fates of Panama and the Panama Canal. One might wonder if it was the best use of the president's time to bother with singing schools for birds and oriole architects.

Most people must have found the whole affair a bit strange—a bunch of grown men, prominent and respectable men at that, arguing over whether porcupines roll downhill or foxes ride across a field on a sheep's back. Some people, such as Lyman Abbott of the *Outlook* magazine, claimed the controversy was too humorous to take seriously. Many, perhaps most, shared the ambivalence displayed by Caspar Whitney, editor of the sporting journal *Outing Magazine*. Burroughs's attack reminded Whitney of the vinegar-bitters forced upon him at prep school: vile, but necessary. The criticism was necessary because "We have grown maudlin over ourselves masquerading as lovelorn rams or unselfish beavers or pacing mustangs or mathematical birds. It has been a veritable carnival of sentimentality." On the other hand, he had considered the "true animal story" to be fiction and kin to Kipling's *The Jungle Book*. As such, these stories were entertaining, in great public demand, and lucrative to writers and publishers alike. Furthermore, they were useful. Whitney pointed out that "'Wild Animals I Have Known' has done more to create real interest in animal life among people at large, young and old, than the entire list of modern scientific naturalists. . . . Not all the Societies for Prevention of Cruelty to Animals, or the Audubon leagues, have done as much. In the light of such work, how insignificant is a lapse in natural history."

He agreed with Long's argument about the importance of animal individuality and the inability of science to acknowledge it. Whitney caught Burroughs with his own words ("Man can have but one interest in nature, namely, to see himself reflected or interpreted there") and hedged his bets by concluding,

> Truth is that I disagree with many of the conclusions of Messers. Seton and Long, and have not seen many of the things they claim to have seen; a too deep tinge of idealism, and animal qualities too suggestively human, have also, I frankly say, sometimes for me marred the narrative. Personally, I prefer less ideal-

ism—that is why the animals stories of Charles G. D. Roberts please me more than any I read. And that may be because Mr. Roberts and I know our animals less intimately than Messers. Seton and Long know theirs—or more intimately; who shall say?[53]

Burroughs and Roosevelt, however, were determined to have their say, and certainly did not share Whitney's tolerance. As the first fires of the controversy cooled, the two men began a protracted war against the sham naturalists. Burroughs wrote articles about natural history misconceptions and animal psychology and sent drafts to the president for his comments. They corresponded often, complaining to each other about new stories by Long and others and calling their opponents all sorts of nasty names. Although they criticized a number of writers, their special animosity was reserved for Long.

However, the two never agreed on one important point. John Burroughs remained adamant in his insistence that animals lived by instinct rather than by parental instruction. For example, in his forthcoming *Century Magazine* article, he wrote, "animals are almost as much under the dominion of absolute nature, or what we call instinct, innate tendency, habit of growth, as are the plants and trees." Theodore Roosevelt advised a more cautious, flexible approach. "I have not the slightest doubt that there is an immense amount of *unconscious* teaching by wood-folk of their offspring," he wrote to Burroughs after reviewing a draft of the article. He urged Burroughs to accept that young animals can learn through the example and imitation of their parents' behavior. When Burroughs protested, Roosevelt argued in the racist parlance of his day that monkeys and salamanders had different mental capabilities:

I think the gap between the highest monkey and an African Bushman is in all respects far less than that between the same monkey and the herring or eft. I should be surprised to find that the salamander or the herring ever in any shape or way did anything that remotely resembled teaching its offspring. On the other hand, I should be rather surprised if it proved true that the higher monkey did not occasionally teach its offspring on some point or other in a way analogous—even if somewhat remotely analogous—to the way in which a Bushman teaches his or her offspring.[54]

Roosevelt avoided becoming publicly entangled in the controversy, arguing that it was inappropriate to use the presidency to attack an individual, although he wanted to "skin Long alive." Nevertheless, he wrote privately to publishers, pointing out their transgressions and those of their authors. Kindly John Burroughs, though, kept urging Roosevelt to go public and "kill" William J. Long in print.[55] He would have to wait four years before his wish was granted.

3.
TELLING THE ANIMALS
FROM THE WILDFLOWERS

As 1903 ended and John Burroughs and Theodore Roosevelt exchanged New Year's greetings, public interest in nature study and wildlife
continued to grow. One author was moved to apologize for writing yet
another bird guide: "In spite of the fact that many excellent books are now
available, the author offers another, both in the belief that there can never
be too many good guides, and in the hope that this book has been especially
adapted to the growing class of beginners in bird study." Nature lovers were
becoming the brunt of popular jokes. One wag claimed that the next
nature book would be entitled *How to Tell the Animals from the Wild
Flowers*, thus spoofing both the sham naturalists (who might be unable to
tell the difference) and the proliferation of nature identification guides. In
1905, *Century Magazine* published a cartoon of a lion strolling along with
a bow on its tail, sporting a frock coat, top hat, cane, and monocle. The
cartoon was captioned, " 'How to Tell the Animals from the Wild Flowers':
A Dandy Lion."[1]

This joke was accompanied by a growing sense of alarm. The magazine
noted that "Hardly a phase of wood or field or marsh or coast life—whether
flowers, trees, mushrooms, insectivora, seashells, big and little game, or
pets—but has had its turn of late years in the scrutiny and classification of
some devoted student," and it described the growing call to return to
nature as taking "on the aspect of a cult which, we fancy, has no
counterpart elsewhere" in the world. This "cult" of nature was becoming

"How to Tell the Animals from the Wild Flowers": A Dandy Lion. By E. W. Kemble. From _Century Magazine_ (June 1905).

ever more attractive to an increasingly urbanized populace. Nature study in the schools and as a hobby continued to grow, and nature books did a brisk business. Urban folk romanticized country life and commuted to the pleasures of the countryside. Meanwhile, ironically, rural professionals were establishing a "country life" movement to improve the poor quality of farmers' lives and to stem the decline of the family farm. Farm children were encouraged to appreciate the natural wonders of their environment and the rewards of rural occupations. School gardens became an important facet of nature education.[2]

Hiking, camping, and other outdoor activities were considered not just fun but also healthy and of benefit to society. The idea that girls did not belong in the outdoors "is a wrong view and an unhealthy one," wrote one woman. "There is no doubt in my mind that it would be better for the growing girls if they were encouraged to indulge more in out-door sports." _Century Magazine_ proclaimed:

> Who can estimate the wholesome and conservative influ-
> ence of this vast employ of our people with the phenomena of
> nature—the healthful rambles over the country, the restful re-
> laxation of the tense mentality of cities, and, to make a paradox,

the humanizing love of animals? It is one feature of American life that may be regarded with unqualified satisfaction—an offset to the hectic winter life of cities, and one of the evidences that, in spite of the alarming growth of sinister influences among us, the heart of the people is sound at the core.[3]

The nature writers helped to establish this phenomenon, and one of them, Ernest Thompson Seton, was creating a youth movement based upon it. His latest book, *Two Little Savages*, was a manual for a generation of boys who wanted to "live as an Indian." His Woodcraft Indians club began out of his efforts to stop vandalism on his Connecticut property. He invited local boys to spend a weekend camping as Indians at Wyndygoul. It was a great success that grew into a national movement as new "tribes" were established in state after state.

Seton was a student and defender of Native Americans, and he made Indian lore the focus of the new boys' club. "To exemplify my outdoor movement," Seton later wrote, "I must have a man who was of this country and climate; who was physically beautiful, clean, unsordid, high-minded, heroic, picturesque and a master of Woodcraft, besides which, he must be already well-known. . . . There was but one figure that seemed to answer all these needs: that was the *Ideal Indian* of Fenimore Cooper and Longfellow." Children, Seton believed, are basically good only if they are given the opportunity, and his child-centered movement was based on this principle. The "Seton Indians" gained social responsibility through self-government, engaged in healthy physical activities in the outdoors, learned woodcraft and natural history, and acquired a sometimes romanticized vision of Native American ways via a multitribal blend of native customs, crafts, myths, and a spirituality rooted in nature.[4]

Americans were in the midst of a complex process of assimilating a new perspective on their relationships with the natural world. This change was expressed in the educational system, recreational activities, and children's activities. The debate about the accuracy of wild animal stories was a literary expression of this process. In the first decade of the twentieth century, American society was contending with a volatile mix of different and often competing values and attitudes regarding nature. For example, the pragmatic, utilitarian view of animals as resources to satisfy our material desires (whether for food, labor, sport, or some other need) was predominant then, as it continues to be today. This view was reflected in more than half the newspaper articles of the time that dealt with animals. Most people, however, viewed animals as individuals with human characteristics. Although only one-third as prevalent as utilitarianism, this "humanistic" or anthropomorphic attitude was unusually common during the first fifteen years of the twentieth century. The attitudes that animals are fearsome and to be avoided or that animals are objects for biological study nearly tied for third and fourth, respectively.[5]

The "realistic" animal stories, which empathized with and anthropomorphized their animal heroes, promoted a feeling of fellowship with wildlife. They frequently preached against the hunter and the trapper, emphasizing the suffering of the hunted and trapped and the tragic loss to their mates and young. This was a popular sentiment, although it was at odds with the predominant utilitarian attitude of the day.

Most often, people harbored conflicting views of wildlife. May Estelle Cook at the _Dial_, for example, strained to resolve the conflict between her desire to see an end to animal suffering and the desire for her own peace of mind in a world of suffering:

> Human nature that is worth anything has to bear a good deal of its own that is pitiful. It should not be weighed down, to no good purpose, with the groaning and travailing of the whole creation. Perhaps by another generation of nature study in school and the reading of nature-books at home, we shall be able to eliminate the man with the gun. But it is not likely, no matter how much nature-writers make us feel the tragedies of the struggle for existence, that we shall take to the woods to do sentinel duty over the victims of that struggle. Nor are we likely to take to the fields to learn our inferiority to the creatures who live there. It is the duty of the naturalists to keep us modest and teach us in this matter; but it is also their duty to teach us without making us over-sad.[6]

Other people had to find their own way through the emotional and philosophical minefield of their time—a time that was giving birth to a new environmental consciousness.

The debate over sham natural history revealed a number of conflicting approaches to nature: Burroughs's mechanistic view of animals as little more than instinctive automatons; Long's vision of the peaceful life of wild animals whose thought processes may differ in degree but not in kind from those of humans; and Roosevelt's more sophisticated view of animal psychology that found a middle ground between the other two approaches while still maintaining the falsity of Long's observations and conclusions. In addition, Long's anthropomorphic view of animals was at odds with the scientific and utilitarian attitudes of his critics. What exacerbated the problem was that Long's emotional and philosophical responses often distorted, rather than informed, his observations and interpretations of nature.

Animal Surgery

At the end of 1903, William J. Long published a new book, *A Little Brother to the Bear*. The *New York Times* liked it and pointed out that "close observation and loving attention to the details of wood life run all through the work."[7] The book, though, advanced a fantastical set of propositions about wildlife, including their methods for treating injuries, that stimulated a great deal of debate during the following few years, mostly behind the scenes and among scientists. This debate reveals a good deal about the conflicts between Long and the scientists and about Long's methods of interpreting the virtues of his woodfolk. In the preface, Long proclaimed:

> Except where it is plainly stated otherwise, all the incidents and observations have passed under my own eyes and have been confirmed later by other observers. . . . I have simply tried to make all these animals as interesting to the reader as they were to me when I discovered them.

This did not satisfy Burroughs and Roosevelt, who began criticizing some of the chapters when they first appeared as magazine articles. One article in *Harper's* told of Canadian lynxes hunting in packs, tracking their prey by scent, and luring a curious caribou within striking range by running in circles to catch its attention. The president had never encountered such behavior, which he placed on the same level as *The Arabian Nights*. When another essay, "Animal Surgery," which described how animals treated their own medical problems, first appeared in the *Outlook*, Burroughs thought it a pack of lies and felt it was immoral for the magazine to print it. Roosevelt simply thought Long was insane, and set off to have a word with the magazine's editor, Lyman Abbott. He left disappointed, because Abbott would not take the matter seriously.[8]

Long's theories about animal surgery caught the attention of the scientific community, but not in the way he might have wished. "That the animals do practice at times a rude kind of medicine and surgery upon themselves is undeniable," Long asserted in *A Little Brother to the Bear*. "The only question about it is," he wrote with a glance over his shoulder for Burroughs's shape on the horizon, "How do they know? To say it is a matter of instinct is but begging the question. It is also three-fourths foolishness, for many of the things that animals do are beyond the farthest scope of instinct."

Having thrown down his gauntlet, Long proceeded to tell how muskrat, beaver, and bear bandaged their wounds and the stumps of amputated limbs by coating them with pine pitch, spruce resin, or clay to keep the injury clean and the flies away. (Aquatic animals do not use clay, he suggested, because it would wash off.) "When a coon's foot is shattered by a bullet," Long wrote, "he will cut it off promptly and wash the stump in running water, partly to reduce the inflammation and partly, no doubt, to make it perfectly clean." He also reported that if an eider duck, which feeds on saltwater mussels, suffers the misfortune of having the mussel

Animal Surgery. By Charles Copeland. From William J. Long, A *Little Brother to the Bear* (Boston: Ginn, 1903).

clamp onto its tongue, it will fly from the ocean to a freshwater pond, dip its head under the water, and let the fresh water kill the mussel, which then drops off. Pondering this tale, Roosevelt wondered why the duck would go to all the trouble of flying inland to a pond, when it might just as well walk onto the shore and wait for the air to kill the mussel. Burroughs argued that the bird stuck its head under the water simply to cool its inflamed injury.[9]

Long was careful to maintain a flexible position when he discussed the issue of instinct versus learning. He argued that birds are "more subject to instinct" than mammals. Of the raccoon's licking its wound, he wrote: "So far this may or may not be pure instinct. For I do not know, and who will tell me, whether a child puts his wounded hand to his mouth and sucks and cleanses the hurt by pure instinct, or because he has seen others do it, or because he has had his hurts kissed away in childhood, and so imitates the action unconsciously when his mother is not near?"

There is no question that an injured animal can find comfort by licking its wounds or that this can have hygienic benefits. The problem arose when Long described the animals' actions as intentional attempts to keep the wound free from infection. He strained credulity when he proposed that animals "bandage" their injuries with pine pitch, despite his use of testimony from an "old Indian" to prove its truthfulness. A few years earlier, Seton had touched on the same theme in his story about a grizzly bear. "The licking removed the dirt," he wrote, "and by massage reduced the inflammation, and it plastered the hair down as a sort of dressing over the wound to keep out the air, dirt, and microbes." However, Seton made a point of describing the bear's actions as "wholly instinctive."[10]

A few years later another writer, Clarence Hawkes, developed the story still further. In his *The Trail to the Woods* he told of a fox that caught its foot in a trap and was forced to chew it off to get free. After reducing the bleeding by soaking his limb in cold spring water, the fox set off "to look for a balsam tree, to apply a favorite remedy that his mother had made use of" when he was young. Finding the tree, he lapped the balsam "up with his tongue and applied [it] to the ragged stump. The balsam was very sticky, and held the ragged ends of skin over the broken bone. . . . In half an hour's time he had stopped the blood and made a very respectable stump with these simple remedies." Hawkes, however, was blind. He had lost both his sight and a leg in boyhood accidents and knew most of his natural history from childhood memories and from books that were read aloud to him. He considered Long a friend and probably derived this story directly from Long's tales of animal surgery. (When Burroughs discovered *The Trail to the Woods*, he threatened to get on Hawkes's own trail, but apparently abandoned the scent.)[11]

Long, though, did not say that either he or his Indian informants had actually seen animals apply the pitch to their wounds, only that pitch was found on the wounds and, thus, that it must have been applied by design. Here lay a big part of the problem. As May Estelle Cook put it in her review of *A Little Brother to the Bear*:

> He asserts with equal confidence that does rather than bucks usually lead the herd, and that the young deer he watched running in circles on the beach are "being taught to twist and double quickly." In each case, the first statement is fact, the second interpretation. It is through failure to make this distinction clear that Mr. Long has laid himself open to criticism by other natural-

ists. . . . Yet it is doubtful if anyone . . . will soon write more entertaining stories than these.[12]

Long continually confused the line between objective reporting and unfounded, even wishful, interpretation, a problem that plagued his writing and continued to invite criticism.

A Woodcock Genius

The animal surgery story that received the greatest attention was about a "woodcock genius" that set and applied a cast to its own broken leg. Long had witnessed the event twenty years earlier, he wrote, when he was in his mid-teens. From the opposite side of a stream he watched a woodcock do an amazing thing:

> At first he took soft clay in his bill from the edge of the water and seemed to be smearing it on one leg near the knee. Then he fluttered away on one foot for a short distance and seemed to be pulling tiny roots and fibers of grass, which he worked into the clay that he had already smeared on his leg. Again he took some clay and plastered it over the fibers, putting on more and more till I could plainly see the enlargement, working away with strange, silent intentness for fully fifteen minutes, while I watched and wondered, scarce believing my eyes. Then he stood perfectly still for a full hour under an overhanging sod, where the eye could with

Long's Woodcock Applying a Cast to its Broken Leg. By Charles Copeland. From William J. Long, *A Little Brother to the Bear* (Boston: Ginn, 1903).

difficulty find him, his only motion meanwhile being an occasional rubbing and smoothing of the clay bandage with his bill, until it hardened enough to suit him, whereupon he fluttered away from the brook and disappeared in the thick woods.[13]

Long believed that the "woodcock genius" was treating a broken leg, but remained silent about it for years until his suspicion was confirmed. First, he found two hunters who had shot birds whose legs had once been broken and had healed perfectly, and finally he chanced upon a lawyer who, when hunting, had bagged a woodcock with a lump of clay on its leg. On removing the clay, Long reported, the man had found a broken bone.

The fact that Long attributed such behavior to "one or two rare individuals here and there more original than their fellows" did not ward off criticism. Scientists went wild. Throughout the spring of 1904, the letters section of the journal *Science* bristled with indignation. The letters revealed the growing, unfortunate polarization between those who believed that nature study was a branch of science education and those who believed that the goal of nature study was first to instill in students an appreciation of nature.

The biologist William Morton Wheeler began the exchange in February. After commending Burroughs's *Atlantic* article, Wheeler described Long's "Animal Surgery" as "a series of anecdotes which for rank and impossible humanization of the animal can hardly be surpassed." Wheeler focused his attack on the woodcock story:

> Mr. Long virtually claims that a woodcock not only has an understanding of the theory of casts as adapted to fractured limbs, but is able to apply this knowledge in practice. The bird is represented as knowing the qualities of clay and mud, their lack of cohesion unless mixed with fibrous substances, their tendency to harden on exposure to the air, and to disintegrate in water. Inasmuch as woodcocks have for generations been living and feeding in muddy places, we could, perhaps, although not without some abuse of the imagination, suppose the bird to possess this knowledge. But the mental horizon of Mr. Long's woodcock is not bounded by the qualities of mud. He is familiar with the theories of bone formation and regeneration—in a word, with osteogenesis, which, by the way, is never clearly grasped by some of our university juniors.

He went on to suggest that it was not unusual to find mud on the leg of a bird that frequented muddy places. Wheeler was particularly distressed to find animal stories such as this used in public schools. Such stories provide amusement, he wrote, "more, in fact, than the authors contemplate, since it not only titillates the fancy of the boys and girls, but adds to the gayety of comparative psychologists. Those who are attacking the fads of our educational system will find plenty of work awaiting them as soon as they turn their attention to the excrescences of 'nature study.' "[14]

Wheeler's letter to *Science* stimulated a flurry of correspondence from others eager to take a shot at Long. Frank Chapman repeated the *Boston Evening Transcript* report of the Andover seminary "I always love to think" incident to demonstrate that Long was not a liar, simply a shoddy thinker. Chapman, too, feared that schoolchildren were being miseducated, a serious problem magnified by the very quality and persuasiveness of Long's writing. "In a well-meant but somewhat ill-considered attempt to stamp out the fire," he wrote, "Mr. Burroughs merely scattered it. From an insignificant smudge, it has become a roaring blaze and its sparks are kindling throughout the land." Chapman called upon naturalists to do their duty and "enlighten the general public, and especially those entrusted with the education of children," to the dangers of Long's stories.[15]

Others wrote to add new accounts of Long's transgressions and those of other writers. William Harper Davis of Columbia University acknowledged that Burroughs, too, made errors of fact: for example, the time he wrote about a snake closing its eyes, although in reality snakes have no eyelids. Long, though, represented a fundamentally different class of writer. "As a romancer," Davis wrote, "[Long] does not stand alone, but as a 'hopeless romancer' he occupies a unique position." Furthermore, Davis saw "Long and his allies" as a threat to rationality and feared that under their influence children faced "growing up with minds perverted and ill adapted to survive as rational beings in a world of fact and law, though they struggle never so hard against both in the supposed interest of their individuality."[16]

W. F. Ganong of Smith College felt that Long and Charles G. D. Roberts "tell about animals, not as they are, but as people like to think they are. . . . To accomplish this end, they have had to cut loose from the trammels of fact which hampered their predecessors, and have given their imaginations full play, thus producing fascinating works of fiction disguised as natural history." The problems were, Ganong wrote, that Long avowed that his stories were true and that Roberts, while not overtly claiming truth, neglected to confirm that they were fiction. Ganon felt that Long's books contained valuable facts but that they were so mixed with untruths as to be "practically valueless for any scientific purpose."[17]

Only one person wrote to *Science* in Long's defense (apart from Long, that is), and she presented a good case. Ellen Hayes admired Long's writing and felt he was being treated unreasonably. In response to Wheeler's incredulous claim that the woodcock surgeon must have known the physiology and theory of bone growth and repair, she pointed out:

> It is [Long's] critic, Mr. Wheeler, who "virtually" affirms that a woodcock could not apply mud to a broken leg without a knowledge of surgery; and it is much as if he should say that a man who blows on his fingers to warm them or on his tea to cool it has a knowledge of the laws of thermodynamics and is ready to discuss entropy or an indicator diagram. It is the merest commonplace fact that in order to avoid danger, to lessen pain, to save life, to gain pleasure, human beings are constantly performing acts the underlying principles of which they understand scarcely any better than a woodcock understands the principles of surgery.

She went on to condemn Wheeler's logical assumptions, which seemed to be: (1) if an animal does something beneficial to itself, then it must understand the principles underlying that action; (2) if a person has not witnessed an event, then no one else could have witnessed it; and (3) "unless an event is of common occurrence it can not occur at all." Hayes scolded the scientists, writing, "Whom the gods wish to destroy they first lure into premises of this sort."[18]

Finally, in May, Long rallied to his own defense. He was understandably upset and suggested that William Harper Davis had demonstrated anything but scientific detachment. To make his point, Long listed three dozen words and phrases used by Davis to describe him. The list began with "Sham, crass, crude, aimless, pitiful, preposterous" and ended with "a facile fabricator, an influence for evil, chief of a tribe, hopeless romancer, incapable of reform, type of his species, intellectual anarchist, wild ass, a sad case." In Long's opinion, all of the attacks were biased and refutable. His critics, he concluded, while cloaking themselves in the mantle of science, were certainly not demonstrating its spirit of objectivity.

"If scientists and comparative-psychologists are honestly looking for new facts in the animal world," he offered, "I have enough to fill several regular editions of *Science*, every one of which is supported not only by my own personal observation, but by the testimony of other honest men whose word can be taken without hesitation." To the question of why he did not present his evidence in proper scientific form, Long responded:

> (1) I am accustomed to be believed when I speak. . . . (2) I have gone into the outdoor world as a nature lover, not as a scientist

. . . to open [people's] eyes to the facts of animal life which the scientist, as well as the vacationist, has overlooked, under the supposition that birds and animals are governed solely by instinct and reflex impulses. And (3) while the scientist deals with laws and generalizations and works largely with species, I have dealt always with individuals, and have tried to understand every animal from moose to woodmouse that I have met in the wilderness.

As for the woodcock story, Long provided an affidavit from an Ohio man who had also shot a woodcock "which had evidently broken its leg above the knee joint. There was a bandage around it, composed of a hard clay-like substance, interwoven with grass or a woody fiber of some kind. The bone seemed to have been set properly and had knit perfectly." The man had shown the specimen to a physician, who said "that it was a better job than nine tenths of the surgeons could do." Long also had a second affidavit from a Connecticut man who reported that he had seen four similar casts. Eighteen years earlier the man was given a woodcock leg with "a clay cast in which some small feathers of the bird and some grass had been interwoven, apparently to make it more adhesive." In more recent years he had handled three similar woodcock legs and casts, and each cast was "made more effective by the interweaving of dry grasses or small bird's feathers."[19] The man had opened one of the casts and found a broken leg. Both men provided statements from other people who confirmed seeing the specimens. Neither man, though, presented any specimens for study and neither had seen a woodcock actually apply a cast. *Science* followed Long's letter with the note, "We hope that this discussion will not be carried further." Frank Chapman later claimed that the editor closed the discussion because he had been "alarmed" by Long's reply.[20]

William T. Hornaday also attacked Long's animal surgery stories, dismissing a similar tale of a cast on the leg of a ruffed grouse as "too absurd for serious consideration." Drawing on his experience with the care of zoo animals, Hornaday pointed out that "In matters involving intelligence, such as in the treatment of wounds, or disease, below the higher Primates there is not more than one out of every hundred which has sense enough to comprehend a relief measure, or which will not fight the surgeon to the utmost . . . [or] will permit a bandage to remain on a broken leg when they have the power to tear it off. 'Animal surgery,' indeed!"[21]

Long was the only person who claimed to have actually seen a bird apply a mud cast, and he had made the observation as a teenager, twenty years before. If we grant that he witnessed the event and that his memory was accurate, there is the question of interpretation—did what he observed support his conclusions, or were his conclusions distorted by his assumptions about the mental capabilities of wildlife? This is always a difficult problem, far more so than Long ever acknowledged.

Take, for example, the case of the swallow with a horsehair bandage reported to the *Medical Record* by a Kansas physician. In 1876 the physician's informant, a Mr. O'Brien, examined a nestling and found that its broken leg was wrapped in horsehair. O'Brien removed the hair and returned the bird to the nest. The next day, the leg was again wrapped in hair. Leaving the bird alone, he discovered two weeks later "that the hairs were being cautiously removed, only a few each day, and finally when all were taken off the callus was distinctly felt, and the union of the bone evidently perfect, as the bird was able to fly off with its mates." This convinced the physician "that the intelligence of animals differs from that of man only in degree and not in kind."[22]

There is, however, another, more plausible explanation of these events. Horses were ubiquitous at that time, and horsehair was a common material in bird nests. It was not uncommon for birds, young and adult, to become entangled and even strangled to death by these long, strong hairs. (This was the fate of a sparrow in one of Ernest Thompson Seton's stories.)[23] Horsehair may well have been included in the construction of the swallow's muddy nest. Perhaps the swallow nestling repeatedly became entangled in it by accident, rather than by design. Loose hairs may have stuck to and wrapped around the leg, especially if there was an oozing wound. Mr. O'Brien, however, could not imagine a way for the hairs to become wrapped around the leg except through parental care. It is most likely, though, that his imagination converted an accidental entanglement into an incident of bird surgery.

A year after the debate in *Science* about Long's woodcock, John Hardy chanced upon a weak, crippled pectoral sandpiper on the edge of the Concord River in Bedford, Massachusetts. Hardy, an amateur ornithologist, picked up the bird and noticed what appeared to be a clump of mud on one of its legs. He knew that the lump was unusual, because he worked for a poultry and wild game company at Boston's Faneuil Hall Market and, although he had handled thousands of birds, until that day beside the Concord River he had never seen anything like what Long described. The lump appeared to be a mixture of mud and feathers. Hardy's specimen eventually came to the attention of the ornithologist William Brewster, of the Harvard Museum of Comparative Zoology, and Harold Bowditch, a young naturalist. The men thought they might have tangible evidence for Long's claims. However, after subjecting the specimen to detailed examinations and even x-raying it, they concluded that the leg was not broken. Brewster consulted with Dr. Arthur T. Cabot, who explained the "cast" as earth and feathers that simply adhered to fluids seeping from the bird's injured leg. Eighty years later, a team of veterinarians examined the specimen and found that the lump was not an applied cast, but a calcified blood clot.[24]

The lump on the sandpiper's leg and the "casts" on all of the woodcock legs may not have shared the same origins. Nevertheless, they were all described in a similar manner and may well have been the same kind of thing. The connection between the mud casts and the sandpiper's blood clot grew stronger in 1907, when Long was again forced, as we shall see, to publicly defend himself against his critics. This time, he finally produced an actual specimen in support of his woodcock story. "Dr. Long took from a case the severed leg of a fowl, around which was bound a jacket of feathers glued together with some adhesive stuff," reported the *New York Times*. "A shot wound could be seen in the bone of the leg underneath the jacket, which had worn loose." Long described this as "the leg of a grouse which has bound up its wounded limb with a bandage of feathers plucked from its own body and cemented with some sticky substance the nature of which we have not been able to discover." William T. Hornaday described the specimen as "a ruffed grouse, having mingled blood and mud on a broken leg," and called Long's claim that this was a bandage "too absurd for serious consideration." Long, though, responded that "there was no blood or mud on the leg or in the record." Despite Long's assertion to the contrary, the mysterious "sticky substance" was most likely dried blood.[25]

Woodcocks are very hardy animals with a remarkable ability to recover from injuries. They can survive a missing leg, missing toes, and even a self-inflicted scalping sustained while trying to escape a trap. They, and other birds, are quite able to recover from a broken leg without the benefit of a cast.[26] William J. Long's "woodcock genius" was the product of his own inventive genius, despite his genuine belief that it was real. In his youth he probably saw a woodcock pecking at a chance lump of mud on its leg, or at a muddy clot over an injury, and assumed that the bird was constructing a cast. This is also the most likely explanation of the "casts" found by the people who rallied in his defense.

Kindergartens for Kingfishers and Schools for Fish Hawks

Long's *A Little Brother to the Bear* did not confine itself to animal surgery. It also described how, in the tradition of his *School of the Woods*, young kingfishers learn to fish:

> The school was a quiet shallow pool with a muddy bottom against which the fish showed clearly, and with a convenient stub leaning

over it from which to swoop. The old birds had caught a score of minnows, killed them, and dropped them here and there under the stub. Then they brought the young birds, showed them their game, and told them by repeated examples to dive and get it. The little fellows were hungry and took to the sport keenly; but one was timid, and only after the mother had twice dived and brought up a fish—which she showed to the timid one and then dropped back in a most tantalizing way—did he muster up resolution to take the plunge.[27]

This is similar to an earlier story in his *School of the Woods* about how fish-hawks (ospreys) are taught to fish. Long claimed that without instruction from their parents, ospreys "would go straight back to the old hawk habit of hunting the woods, which is much easier." In his story, a young osprey's mother prevented this by coaching and encouraging it to fish, but her young student had no success on its own. Then the dutiful mother had an idea:

> Gripping her fish tightly, she bends in her slow flight and paralyzes it by a single blow in the spine from her hooked beak. Then she drops it back into the whitecaps, where, jumping to the top of my rock, I can see it occasionally struggling near the surface. *Cheecep!* "try it now," she whistles. *Pip, pip!* "here goes!" cries the little one who failed before; and down he drops, *souse!* going clear under in his impatient hunger, forgetting precept and example and past experience.
>
> Again the waves race over him; but there is a satisfied note in the mother's whistle which tells me that she sees him, and that he is doing well. In a moment he is out again, with a great rush and sputter, gripping his fish and *pip-pipping* his exultation.[28]

Perhaps kingfishers and ospreys do become more skilled with experience. One begins to balk, though, when it comes to parental coaching and practice sessions with intentionally injured or killed targets. Burroughs, for one, rejected the whole notion. "If [Long] had said that he saw the parent birds fishing with hook and line," he wrote in the *Atlantic*, "or dragging a net of their own knitting, his statement would have been just as credible." In his 1903 *North American Review* article, though, Long defended these stories and claimed that "Mr. Mauran Furbish, who probably knows more of the New Brunswick wilderness than any other man, has told me since my book was written that he had seen the same thing." The full account of Furbish's experience reveals a good deal about Long's abilities as a naturalist.[29]

Mauran Furbish and William J. Long had been good friends and neighbors, often taking Sunday dinner together. Nevertheless, Furbish did not consider Long a reliable observer, despite the pastor's firm belief in his own truthfulness, and this was a case in point. W. F. Ganong, who had fished in New Brunswick with Furbish, asked the man to substantiate Long's claim. "[Furbish] replied that he had simply told Mr. Long of our finding one day a wounded gaspereau [alewife] floating at the foot of a lake and that Mr. Long 'had furnished all of the romance and the reason for their being there.'" William Brewster later chanced upon Furbish and learned more details. The gaspereau had a crippling cut along the side of its head that Furbish thought came from hitting against a sharp rock. When Furbish returned to Connecticut and discussed the matter with Long, the latter asked whether there were any fishhawks in the region where the fish had been found. Yes, answered Furbish, but not in the immediate area where the fish was found. Long said that there must have been a family nearby, for an adult had caught the fish at sea and carried it back to the lake so the young fishhawks could practice catching fish. There were, though, no talon marks on the fish where the hawk would have grasped it during the flight. It appears that Long was so sure of what had happened that he did not need to be encumbered with confirming facts. And he was so convinced by his own conclusions that he, with all good intentions, sent his critics to Mauran Furbish to confirm his story.[30]

Long defended himself after Ganong first reported the story in New Brunswick's _Saint John Globe_ in March 1904. He condemned Ganong's attack and implied that the scientist's own work was unsound. He did, though, acknowledge that Ganong had caught him in one error. "My use of [Furbish's] name may have been unwarranted," Long wrote, "and I cry mea culpa sincerely." In any event, he wrote, the error was insignificant. "My fish-hawk article was already in print, and was based solely upon my own observation, backed up by that of Indians and hunters. At the time of my conversation with Mr. Furbish, the article had not been criticized nor questioned, and was not attacked for more than a year afterwards.... If my impression [from Furbish's comments] were wrong, it is simply one bit of supplementary evidence the less, and I regret having used it."[31]

The error, though, was significant. It revealed how quick Long was to grasp at any straws that might support his conclusions. He believed Furbish's account confirmed his fishhawk story because he wanted to believe the story himself. He seemed unable to evaluate his wildlife observations or those of others with any skepticism or detachment. Long's stories humanized animals because he believed they were akin to humans. John Burroughs, on the other hand, believed nothing of the sort, because he understood animals to be instinctive machines. Each was blinded by his bias.

While the scientists were getting their licks in at Long, Burroughs began to focus on animal psychology with a series of articles in *Century Magazine*, arguing that animals functioned with little more than instinct and a limited ability to learn from experience. He reported with amazement a letter printed in a newspaper from someone who claimed (Burroughs was unsure whether it was written in seriousness) to have witnessed a group of crows try, convict, and execute one of their own—the victim's wings were even tied behind its back with bark! Burroughs also attacked the errant Hermit, publishing the private criticisms that he and Roosevelt had exchanged earlier, and illustrated his points about animal psychology with numerous examples of animal behavior and nature observations. (His articles, though, often repeated the same things over and over again, with little more than changes in his illustrative examples.) Burroughs continued to attack the natural history romancers and shoddy observers. In his view:

> Most of us, in observing the wild life about us, see more or see less than the truth. We see less when our minds are dull, or preoccupied, or blunted by want of interest. This is true of most country people. We see more when we read the lives of the wild creatures about us in the light of our human experience, and impute to the birds and beasts human motives and methods. This is too often true of the eager city man or woman who sallies out into the country to study nature.

Burroughs believed that science was our window to the truth, for "only a person with the scientific habit of mind can be trusted to report things as they are."[32]

Century Magazine provided its own spoof of Long's *School of the Woods* with a full-page illustration entitled "A Lesson in Wisdom." It showed Mother Nature sitting in a field with five foxes gathered around and staring intently at her book, *The Fox Who Lost His Tail in the Trap*. The magazine also published, in the same issue as one of Burroughs's articles, Ernest Thompson Seton's only public response to Burroughs's *Atlantic* attack. It was a lighthearted and oblique fable about a critic named Little Mucky who climbed to the top of a hill named Big Periodic and threw mud at a newcomer who was drawing attention away from him: "MORAL: Notoriety is a poisonous substitute for fame."[33]

"A Lesson in Wisdom." By Frederick A. Church. From *Century Magazine* (March 1904).

Despite these minor skirmishes, the public debate died down in 1904. The *Atlantic Monthly* found so little controversy that it published Burroughs's article "The Literary Treatment of Nature." The article was a more detached journey over by now familiar ground in which Burroughs publicly made peace with Seton. Burroughs's correspondence with Theodore Roosevelt slowed to a trickle, and the president complained about little more than the sorry state of the Yellowstone bears, which were getting their feet caught in tin cans. Civilization had found the Yellowstone wilderness.[34]

A Philosophical Brier Patch

In December 1904, after nearly two years of debate over his abilities as an observer of nature, William J. Long went blind. Page one of the *New York Times* carried a brief report:

> Stamford, Conn., Dec. 9—The Rev. Dr. William J. Long, prominent as a writer and lecturer on animal life and kindred subjects, has been stricken totally blind and the chances of his ever recovering his sight are poor.
>
> For years one of his eyes was weak, and chiefly on that account he retired from the ministry in 1903. Last week he lost the sight of both eyes. He is confined in a dark room and bears his affliction with cheerfulness.

Despite his illness, Long continued writing. In January 1905 he wrote a preface to *Northern Trails*, a forthcoming book about wildlife in Newfoundland and Labrador. He also began writing a series of *Harper's Monthly* essays under the pseudonym Peter Rabbit. He accomplished this in the midst of blindness by writing between his fingers to guide the pen along the line. "The darkness was good for thinking," he later wrote, "but bad for writing, and it made proper revision impossible." Long's physician predicted that his sight might return, and so it did after some months.[35]

Almost a year later, Long delivered a sermon at the Park Congregational Church in Hartford, Conn. "He is preaching with his old time power and eloquence," a reporter announced, "and we rejoice with him that he can again do the work of his choice." But the rejoicing was premature, for this was one of at least three bouts with blindness that Long faced during his life. "Hardly had my work [as a minister] well begun," he wrote years later, "when Blindness stood beside me with the grim order, 'Give up preaching and public speaking, or go in darkness for the rest of your life.'" This was a severe blow for Long, who was dedicated to the ministry. Although he delivered occasional lectures and sermons, he never returned to the ministry except on an informal basis. Long's illness bore the marks of hysterical blindness brought on by emotional stress, but whatever the cause, he persevered.[36]

Long's Peter Rabbit essays presented a rabbit's view of the human condition, animal intelligence, and the sham natural history controversy. They revealed a new side of Long: his gentle sense of humor and his skills at social satire. When the collected essays were published in 1906 as *Brier-Patch Philosophy*, the book included this dedication: "To those who have found Their Own World to be something of a Brier-Patch the Rabbit Dedicates his little book of Cheerful Philosophy." The book began, "There is this difference between a man and a rabbit: the rabbit lives in a brier patch, and his philosophy makes his little world a good place; the man lives in an excellent world, and by his philosophy generally makes it over into the worst kind of brier patch, either for himself or for his neighbors." The voice of Peter Rabbit provided an opportunity to address the issues with wit and detachment. "[T]his is not an animal story or a book for children," Long wrote. "Though more or less disguised, it is nevertheless an effort to understand the common life of animals and men."[37] It did little more than restate Long's well-established views about animals, but it was the most delightful statement he had yet made.

Theodore Roosevelt, however, did not like the Peter Rabbit articles and felt magazines such as *Harper's* were irresponsible in publishing such things. On the other hand, he chastised John Burroughs about holding such an extreme position in favor of instinct and warned:

> Long and his crew have been only too glad to divert attention from the issue, which was their untruthfulness in reporting what they purported to have seen, to the issue of how much intelligence animals display—as to whether they teach their young, and so forth. Some of the closest observers I know—men like Hart Merriam, for instance—feel that animals do teach their young in certain cases and among the higher forms; and feel very strongly that the higher mammals, such as dogs, monkeys, wolves, foxes, and so forth, have mental faculties which are really far more akin to those of man than they are to the very rudimentary faculties out of which they were developed in the lower forms of life. I am inclined to sympathize with both of these views myself. I think there has been preposterous exaggeration among those who speak of the conscious teaching by animals of their young; but I feel that the balance of proof certainly is in favor of this being at least occasionally true. . . . all I mean is that I would be careful not to state my position in such extreme form as to let them shift the issue to one in which they will have very excellent observers on their side.

Burroughs still did not accept this position, although he did grant that dogs had some limited ability to think. For his part, Roosevelt gave in to Burroughs's arguments against the notion that animals teach their young to avoid traps.[38]

Burroughs continued his jabs regarding animal reasoning, often making it the theme of a natural history column he was writing for *Outing Magazine*. The magazine also published a pair of articles debating the theme "Do Animals Reason"; Burroughs penned the one against the idea. He assembled many of his sham natural history articles in *Ways of Nature*, which was published late in 1905. He hoped that this would end his involvement with the topic, but it did not.[39]

Burroughs's essays on animal psychology were quite different from the more poetic treatment of animals that characterized his writing before 1903. In his preface to *Ways of Nature*, he wrote, "My readers will find this volume quite a departure in certain ways from the tone and spirit of my previous books, especially in regard to the subject of animal intelligence. Heretofore I have made the most of every gleam of intelligence of bird or four-footed beast that came under my observation, often, I fancy, making too much of it, and giving the wild creatures credit for more 'sense' than they really possessed." The willful misrepresentations of recent writers, however, "led me to set about examining the whole subject of animal life and instinct in a way I have never done before." Now, Burroughs asserted, "Of our faculties I concede to [animals'] perception, sense memory, and association of memories, and little else."[40]

However, Burroughs felt that William J. Long's position was moderate when he saw it stated outside of the nature story format. Long had published such a piece in *Harper's*. "Most of our difficulty in the past has been due to the fact that, like the theologians, we have drawn lines of distinction where none have any right to exist," Long wrote. "We have gone on the general supposition that reason guides man and instinct guides the animal, and that between the two a sharp line is drawn. Probably no such line exists between instinct and reason; and what separates man from the animals is not a line, but a million years of development. As Quinet observes, 'Between man and the brutes there intervenes all history.'" Long appealed to no less an authority than Darwin and Darwin's "effort to establish the fact that all of man's faculties without exception are evolved by gradual process from the faculties of the animals" and argued that:

> instinct is not the animal, and reason is not the man. With man's reason are his will and emotions—love, fear, courage, generosity,—none of these separate and distinct entities, but all combined together to make the man. With the animal's instinct are other things that we must consider—something which looks like will, and emotions of love, fear, courage, and self-denial, which are undeniably like those in our own hearts, however much they differ in degree. Since we share so much in common of the physical and emotional life, it is hardly more than to be expected that the animal himself, apart from his instinct, should share something of our rational facilities.[41]

Theory and practice, however, are two different things. The finest theory does not necessarily insure sound action. Long was still open to attack for the way he translated his theories into animal stories.

Wayeeses the Strong One

In September 1905, George H. Locke had a pleasant thought. Locke, a member of Ginn & Company's editorial staff, knew of Theodore Roosevelt's love of the outdoors and felt the president was certain to enjoy the company's latest nature book as much as he had. With Ginn & Company's compliments, he sent Roosevelt the first copy of William J.

Long's book *Northern Trails*. The gesture, it appears, was made in good faith, for Roosevelt had yet to publicly announce his views about Long. Locke soon discovered what those views were after the president fired off a four-page, typed letter to his unsuspecting benefactor.[42]

Roosevelt enjoyed the book and read it to his children. He cautioned them, though, to judge it on the same basis as Kipling's *The Jungle Book*. The caution had merit, despite Long's assurance that "Every smallest incident recorded here is as true as careful and accurate observation can make it." (Mabel Osgood Wright described *Northern Trails* as a product of Long's "old formula, which was made into kindling, burned, and the ashes scattered to the four winds" by Burroughs's earlier attacks.) Although it was a collection of stories based on Long's travels in Canada, nearly half of the book was occupied by a single narrative involving the great white wolf Wayeeses. Again, Long asserted that "every incident in this wolf's life, from his grasshopper hunting to the cunning caribou chase, and from the den in the rocks to the meeting of wolf and children on the storm-swept barrens, is minutely true in fact, and is based squarely upon my own observations and that of my Indians." The wolf, though, was not great enough to withstand Roosevelt's attack. It provided an opportunity for him to strike at the accuracy of Long's observations without entering into the confused territory of animal intelligence.[43]

The story, actually a 170-page novel of six chapters, followed the life of a wolf as she raised her young; hunted rabbits, mice and other small game, and caribou; and eventually assisted two lost Indian children by guiding them back to their home.[44] Roosevelt was particularly upset by the account of how wolves killed caribou. "Like a flash he leaped in on the fawns," reported Long. "One quick snap of the long jaws with the terrible fangs; then, as if the whole thing was a bit of play, he loped away easily [and waited] . . . one quick snap of the old wolf's teeth just behind the fore legs having pierced the heart more surely than a hunter's bullet." Another kill involved a young bull caribou: "A terrific rush, a quick snap under the stag's chest just behind the fore legs, where the heart lay; then the big wolf leaped aside and sat down quietly again to watch." The caribou moved off with "a swaying, weakening trot." The wolf followed, "but holding himself with tremendous will power from rushing in headlong and driving the game, which might run for miles if too hard pressed," until the animal fell.[45]

"Now this is sheer nonsense and must come from a complete misunderstanding of how game acts when hurt," Roosevelt wrote confidentially to George Locke. Drawing upon his extensive hunting experience, he pointed out that "A gut-shot or broken-legged caribou will, if hard pressed, go for miles whereas if not hard pressed it will lie down. . . . But if an animal is hurt in the heart or around the heart, as here described, it makes not the slightest difference whether it is hard pressed or not, any more than it would make if it were hurt in the brain or spine. Such a heart struck animal will usually make a short, rapid dash, but it is a physical impossibility for it to continue that dash."[46]

If this was not enough, the very method of the kill, a snap to the heart, strained beyond belief. "Now not only is this not the usual way in which a wolf kills, but it is so very unusual that I am tempted to doubt if it is a mortal way at all, it certainly can not happen normally as described. . . . I have never known of one instance in which the heart was the point of the

A Quick Snap Where the Heart Lay. By Charles Copeland. From William J. Long, *Northern Trails* (Boston: Ginn, 1905).

wolf's attack." There were three difficulties. First, a wolf's jaw cannot open wide enough to take a caribou's chest in its mouth, and such a wound could not be inflicted from the side. Second, a wolf's teeth are too small to penetrate through the chest, beyond the ribs, and into the heart. Finally, "If a caribou were standing or running the wolf would have to turn upside down, like a shark, in order to deliver such a bite," an awkward and potentially dangerous position for the wolf. "It is possible," Roosevelt wrote, "although most improbable that under exceptional circumstances a wolf might kill a fawn in this very clumsy way, but I am inclined to think that with an old caribou it would be a physical impossibility." (Even artist Charles Copeland had a difficult time depicting the act in the book's full-page illustration, "A quick snap where the heart lay," which looked more like the wolf was about to bite the caribou's leg.) "Wolves normally kill large animals by biting at the flanks and haunches," Roosevelt informed Locke. "Occasionally, but much more rarely, they seize by the throat."[47]

Roosevelt dismissed the tale of the wolf helping the lost Indian children find their way home as a fairy tale in the class of Kipling's _The Jungle Book_ or Jack London's _The Call of the Wild_, as was the entire book. (Indeed, Long's version of wolf kill behavior may have been influenced by London's book, which referred to "the quick wolf snap" and "The wolf manner of fighting, to strike and leap away." But even Roosevelt wrote of wolves killing "with a few savage snaps.") Aside from the obvious problem of the story itself, Roosevelt was also unprepared to accept Long's premise that wolves were peaceable creatures. The prevailing image of wolves was that they were bloodthirsty beasts, "man-killers" intent upon destruction, and savage even to each other. The president knew better and was reluctant to accept the notion that wolves had a taste for human flesh, recognizing that wolves "preferred to prey on young animals, or on the weak and disabled." Nevertheless, he did see them as ferocious and described them as "the archetype of ravin, the beast of waste and desolation."[48]

Long's image of wolves, on the other hand, was similar to the more gentle predator popularized more than half a century later by authors such as Farley Mowat (_Never Cry Wolf_) and Barry Lopez (_Of Wolves and Men_). "As for the wolves," Long was later quoted as saying, "the ferocious stories we hear about them are just hunters' yarns. Oh, yes, I have had them howling around my camp, and have had them follow my trail; but I have yet to find one that seems to me as dangerous as a house dog." Roosevelt's view is not surprising, since his knowledge of wolves was limited largely to their behavior as predators or as objects of his hunt, whereas Long's interest was more in their family life and individual stories, with predation but one facet of the individual wolf's story. Still more important, Long began with the assumption that all of nature is fundamentally a place of peace rather than conflict.[49]

Wolves were objects of fascination for many nature writers and appeared in a number of their stories. Ernest Thompson Seton felt a personal identification with wolves and adopted a wolf pawprint as a part of his signature. Both Seton and Jack London went by the nickname of "Wolf." Many of the stories, with the notable exception of London's, presented a kinder view of wolves than had traditionally been the case. Although Seton had done lurid paintings of a wolf gnawing on a human skull and of a ravenous pack of chasing wolves as viewed from a fleeing sleigh, his classic story about Lobo emphasized the wolf's skill in avoiding and outwitting the wolf hunter and its loyalty to its mate. Charles G. D. Roberts's story "The Homeward Trail" took the archetypical tale of wolves chasing a sleigh across a winter landscape and turned it into a Christmas story that dulled the traditional terror of the situation. One night, on their way home for Christmas, a father and son were chased by wolves through the Canadian woods. The wolves, though, kept their distance, frightened by the sound of the sleigh bells and "evidently unacquainted with horses or men, and shy about a close investigation." Arriving safely home, the father exclaimed, "I reckon they were extry-ordinary civil, seein' us home that way through the woods!"[50]

Theodore Roosevelt thought Burroughs would find his letter to George Locke regarding *Northern Trails* amusing, and sent his friend a copy. He invited the old man to come and visit so they could continue discussing their own differences about animal psychology. Burroughs wrote at the end of September, 1905, to say how delighted he was to see that the president was not entirely silent on the matter, but urged him to speak publicly. Burroughs, too, thought the notion of killing a caribou with a bite to the heart was fanciful—the wolf would need teeth like a walrus's tusks! He seemed pleased to report that, just a week before, he had met a Stamford, Conn., physician who said that William J. Long was known around town as a liar. Roosevelt later complained that Locke did not respond to his letter, nor did Long or anyone at Ginn & Company. "I wish to Heavens," Roosevelt wrote, "I had some legitimate opportunity to skin that gentleman."[51]

Imagine how much it would have delighted the two friends to have known the following story. By one account, Long did not travel alone to the Canadian barrens. He brought along a companion, Dr. Worcester. A few years later, Worcester reported that they had not encountered any wolves or caribou during this, Long's only visit to the area. He also reported that Long had not visited Canada's northern woods. How, then, one wonders, could the stories in _Northern Trails_ be based on Long's experiences? Dr. Worcester also mentioned that Long had difficulties with his eyesight. At one point on the trip, Long mistook a seagull for an eagle and began taking notes on its behavior.[52]

In October 1905, Theodore Roosevelt published _Outdoor Pastimes of an American Hunter_. It was dedicated to John Burroughs. The elder naturalist had tears in his eyes as he sat by the fire at Slabsides and read the president's words: "It is a good thing for our people that you should have lived; and surely no man can wish to have more said of him." Roosevelt also used the dedication to make his first public pronouncement in the nature faker controversy.

> I wish to express my hearty appreciation of your warfare against the sham nature-writers—those whom you have called "the yellow journalists of the woods." . . . [Animal] fiction serves a useful purpose in many ways, even in the way of encouraging people to take the right view of outdoor life and outdoor creatures; but it is unpardonable for any observer of nature to write fiction and then publish it as truth, and he who exposes and wars against such action is entitled to respect and support. You in your own person have illustrated what can be done by the lover of nature who has trained himself to keen observation, who describes accurately what is thus observed, and who, finally, possesses the additional gift of writing with charm and interest.[53]

The Nature Fakers' Foxes

As the year came to a close the _Dial's_ May Estelle Cook proclaimed that "No Christmas-tree is fully equipped which has not a flowering of animal story-books somewhere among or beneath its branches, and no child counts his gifts complete without some new tale of outdoor life." She went on to review, side by side, Seton's _Animal Heroes_, Long's _Northern Trails_, Charles G. D. Roberts's _Red Fox_, William Beebe's _Two Bird-Lovers in Mexico_, Burroughs's _Ways of Nature_, and others. She felt that Seton's powers "increased as his style has become more simple and his allegiance to plain facts more indisputable." Long's stories had "a charm and an excellence of their own." Roberts's new book was not dull, but "[the fox's] 'calculations' about avoiding traps, stalking partridges, leading dogs over rotten bridges that will not hold them, and escaping detection by riding in a farmer's wagon, may seem a trifle incredible." Cook judged Burroughs's volume the most significant of the lot, and of the furor he started she remarked, "Undoubtedly the controversy has been a good thing, calling for confession on the part of writers and readers alike that animal psychology is a practically unknown subject, and increasing the desire of both parties in the argument for greater knowledge and greater fidelity to truth."[54]

Burroughs kept up his friendship with Ernest Thompson Seton, although Seton's wealthy lifestyle was not to his liking. "His way of loving nature is not mine," Burroughs wrote, "but doubtless it is just as genuine." He approved of the Connecticut naturalist's new book, *Animal Heroes*, and now felt that he was the best animal story writer. Seton's boys' Indian camp program was growing, and in 1906 Burroughs urged Roosevelt to give it encouragement. At the suggestion of Richard Watson Gilder, editor of *Century Magazine*, Burroughs later recommended that the president and Mrs. Roosevelt visit Seton's Connecticut camp. This was really an invitation from Seton, it turned out, who did not know Roosevelt well enough to approach him directly. But the president declined.[55]

Although he had made peace with Seton, Burroughs's opinion of Charles G. D. Roberts was on the decline. In his original "Real and Sham Natural History" article in the *Atlantic*, Burroughs had spoken well of Roberts, describing his *Kindred of the Wild* as "in many ways the most brilliant collection of animal stories that has appeared."[56] He was not as generous about Roberts's new book, *Red Fox*.

Roberts had paid close attention to Burroughs's 1903 *Atlantic* article; he also had faith in his own writing. A year later, referring to Burroughs, he wrote:

> A very distinguished author—to whom all contemporary writers on nature are indebted, and from whom it is only with the utmost diffidence that I venture to dissent at all—has gently called me to account on the charge of ascribing to my animals human motives and the mental processes of man. The fact is, however, that this fault is one which I have been at particular pains to guard against. The psychological processes of the animals are so simple, so obvious, in comparison with those of man, their actions flow so directly from their springs of impulse, that it is, as a rule, an easy matter to infer the motives which are at any one moment impelling them. . . . Where I may have seemed to state too confidently the motives underlying the special action of this or that animal, it will usually be found that the action itself is very fully presented; and it will, I think, be further found that the motive which I have here assumed affords the most reasonable, if not the only reasonable explanation of that action.

More than most, Roberts tried to avoid giving his animals human personalities and human names.[57]

Roberts was perhaps the most literate of the animal story writers, and with good reason. Born in New Brunswick in 1860, Charles G. D. Roberts grew up on a farm at the edge of the Canadian wilderness, where he acquired both the experience and love of wildlife and nature.[58] His professional interests, though, turned to literature and he published a half-dozen volumes of poetry and three of fiction before his first nature book, *Earth's Enigmas*, appeared in 1896. In the process, he established an important place for himself in Canadian literature, especially as a poet. He was a scholar who held professorships in literature and economics at King's College in Nova Scotia from 1885 to 1895, when he left to make his living as a writer.

Roberts was not a naturalist in the way that Burroughs, Seton, Roosevelt, or perhaps even Long were. As W. F. Ganong put it:

> those who know Mr. Roberts are aware that the requirements of his literary work for several years past have not permitted him to make those journeys into wild New Brunswick essential to the study of its animal life, and that his few earlier trips had not this object in view, and were not of a character to permit it. The experiences of his boyhood in the wilderness about his home . . . must necessarily have been confined to the smaller and commoner forms found near the settlements, and could not have included the moose, caribou, bear, lynx, and other great animals about which he chiefly writes.

Thus, Ganong concluded, Roberts's stories must be based on his studies in libraries, museums, and zoos and the resources of his own imagination. Nevertheless, Roberts was a careful writer. He described his own standards when he wrote, "In my desire to avoid alike the melodramatic, the visionary, and the sentimental, I have studied to keep well within the limits of safe inference."[59] In some cases, however, he did wander beyond these limits; *Red Fox* was such a case.

Red Fox differed from Roberts's other animal books, which were collections of short stories. This one was more like a novel. It was a book-length, integrated sequence of stories following the life of a single animal. The book had some fine descriptive passages, including a moving chapter about the forest animals' response to a forest fire, and made a serious effort to carefully interpret the mental life of the fox without overly humanizing the creature. Roberts was at his best when interpreting the fox's actions in emotional rather than rational terms. Red Fox was, though, a remarkable fox indeed, despite Roberts's assertion that "The hero of the story, Red Fox, may be taken as fairly typical, both in his characteristics and in the experiences that befall him, in spite of the fact that he is stronger and cleverer than the average run of foxes." Red Fox was not just clever, he was brilliant, and he had a brightness of personality that reflected the author's obvious love for his character. (He was, as were so many animal heroes, what Dallas Lore Sharp called a "*cum laude* pup.") Roberts left himself wide open to Burroughs's attack when he went on to certify that "The incidents in the career of this particular fox are not only consistent with the known characteristics and capacities of the fox family, but there is authentic record of them all in the accounts of careful observers." Perhaps this was true of many of the outward events, but he could scarcely claim such certain knowledge of the animal's thoughts, motives, and emotional life.[60]

John Burroughs's critique of the book, published in July 1906, began by claiming "genuine admiration for Mr. Roberts' genius," but cautioned that the quality of the writing could lull one into the easy belief that the fox was real, rather than "the author himself who is playing the part of Red Fox now." Once again Burroughs argued that animals are governed by instinct alone. How could Red Fox's mother know not to poach poultry from nearby farms (distant farms were fair game) for fear of drawing attention to herself, and could she have taught this to her son? Burroughs did not believe the incident when the fox escaped the hounds by running across a field over the backs of closely huddled sheep: "fancy a flock of sheep standing in a compact body with a wild animal racing across their backs!" How could Red Fox have known when it saw a sick muskrat that "a single one of its venomous bites might be fatal" to his young? Then there was the time when the fox feigned death and allowed itself to be carried off, planning to escape at the first opportunity. No wonder John Burroughs felt a need to complain.[61]

However, Burroughs's criticism did not all ring true, unless one accepts his notion that foxes are little more than instinctive machines. For example, there was the time the young fox first encountered snow:

At his first sight of a world from which all colour had been suddenly wiped out, Red Fox started back—shrank back, to the very bottom of his den. The universal and inexplicable whiteness appalled him. . . . Cautiously thrusting his head out, he stared in every direction. What was this white stuff covering everything but the naked hardwood branches? It looked to him like feathers. If so, there must have been good hunting. But no, his nose soon

97

informed him it was not feathers. Presently he took up a little in his mouth, and was puzzled to find that it vanished almost instantly. At last he stepped out, to investigate the more fully.[62]

Burroughs's response to this episode was, "Now I think it quite certain that the animals, wild or domestic, are not at all curious about the general phenomena of nature, nor disturbed by them. A sudden change from a brown world to a white world does not apparently attract their attention at all." Roberts's fox, though, was not curious about general phenomena of nature. He was dealing with an immediate, novel event, which he tried to understand in terms of his own past experience.

Roberts's exploration of the sensory world of the fox, a world different from our own, was both admirable and rare in the genre. In his account of a boy who observed the fox by sitting motionless in the woods, Roberts wrote:

[The fox] would come suddenly upon a moveless gray shape, to his eyes not altogether unlike a stump, sitting beside a stump or against the trunk of a tree. Stiffening himself on the instant into a like immobility, he would eye this mysterious figure with anxious suspicion and the most searching scrutiny. As his gaze adjusted itself, and separated detail from detail (a process which the animals seem to find difficult in the case of objects not in motion), the shape would grow more and more to resemble the Boy. But what he knew so well was the Boy in motion, and there was always, to him, something mysterious and daunting in this utterly moveless figure, of the stillness of stone. Its immobility always, in the end, outwore his own. . . . Little by little circling about, and ever drawing closer and closer, he would presently get around into the wind and catch the scent of the strange, unstirring object. That would end the little drama. The testimony of his nose always seemed to him more intelligible and conclusive than that of his eyes.[63]

This event, the account of the fox's encounter with snow, and many others were deftly handled. This sort of exploration of the inner experience of animals may not have been Burroughs's cup of tea, but it was legitimate ground for literary exploration, and Roberts generally covered the terrain carefully.

Some of the fox's actions did strain beyond belief. There was, for example, the following incident: Red Fox was being chased by dogs and he came upon a herd of frightened sheep huddling together in a field. "Leaping lightly upon the nearest," Roberts wrote, the fox ran "over the thick-fleeced backs of the whole flock, and gained the top of the rail fence, from which he had sprung easily to the cleft in the rock," thus confounding the dogs. Such an incident (although somewhat plausible, given the agility of foxes and the placid nature of sheep and discounting the suggestion that the fox did this as a matter of strategy) seemed far-fetched. It was similar to Ernest Thompson Seton's still more fanciful account of the fox that sprang on the back of a sheep: "The frightened animal ran for several hundred yards, when Vix got off, knowing that there was now a hopeless gap in the scent, and returned to the den."[64] These were wonderful stories, but were they true?

Seton did not defend his sheep-riding fox story, but William J. Long made an effort to do so. In 1887, Long found tracks in a field in Boothbay, Maine, that proved the matter to his satisfaction. "A fox-trail came down to where the sheep were standing and ended there; nor was there any further track [in the snow] that my own eyes or the hound's nose could discover. On the other side of the field I found the fox track again beside that of a frightened sheep." On its surface, this account might sound convincing—but perhaps the fox simply ran through the flock and its tracks were obliterated by those of the sheep. It was very weak proof, based on a pattern of tracks that was open to more than one interpretation.[65]

Foxes have a time-honored reputation for being wily, intelligent, and resourceful. It is not surprising that people tend to interpret their behavior in the slyest terms. Both Roberts and Long told stories of foxes intentionally playing dead when cornered by people. Perhaps, though, the foxes were simply unconscious from an injury or shock, then recovered and ran off in an unguarded moment; if so, the escape was not the result of strategy but of circumstance. Similarly, the stories of foxes intentionally leading dogs into the path of railroad trains may well be simply the result of hopeful interpretation. Seton told how his fox would "lead the hounds straight to a high trestle just ahead of the train, so the engine overtakes them on it and they are surely dashed to destruction." Defending Seton, Long reported that a fox had killed two of his dogs in the same way. However, neither man reported actually seeing these events. It is not surprising that a fox may run along or across railroad tracks as it tries to escape hounds, nor is it surprising that a dog may be killed in the process.[66]

In 1906, May Estelle Cook included Long's *Brier-Patch Philosophy* in her list of recommended Christmas books, although she cautioned that Long's reasoning was based on analogy and, thus, would not be acceptable to all. Nevertheless, she enjoyed "the cleverness with which he defends his beliefs," and concluded, "At least 'Peter Rabbit' asks questions that are hard to answer, and in the end wins gratitude for letting poor humans off as easily as he does." The *Nation* considered the book a defense "of the anti-science group of nature writers," although it acknowledged that the scientists had responded to the controversy "with more heat than caution." Nevertheless, it did find value in the book and the controversy:

> Doubtless the very controversy which has been stirred up by Mr. Long's writings will secure from scientists themselves more careful study of such rudimentary intelligence as animal life does possess. For this quickening Mr. Long is entitled to some credit, but we may take it for granted that any substantial gains in this field will come from the application of a rigidly scientific method, and not from the bald assumption of a detailed parallelism between the mental processes of widely separated forms of sentient life.[67]

This was mild praise, but perhaps it gave Long some comfort. He would need it. After the first year or two of noise, the controversy had quieted and, although Long was not vindicated, 1906 was a year of relative calm (Burroughs's pot-shots aside). The quiet, though, was about to end, and in the year ahead William J. Long was to find himself in the eye of a wilder storm than any he had faced before.

4.
ROOSEVELT'S WAR
WITH THE NATURE FAKERS

Theodore Roosevelt, the war hero, demonstrated that he was also a man of peace by mediating an end to the Russo-Japanese War in 1905. In December 1906, he received the Nobel Prize for peace, the first granted to an American. However, he brooked no peace with William J. Long.[1]

In March 1907, John Burroughs received a letter that must have warmed his heart. "You will be pleased to know," the president wrote, "that I finally proved unable to contain myself, and gave an interview or statement, to a very fine fellow, in which I sailed into Long and Jack London and one or two other of the more preposterous writers of 'unnatural' history." The "very fine fellow" was Edward B. Clark, a journalist with the Chicago Evening Post. He and Roosevelt had struck up a friendship when they first met in 1903 and the president learned of Clark's interest in birds. Their conversations inevitably turned to nature books and Roosevelt's opinions of the sham naturalists. Over the following years they kept returning to the subject. Clark, a good journalist, kept urging the president to make his views public.[2]

Clark finally succeeded in February 1907. They had discussed Long's tale of Wayeeses, the white wolf, and the reporter, perhaps unaware of Roosevelt's heated letter to Ginn & Company less than two years earlier, sent the president a copy of Northern Trails. Clark pointed out Long's assertion that the tales were truthful and asked Roosevelt to dictate an article to a stenographer. A short time later, the two spent an evening together discussing the matter in the president's White House study. There Roosevelt recounted, one after another, the shoddy and unacceptable nature stories that had found their way into print. Clark pressed again and finally convinced him to act. Roosevelt would not dictate an article, but he allowed Clark to write up their conversation in the form of an interview. After the president had reviewed the manuscript and made extensive corrections and revisions, Clark sent his article, "Roosevelt on the Nature Fakirs," off to _Everybody's Magazine_, confident that he had pulled off a journalistic coup. "I know that as President I ought not to do this," Roosevelt told Burroughs, "but I was having an awful time toward the end of the session and I felt I simply had to permit myself some diversion."[3]

For years, Burroughs and others had urged him to make his views public. Why now, after four years of silence, did Roosevelt finally jump into the fray? It was not simply a matter of giving in to pressure. The need for a bit of amusement may well have been an important motivation; as well, he certainly enjoyed the heat of battle. His frustration with the persistence of the errant writers must also have played an important role. Especially upset that their books were used in public schools, he worried about the damage they were doing through miseducation. "I am not sure that it was wise for me to attack him," Roosevelt later wrote to Caspar Whitney. "But when I found that his books were being read by school boys even in the District of Columbia, I thought I really ought to make a protest."[4] The stage had been set. Burroughs and other people of substantial prominence and credibility were on his side and all the issues had been aired. Clark now provided a forum and all Roosevelt had to do was deal the killing blow.

The president's concern fit within a broader and growing sense of alarm with the "back to nature" movement, of which the nature books were a part. For example, a _Nation_ article, "Hobbling Back to Nature," warned, "Whenever the flood-tide of prosperity subsides sufficiently to give us time and occasion to think, we begin to study our falling birth-rate, our increasing slum and criminal population, the iniquities of the food adulterator and the yellow press, and become convinced that we are well on the way to ruin, and that the city is responsible for it all. Check the drift to the city, return to the poor, old, hackneyed 'simple life.'" However, the article argued, the problems of city life cannot be solved by turning slum dwellers into farmers. Indeed, many of them had grown up on farms and abandoned them for the city. Furthermore:

> Nature, we admit, appeals strongly—to the mentally tired. They, however, do not as a rule live in the slums. They are tired, in fact, from making more or less money, and the country to them suggests

rest. It does not really impugn the sincerity of their emotions that they do their longing for a bit of black soil of their own, as the phrase goes, beside a steam radiator and with an electric push-button at their elbow. Visions will come then of green spaces, where the asphalt ceases from melting, and the subway guard is at rest; of cool, moist earth-clods, where repose the luscious red or green of tomatoes and cucumbers that need no Pure Food law, but are an end in themselves; of delightful delving with the hoe and the spade in early morning hours.[5]

In short, the middle and upper economic classes' return to nature and a simple life on the farm was little more than a selfish, romanticized escape from social responsibility.

Meanwhile, Burroughs had been busily keeping up his end of the battle. "The quack nature writers are on the increase," he warned in the February issue of *Outing Magazine*. "Nearly every month a new one turns up somewhere, falsifying natural history and humbugging their eager and gullible army of nature readers; humbugging also the editors of the popular magazines." This was a new strategy: placing responsibility on the editors. Burroughs reported that the editor of *Country Life* had been deceived by a writer who claimed that grouse made their drumming sound not with their wings but vocally and even provided faked photographs to prove it. Burroughs also pointed to lapses on the part of the editors of *McClure's* and *Century*, but singled out the editor of *Harper's Monthly*, which had published a number of Long's articles, for special attention.[6]

Harper's had published two essays by Harold S. Deming about a place he called "Briartown," of which Burroughs wrote, "As fiction, they are dull and uninteresting; as natural history, they are entirely false. . . . They are probably written by some young man fresh from reading the books of Rev. Wm. J. Long, and who has said to himself, 'I will go and do likewise.' " Deming, he complained, reported that crows use their feet rather than their beaks to carry food and nest-building materials; that male humming-birds help the females build the nest and incubate the eggs; that these birds use a pulp of rotten wood to build their nests, which are so tight that they hold water, sometimes causing the eggs to drown when it rains; and that red-winged blackbirds nest in colonies. "It is so much easier to invent your natural history," Burroughs offered, "than to discover it by actual observation."[7]

Whatever truth there was in Burroughs's attack, his own dogmatism and carelessness left him wide open for counter-attack. *Harper's* responded by asserting that all of John Burroughs's charges were groundless and printing a letter defending Deming.[8] The letter, written by an anonymous "Connecticut," pointed out that, contrary to Burroughs's assertion that Briartown was in New Jersey, the essays never mentioned the state in which Briartown was located. Burroughs had asserted that wood lilies and wild grapes do not bloom in the same season, "Yet in the region with which I am familiar," wrote Connecticut, "it is a matter of common observation that the blooming seasons of the lily and the grape overlap." Burroughs took issue with Deming's claim that chipmunks will store food in a hollow tree, writing that chipmunks are ground squirrels and therefore store their food in the ground. Connecticut, though, argued that, nevertheless, an occasional chipmunk may use a convenient tree, and then jabbed, "The chipmunk is not an earthworm, Mr. Burroughs." Furthermore, he observed that red-winged blackbirds can be found nesting very near each other. And if the Briartown writer saw a male hummingbird assisting with nest building and incubations, even if this is not generally true of the species, why could it not be true in this instance? Connecticut concluded:

> One who, after reading Mr. Burroughs's savage attack, turns to the Briertown sketches themselves, will have no doubt whose are the real "inventions." They are Mr. Burroughs's own perversions of the Briertown writer's statements and the wonderful laws of nature which Mr. Burroughs promulgates. The more one studies this Burroughs article, the more one is amazed alike at its intolerant tone, its unwarranted aspersions of another writer's good faith, and its reckless display of dogmatic ignorance. As an exhibition of truculent temper and hopelessly bad logic it is absolutely unique.

Having initiated this flare-up by giving Burroughs his say, *Outing Magazine*, in March, gave equal voice to Deming, who countered with an aggressive self-defense. Burroughs, he pointed out, did not question or criticize, he denounced. Deming accused Burroughs of distorting his statements and of establishing dogmatic general "laws" of nature and then attacking him on this basis. When this did not work, he argued, Burroughs took the stand, "I don't believe you; therefore, you lie." "Though to the ordinary eye it would seem clear enough that these are not scientific monographs, but literary sketches," he wrote, "Mr. Burroughs is unwilling to permit in them any latitude of descriptive phrase; but has demanded of them an exactness of statement and a nicety of description like that in a scientific treatise." He suggested that readers compare the Briartown sketches and Burroughs's criticism side by side and observe the inexactness of Burroughs's methods.

Deming pointed out that, indeed, New Jersey had never been identified as the location of the mythical Briartown; the essays had actually been written in southern Massachusetts. In fact, the first sentence of one essay established the site as "a hillside by the Quinebaug River." As for the hummingbird's nest, he had not written that the bird made a pulp from rotten wood, but that it extracted fibers from rotten and "pulpy wood." He had written, "In the alders almost countless pairs of red-winged blackbirds build their nests," and it was Burroughs who turned this into a colony. Also, he had not written of wild grapes and wood lilies blooming at the same time. He wrote, instead, of the scent of grape leaves and of nearby flowers mingled in the air. Deming concluded:

> Mr. Burroughs's position is untenable. The Briartown Sketches are not the product of a morbid imagination; they are based upon actual observations honestly made and honestly recorded. I may have misobserved or through faulty recollection misreported; and I have no wish to deprecate fair criticism of any of my statements. But, as we have seen, Mr. Burroughs's article is not only not fair criticism, it is not criticism at all, but a blend of faulty logic, frequent misstatements and heated temper, strangely out of tune with the good sense and kindliness which so distinguish his writings when he is not in this curious bellicose mood.[9]

A month later, in a letter to the *New York Times Saturday Review of Books*, John R. Spears ventured, "Hoping I may say it without offense, it seems to me that Mr. Burroughs has done much in the last two years or so to destroy the good work of his early years." Spears added, "I fear that the gun kept behind the door at Slabsides has blinded Mr. Burroughs," perhaps referring to the old man's eternal battle with woodchucks.[10]

We do not know how John Burroughs responded to these reprimands. He had been ill with influenza at the end of February, and this was followed by a heart problem and persistent cough. Nevertheless, he was able to travel to Atlantic City, where he celebrated his seventieth birthday on April 3. His New York friends made much of the event and held a larger birthday celebration eight months later in New York City. Burroughs attended this "sham birthday," but refused to return to the city for the American Academy of Arts and Letters dinner. He preferred instead to dine at Slabsides with his dog.[11]

William J. Long's birthday, which also fell on April 3, must have been a very happy occasion. Burroughs had been trounced in print and, still more important, Long's third child had been born two weeks earlier. He had wanted a boy (when his second daughter arrived in 1905, he had stubbornly refused to look at her for several weeks) and now, with the birth of Brian, he had a son.[12] Life must have seemed very sweet—at least for a short while.

Edward Clark's interview with the president was published in the June issue of *Everybody's Magazine*. The article began with a high tone set by the magazine's editor in justifying Roosevelt's involvement:

> It is about time to call a halt upon misrepresentative nature studies. Utterly preposterous details of wild life are placed before school children in the guise of truth. Wholly false beliefs have been almost standardized. Only by an authoritative protest can the fraud be exposed. At this juncture it is fitting that the President should come forward. From every point of view he is the person in the United States best equipped for the task, and we are fortunate in being able to fire the first gun, so to speak, with a charge of Mr. Roosevelt's vigorous, clear-cut English.

Then Clark stepped in to establish the president's credentials. He quoted the director of the United States Biological Survey, C. Hart Merriam: "Theodore Roosevelt is the world's authority on the big game mammals of North America. His writings are fuller and his observations are more complete and accurate than those of any other man who has given the subject study." Next, Clark described Roosevelt's field study and birding skills and the extensive collections of specimens that he had donated to the Biological Survey, including "the only cougar series extant in the museums of the country—a series of males, females, and immature specimens which has been the greatest value for comparative purposes."

Finally, Clark set the scene—an evening in the White House sitting by a fire ("suggestive of the camp"), as the president explained his concerns:

> "I don't believe for a minute," said Mr. Roosevelt, "that some of these men who are writing nature stories and putting the word 'truth' prominently in their prefaces know the heart of the wild things. Neither do I believe that certain men who, while they may say nothing specifically about truth, do claim attention as realists because of their animal stories, have succeeded in learning the real secrets of the life of the wilderness. They don't know, or if they do know, they indulge in the wildest exaggeration under the mistaken notion that they are strengthening their stories.

"As for the matter of giving these books to the children for the purpose of teaching them the facts of natural history—why, it's an outrage. If these stories were written as fables, published as fables, and put into the children's hands as fables, all would be well and good. As it is, they are read and believed because the writer not only says they are true but lays stress upon his pledge. There is no more reason why the children of the country should be taught a false natural history than why they should be taught a false physical geography."

Roosevelt went on to critique specific writers and their stories. He spent little time on issues of animal psychology, focusing instead on the clearer questions of accurate natural history. Then he launched into his attack. The bulldog, the president said, should have quickly lost the fight with the wolf in Jack London's recent book *White Fang*, and the Canada lynx should have lost the battle with the dog-wolf. "Nobody who really knew anything about either a lynx or a wolf would write such nonsense," he protested. Similarly, the lynx in one of Charles G. D. Roberts's stories would not have been able to hold its own against a pack of wolves. After describing the weight and fighting behavior of the lynx and actual battles between lynx and dog, Roosevelt concluded that "Real wolves would have made shreds of a real lynx within a twinkling of the time they closed in to the attack." William J. Long, too, had misrepresented the lynx's threat.

The president gave special attention to Long's story of Wayeeses the wolf and the way it killed caribou with a snap to the heart. After repeating the same criticisms he had made two years earlier in his letter to George Locke of Ginn & Company, Roosevelt argued that Long obviously did not know the length of a wolf's teeth. The task of biting through the rib cage into the heart was, he said, similar to biting through a keg of flour into a grapefruit. "If Mr. Long wants us to believe his story . . . he must produce eye-witnesses and affidavits." He condemned Long's notion that animals consciously teach their young, and concluded:

The preservation of the useful and beautiful animal and bird life of the country depends largely upon creating in the young an interest in the life of the woods and fields. If the child mind is fed with stories that are false to nature, the children will go to the haunts of the animal only to meet with disappointment. The result will be disbelief, and the death of interest. The men who misinterpret nature and replace fact with fiction, undo the work of those who in the love of nature interpret it aright.[13]

Long Strikes Back

"ROOSEVELT ONLY A GAMEKILLER—LONG. Stamford Naturalist Strikes Back at Criticism of His Nature Books," shouted a headline in the *New York Times*. William J. Long was upset, and he responded quickly and with a vengeance. Right after reading Roosevelt's interview, Long mounted an energetic defense—perhaps "offense" is a better description of his stance. On Wednesday, May 22, Long fired off a letter informing the president that he would live to regret his own "foolish words." "With all my soul I regret this necessity and shrink from it," Long wrote, "but you have brought it upon yourself." He promised, though, to send an advance copy of his response, underscoring that this was a courtesy the president had not seen fit to extend to him.[14]

The next day the *New York Times* and the *Washington Post* carried an interview with Long. He had done his homework, and told the reporter that Roosevelt had arranged the *Everybody's* interview and revised its text. He called the article "venomous," labeling the president "cowardly" to hide behind the journalist Clark. Long also alleged that the president was upset with by Peter Rabbit articles, in which the rabbit had the temerity to criticize hunting. "Mr. Roosevelt has never forgiven the poor animal who dared to criticize his hunting," he said, "and twice to my knowledge has declared to his associates that he would 'get even' and would even 'do me up.'" Long saw the *Everybody's* article as the fulfillment of this pledge. He then turned to the president's record as a "gamekiller." "I suggest that one who would understand Roosevelt's attack read Roosevelt's 'Wilder-

Heroes Who Hunt Rabbits. By Charles Copeland. From William J. Long, *Brier-Patch Philosophy* (Boston: Ginn, 1906).

ness Hunter,' and then read 'Wild Ways' [*sic*], which he condemns." This would explain "why he has no sympathy with any brand of nature study except his own."[15]

Long also told the *Times*, "The one thing [the president] declares to be a mathematical impossibility is that a huge wolf should kill a small deer by biting into the deer's chest." Long argued that this statement was absurd, which prompted Edward Clark to warn the president that Long was trying to redefine the wolf/caribou debate. Roosevelt had not talked about a "small deer." What he really said was, "That Wayeeses tore the heart of the bull caribou in the way that Mr. Long describes ['a quick snap'] is a mathematical impossibility." There is a difference between a small deer and a bull caribou, one that Long continually obscured. The president had already acknowledged in his letter to Ginn & Company's George Locke, a year and a half earlier, that a wolf could conceivably kill a fawn this way.[16]

The press was having a great time with the whole affair. Roosevelt was not inclined to respond to Long's criticism, considering him "too small game to shoot twice." Long responded to this insult by releasing the text of his private letter to the president. The next day, Friday, May 24, the *Times* editorialized on the issue. The author questioned the president's standing as a world authority on mammals and found it difficult to believe that Roosevelt had intended, as Long reported, that his views be quoted publicly. "Thinking it, as we do, something less than becoming for the, or, rather, for a, President of the United States thus to start what he must have known would be a bitter personal controversy over a matter of no great importance, we cannot help hoping that Dr. Long has been misinformed." Nevertheless, the *Times* was of "the opinion that in every detail of the dispute the President is right and the doctor wrong."[17]

A day later the *Times* reported that Long had attacked Caspar Whitney of the *Outlook*. The reporter had shown Long some unflattering interviews with John Burroughs and Whitney. Long pointed out that Whitney's criticism flew in the face of the fact that the editor repeatedly purchased Long's stories for his magazine. Long produced a letter from Whitney that read: "Dear Dr. Long: Will you do the cougar, lynx, wolf, and fox volume of the American Sportsman's Library, which I am editing? Dr. Merriam has done the bear family, George Grinnell is doing the buffalo, Dr. Elliott has done the caribou, &c. The Macmillan Company pay —— —— for these volumes. I might induce them in your case to pay —— more. Will you undertake the volume?" This, said Long, hardly needed further comment. "It is up to Mr. Whitney to explain. Only he must be careful," he added ominously. "I have more letters."[18]

On Sunday, May 26, the *Times* published the news that Long had an affidavit from a Sioux Indian proving that wolves kill by biting an animal in the heart. The document, Long announced, would be published in the next week, at which time he expected "Mr. Roosevelt, as an honest man, to come out and admit his mistake." The *Times*, however, buried the news at the end of an article entitled "London Zoologist Upholds Roosevelt." This article reported that news of the affair had traveled to London and the secretary of the London Zoological Society had spoken in Roosevelt's defense, branding some of Long's statements as "perfectly silly."[19]

Silly or not, William J. Long persisted. On Tuesday, two days later, he made public an open letter to the president, sending it to newspapers throughout the nation. (He traveled up to Boston to personally deliver the letter to George Gavin of the *Globe* and garner support from a former Nantucket high school pupil who was on its staff.) "The issue between you and me," Long wrote in his letter, "is no longer one of animals, but of men. It is not chiefly a matter of natural history, but of truth and personal honor." He provided a copy of an affidavit from the Indian and claimed that he, Long, had personally seen a deer that had been killed by a wolf bite to the chest. "If your talk of a square deal is not all a sham, if your frequent moral preaching is not hypocrisy, I call upon you as president and as a man to come out and admit the error and injustice of your charge in the same open and public way in which you made it."[20]

The next day Long mailed Roosevelt a proof copy of the open letter and enclosed the affidavit from the Sioux Indian, Stephen Jones. The Indian reported seeing wolves in Nebraska and Dakota kill horses by nipping at their rear legs, spinning them around until they fell and then biting their chests. He had seen a carcass that had been chewed open to the heart, but did not mention whether the wolves bit into the heart. He had also witnessed one kill, but he did not know if the heart was reached, although the first snap once the horse had fallen was to the chest area. The affidavit was witnessed by a C. J. Ryder, who testified to Jones's trustworthiness and truthfulness. Long urged the president to do the gentlemanly thing and publish a retraction. (Unknown to Long, a Vermonter also wrote Roosevelt, reporting that he, too, had witnessed a similar event. One night he heard a deer bleat just before it was driven by a pack of wolves through his camp. The next morning he found the deer dead and its side ripped open to and into the heart.)[21]

Scientists and naturalists wrote to Roosevelt in support of his position. John Burroughs was incredulous at Long's apparent ability to produce affidavits on demand. William T. Hornaday told the president that he was performing a public service. George Shiras described Long's response as "splenetic." On the other hand, one letter-writer to the *New York Times* took the president and Burroughs to task for criticizing "the gentlest, keen-eyed, and most loving student of wild life in America" and reported an effort to bar Long's books from the Library of Congress. Another letter in the *Times* told of a dog that stood "on the brink of the mighty Hudson," his heart broken by cruel treatment: He "once more lifted his face to the sky, and protested with pitiful howl against the cruelty of the world; and then deliberately committed suicide" by holding his head beneath the water.[22] Long continued his defense, and the press and the public did their best to make sense, or make hay, of the affair.

An article in the *Minneapolis Journal* underscored an issue that was at the heart of the president's concern. "While President Roosevelt and Rev. William J. Long are calling each other 'nature fakirs' and other polite names," it pointed out, "more than half a million school children in New York City are being taught natural history and the lore of the woods from the books of Dr. Long.... Four of Dr. Long's books are on the list of books

Long on the Attack. By Frank Wing. Courtesy of Theodore Roosevelt Collection, Harvard College Library.

for the school children of Brooklyn and the other boroughs of New York to read." The article then described some of the absurdities of the two most popular books, *Wilderness Ways* and *Wood Folk at School*, noting, "An hour at the zoological gardens in Bronx Park will make almost anybody begin to feel incredulous of some of the tales in the Long books."[23]

William J. Long's next and biggest blow aimed at the president followed on the heels of his open letter. He wrote a major article, which he sent to newspapers in New York, Boston, Chicago, Philadelphia, and other cities for publication on Sunday, June 2. "I PROPOSE TO SMOKE ROOSEVELT OUT," read the headline quoting Long in the *New York Times's* version. "LONG WILL COMBAT ROOSEVELT UNTIL LATTER IS WHIPPED," quoted Philadelphia's *Public Ledger*. "PRESIDENT A SLAYER NOT LOVER OF ANIMALS," announced the headline in the *Boston Globe's* version.[24] Long's attack even turned Roosevelt's own hunting books against him. "Mr. Roosevelt is a man who takes savage delight," he wrote, "in whooping through the woods killing everything in sight." Some newspapers revised Long's article to make it appear as if it were an interview with one of their reporters, while the *Globe* printed it under Long's own byline. The *New York Times* began by describing Long's academic accomplishments and providing a sympathetic portrait of the man:

> He is six feet tall, and would weigh about 175 pounds. He has an open and engaging, a rather boyish face; is nervous, and swift of foot and hand; looks you in the eye and talks with immense frankness and rapidity. He is full of his experiences with the animals, is apt to run off every few sentences into an anecdote, told with striking vividness of detail, and marked by certain simplicities of narration. It is impossible to talk five minutes with this man without concluding that what William J. Long says he saw he did see.
>
> It is also impossible to doubt but that Mr. Long will keep after President Roosevelt until he gets some sort of satisfaction. The nature writer appears to have no animosity against the President, though he abominates what he freely calls his "brutal" and "bloodthirsty" and "barbarous" methods in hunting the beasts. But Mr. Long is immensely in earnest in his conviction that where two gentlemen are concerned, a question of veracity cannot remain unsettled.

To support his woodcock surgery story, Long showed the reporter a severed grouse leg that a friend had sent to him from Scotland. There was "a jacket of feathers glued together with some adhesive stuff" covering a wound on the leg. He asserted that under some circumstances a lynx can win out in a battle with a wolf. Long demanded that Roosevelt hold to the same standards of documentation that the president required of him, asking for "eyewitnesses and affidavits to support his statement [that it is impossible]. This is simply because only Mr. Roosevelt and God know all about lynxes, and God is modestly silent." Long supported his story of a wolf killing caribou with a bite to the heart by reporting that he "once found a small deer lying in the snow, still bleeding, with wounds on the lower chest as if made by long fangs. One of these had ripped into the chest and touched the heart." He also reported that one of his Indian guides had witnessed caribou kills:

> Sometimes they spring at the front chest; one snap tears into the cartilage, and a wrench lays the heart bear [*sic*]. If the first snap fails, others follow quicker than a man can open and shut his hand, and the heart is cut open before the caribou is fairly aware that he has been gripped. That this is an unusual method of killing goes without saying, but that a big wolf who had learned the trick could kill a deer in this way is both possible and probable.

Long described a wolf as often "more like a big, shy, independent dog, than any other creature I know," rather than the savage creature that the president knew. But, he argued, Roosevelt could not learn this while "Chasing wolves with a pack of dogs and half a dozen yelling hunters." Long even claimed that, while a student in Paris, he had bribed a zookeeper to let him into a cage with a pack of wolves. The wolves were well fed and simply retired to the other end of the cage, except for one that eventually sniffed his hand and let him scratch behind its ear.

As before, Long's principal issue with the president was that the latter did not pay attention to the individuality of animals or acknowledge the possibility of individual learning or genius. Now Long went even farther:

> The idea of Mr. Roosevelt assuming the part of a naturalist is absurd. He is a hunter. . . . Who is he to write "I don't believe for a minute that some of these nature writers know the heart of the wild things." As to that, I find after carefully reading two of his big books that every time Mr. Roosevelt gets near the heart of a wild thing he invariably puts a bullet through it. From his own records I have reckoned a full thousand hearts which he has known thus intimately. In one chapter alone I find that he violently gained a

knowledge of eleven noble elk hearts in a few days and he tells us that this was "a type of many such hunts."

The Philadelphia *Public Ledger* softened the impact of Long's attack by printing it alongside an article entitled "Roosevelt's Shack: Only a Genuine Lover of Nature Would Care for the Place." Describing the president's rustic Virginia retreat of four rooms, kitchen, and bark-covered poles holding up the roof over the porch, the piece emphasized the shack's closeness to nature and local mountain folk. "In this Piedmont region of Virginia," concluded the article, "the president of the United States is 'Neighbor Roosevelt' whenever he may wander around 'Plain Dealing Plantation.' "[25]

The *New York Times* acknowledged that Long's defense was winning him supporters. The newspaper seemed to relish the controversy and even to stoke the fire. "The question is," it editorialized, "Will the good impression created by DR. LONG survive the publication in THE TIMES to-morrow of a reply by MR. JOHN BURROUGHS? . . . to-morrow's issue of this paper will be exceptionally interesting in many features."

A day later the *Times* treated its readers to an interview with Burroughs. The reporter wrote that Burroughs

> tried, he conscientiously tried, to speak as well of the Stamford man as possible. . . . "I would not be quoted as charging Dr. Long with conscious falsehood," Mr. Burroughs would pleasantly remark, and then proceed to a series of variegated and vigorous descriptions of a liar. The white-bearded patriarch of Slabsides is kindly disposed toward all mankind, but try as he may to be polite about it, [it] is clear that he looks upon William J. Long as a man who is without the fear of the Lord before his eyes.

Burroughs proceeded to defend Theodore Roosevelt, condemn Long and his affidavits (arguing that people will testify to anything for the sake of notoriety), and once again dispose of woodcock surgeons and oriole architects.[26]

At this point Charles G. D. Roberts spoke out in his own defense. He had been in Naples when Roosevelt made his attack, and a reporter was waiting when he returned to New York on the liner *Adriatic*. Roberts stood by his stories. "I am of the opinion," he said, "that the whole question is not one of veracity but of judgment." He underscored the conflict between those who viewed animals as mere bundles of instincts and those who believed that they reason. "Mr. Hornaday is one of this last class," he said.

"Animals are actuated in varying degrees by a process akin to reason. They do think and compare."[27]

Two days later the enterprising *New York Times* published an interview with William T. Hornaday, who criticized both Long and Burroughs. Sitting in his office behind the Bronx Zoo reptile house, he explained that a study of zoo animals revealed that animals do have the ability to reason. He took the reporter on a tour of the zoo's animals to prove his point. Nevertheless, he characterized Long as a man of "vaulting imagination which places upon the acts of wild creatures only the most farfetched and wonderful interpretations" and dismissed his work as excellent fiction.[28]

Long fired back with a letter to the *Times*. First, he took on John Burroughs. "The underlying reason for his enmity is simple," Long wrote. "Since my little books have appeared, his have fallen into the background; and where his were once found in a few scattered schools, now mine are read in a thousand." (This hit Burroughs where it hurt, and he wrote to his publisher asking whether his book sales really had declined.) Long also accused the elder naturalist of attacking "every naturalist whose articles were more interesting and successful than his own." As he had done with Roosevelt, Long tried to turn Burroughs's own writing against him. Long then branded William T. Hornaday and Stewart Edward White, another defender of the president, as self-serving and untruthful.[29]

Pigs Make Their Nests in Chicago

The press had a field day. Delighted newspapers around the country published interviews with Long, while New York papers were printing fake interviews with John Burroughs, much to Burroughs's distress. The humor of the situation was not lost on many. The *New York Evening Journal* published a cartoon showing new members approaching the "Ananias Club," a mythical society named after a biblical character known as a liar to which Theodore Roosevelt routinely assigned his opponents. Long was at the head of the line, pig under arm, saying, "Pigs make their nests in Chicago." Jonah, saying, "I'm a nature writer," was driving up in an automobile dragging a whale labeled, "Whales are not steam heated and have no janitors." Ernest Thompson Seton approached, dragging a Teddy Bear labeled, "Teddy Bears will not follow you into the woods if you do not offend them."[30]

Mr. Dooley, the character in F. P. Dunne's widely read newspaper column, reported that "me frind Tiddy Rosenfelt has been doin' a little lithry criticism, an' th' hospitals are full iv mangled authors. Th' next time wan iv them nature authors goes out into th' woods lookin' f'r his prey he'll

The Ananias Club. By T. E. Powers. From *New York Evening Journal*, 24 May 1907.

go on crutches." This meant that "Th' wild animiles can go back to their daily life iv doin' th' best they can an' th' worst they can, which is th' same thing with thim, manin' get what ye want to eat an' go to sleep with ye're clothes on." On the other hand, Mr. Dooley (whom Long read faithfully) seemed to question whether, to the urban poor, the whole ruckus was worth the effort:

> In me heart I'm glad these neefaryous plots iv William J. Long an' others have been defeated. Th' man that tells ye're blessed childher that th' way a wild goat kills an owl is be pretindin' to be an alarum clock, is an undesirable citizen. He aught to be put in

an aquaryum. But take it day in an' day out an' Willum J. Long won't give anny information to ye'er son Packy that'll deceive him much. Th' number iv carryboo, deers, hippypotamuses, allygators, and muskoxes that come down th' Ar-rchey Road in th' course iv a year wudden't make anywan buy a bow an' arrow. It don't make near as much difference to us how they live as it does to thim how we live. They're goin' an' we're comin', an' they ought to investigate an' find out th' reason why. I suppose they don't have to go to school to larn how to bite something that they dislike so much they want to eat it. If I had to bring up a flock iv wild childher in Ar-rchey Road, I wudden't much care what they larned about th' thrue habits iv th' elk or th' chambok, but I'd teach thim what I cud iv th' habits, the lairs, an' th' bite iv th' polisman on th' beat.[31]

The Cow Bird. The Cowslip.

Growing in mires, in gold attired,
The Cowslip has been much admired,
Altho' its proper name, we're told,
Is really the Marsh Marigold:
The Cow Bird picture, I suspect,
Is absolutely incorrect,
We make such errors now and then,
A sort of cow slip of the pen.

The Cow Bird and the Cowslip. From Robert Williams Wood, *How to Tell the Birds from the Flowers* (San Francisco: Paul Elder, 1907).

The mythical *How to Tell the Animals from the Wild Flowers* became a reality under the title *How to Tell the Birds from the Flowers*. It was a small, humorous collection of illustrations, each pairing a bird and a plant, emphasizing their visual similarities. The author concluded:

> Not every one is always able
> To recognize a vegetable,
> For some are guided by tradition,
> While others use their intuition,
> And even I make no pretense
> Of having more than common sense;
> Indeed these strange homologies
> Are in most flornithologies,
> And I have freely drawn upon
> The works of Gray and Audubon,
> Avoiding though the frequent blunders
> Of those who study Nature's wonders.[32]

This was not the only doggerel spawned by the nature fakers affair. Another writer penned:

> I think I've read about enough
> of this denatured "Nature" stuff;
> I don't desire no city chap
> That's never set a woodchuck trap
> To write a piece for me that tells
> That woodchucks lay their eggs in wells;
> That eels are fond of pusly greens,
> And Chipmunks live on pork and beans.

Still another wit offered:

> Remember, little children, then,
> 'Tis wrong to tease the bat;
> Embrace the adder in his den,
> And feed the pleasant rat;
> Vex not the birds with scarecrow men;
> Be gentle to the gnat.

> Oh, rub the friendly wild-cat's nose;
> Be civil to the bass;
> And study Nature as she grows,
> With sister's opera-glass;
> Then write your book, and you can pose
> As brother to the ass![33]

The *Independent* magazine was lucky enough to have articles on hand by both Long and Burroughs, and it published them together. Long's was about fishing, a pursuit he enjoyed throughout his life. It was a pleasant account of his fishing methods and experiences on the lakes and streams of the northeastern United States and Canada, completely uncharacteristic of the stories that were at the heart of the controversy. (The *New York Times* reviewed the essay with admiration.) Burroughs's essay was a now familiar slap at the nature writers. "No sooner does one of these observers step out of doors," he wrote, "than the wild creatures proceed to get up private theatricals for his especial benefit." He did, though, soften his position by

Roosevelt the Hunter. Statue by Paul Nocquet. From *Current Literature* (July 1907).

acknowledging that wild animals could adapt their nesting and foraging behavior to the presence of humans, "but they are still in the main guided by instinct, and not by reason."[34]

By pairing the articles, the _Independent_ appeared to avoid taking a position in the conflict. _Literary Digest_ and other magazines also chose to maintain their independence and report the events without taking a position. Some added a note of amusement, as did _Canadian Magazine_ when it noted, "Decidedly President Roosevelt has raised a hornet's nest about his ears, but as a lover of nature, he will hardly object to this." _Current Literature_ gave the president the last word, but illustrated its article with a photograph of a marble figure, "Roosevelt the Hunter," depicting him with rifle over shoulder, gleefully holding a dead bear cub high in one hand and clutching an adult carcass with the other. (The magazine made a point of mentioning that the president had expressed "amusement" on seeing the statue.) The _Bookman_ took a different approach, pointing out that "the entire question of bogus natural history was pretty well threshed out four years ago, with Mr. Burroughs as chief thresher, and Mr. Long and Mr. Seton, the principal threshees." It did, though, agree with the president and even commended his hunting stories, which "are not at all like his messages to Congress. In the first place, they are shorter," and furthermore they were not burdened with patriotic exhortations.[35]

A Washington _Herald_ editorial accused Edward Clark of hawking the Roosevelt interview for the highest bid. (Clark was quick to assure the president that this was not true. Rather, he had offered it right off to _Everybody's_ and was paid his normal rate of six cents a word.) The St. Louis _Republican_, no friend of the president, proposed that "Dr. Long is deserving of the Carnegie Medal, the Garter, the Cross, and every other mark and symbol of unusual and remarkable personal bravery." May Estelle Cook took an indirect swipe at Roosevelt in one of her book reviews. She wrote, "The three books in our present group strikingly bring out the fact, pertinent to some current newspaper discussion, that the man who goes to the woods to learn gets more permanent value, both for himself and others, than the man who goes to hunt. The steel-cold click of the hunter's gun sounds in all his facts, because he had shown disrespect for the greatest fact of all—life. Even a little romancing is preferable to that." She hastened to add, though, that "there is no real danger of romancing" on the part of the authors she was reviewing, including Charles G. D. Roberts.[36]

"The greater the man, the more likely he is to have the defects of his virtues," wrote Lyman Abbott in the _Outlook_ on June 8. Abbott could not take the matter seriously when Burroughs had first attacked the nature story writers, and now he wrote publicly to chastise Roosevelt for both taking it too seriously and responding inappropriately. He pointed out that the president was not being very scientific when he claimed that it was a "mathematical impossibility" for a wolf to kill a caribou as Long claimed. Perhaps even more important, "Whether Dr. Long or Mr. Roosevelt is right is not very material; and we have no judgment to express on that question," he wrote. "It is much more material that the president of the United States should not add to the controversies which are essential to his political leadership other controversies which have nothing to do with that leadership." Getting to the substance of the controversy, Abbott wrote:

> We quite agree that fiction ought not to be palmed off on school-children as fact; but we do not agree with what is implied, that imagination may not be used in interpreting and narrating facts. Men see through their temperaments; the imaginative man sees through his imagination; and he is telling the truth if he tells what he sees as he sees it. . . . The question whether animals possess a certain measure of *quasi* human reason, or are purely the creatures of a mechanically formed habit, is not to be settled by the short and easy method of denying the possibility of all the phenomena which point to a human kinship in animals. The question is really one rather of psychology than of natural history, and cannot be closed by either an appeal to past tradition or a dogmatic declaration upon the authority of any observer, however wide his observations.[37]

Abbott's view of the issues seemed a bit confused. If Long or anyone else, regardless of how fruitful their imagination may be, honestly reports what they believe they saw, then they are being truthful. They are also being accurate in their report of their beliefs. However, this does not necessarily mean that they are being accurate or factual in their reports of the lives led by wildlife apart from their own imaginations. The issue was whether Long's stories accurately described wildlife, not whether they accurately described Long's imagination. Abbott did, though, hit the target when he criticized dogmatism and identified the extreme positions—whether animals should be described as similar to humans or to machines.

Both Theodore Roosevelt and John Burroughs were upset by Lyman Abbott's editorial. Burroughs felt it reflected Abbott's intellectual limitations, and at Roosevelt's suggestion he wrote a letter to the editors of the *Outlook*. It was quite unlike his other writing on the subject, for he did not directly address issues of animal psychology. Instead, he focused on the issue of accuracy. He wrote that he did not object to imagination in the interpretation of natural history:

> There can be no good literature without it. But it is one thing to interpret facts and quite another thing to invent them. With Mr. Long's interpretation of the facts of natural history neither the president nor myself has any quarrel; all we contend for is for the fact—we dispute his statement of fact. Mr. Long may find in the croaking of the frogs a key to the riddle of the universe if he can, and be entirely within his rights. All that I demand of him is that he be sound upon his frogs.

Burroughs then went through a litany of Long's errors, and concluded:

> Is there, then, not such a thing as seeing truly and seeing falsely? True it is that the report of every man of what he sees in nature and in life will be colored more or less by his temperament, or by his personal equation—colored, I say, but not necessarily distorted or falsified. The poet and the artist see nature through the imagination, but the natural history observer sees through his eyes, or else his observations have no value as natural history. With him it is not a question of temperament, but a question of accurate seeing and of honest reporting.

This was the distinction that Roosevelt wanted made. "We have no quarrel with Mr. Long for the conclusions he draws from the facts," he wrote to Burroughs. "Our quarrel with him is because he invents the facts."[38]

It was not a distinction, it seems, that the *Outlook* accepted. After writing his initial editorial comments about the controversy, Lyman Abbott left for a trip to Europe. His son, Lawrence, was left in charge and acted to uphold his father's original position by appending a note to Burroughs's article. It restated their view that it was not appropriate for the president to enter the controversy and that Roosevelt overstated his case about "mathematical" impossibilities. It also argued that Long's books had the value of interesting children in nature, while Burroughs's were of interest to adults. Finally, "The President and Mr. Burroughs support the theory of instinct as governing the acts of the so-called brute animals. Mr. Long supports the theory of reasoning intelligence [with which the *Outlook* agrees].... Is not this really the basis of the antagonism to Mr. Long on the part of many students and authorities of natural history, rather than his alleged distorted misstatement of specific animal acts?"[39]

Burroughs was hurt by the suggestion that children did not like his books and wrote unkind things to the president about Lyman Abbott. For his part, Theodore Roosevelt was distressed by the *Outlook's* position, because he was genuinely fond of the magazine (he would become a contributing editor after leaving the presidency). Although he did not feel compelled to respond to the *Evening Post*, which took a similar position, he had to write to the *Outlook*.

It was a long confidential letter addressed in a friendly yet forceful way "To the Editors," since he did not know which "one of my friends among the editors" had written the note appended to Burroughs's article. If his criticisms of Long seemed rude, Roosevelt wrote, this was because "every competent observer regards Mr. Long with utter contempt as a cheap imposter" and he found it difficult to contain himself. He agreed that, in general, a president should not become involved in such a controversy, but because of his deep involvement with outdoor life he could not help himself. Besides, it was not a personal attack. "I was not thinking of him personally at all, any more than I am thinking of the other 'fakers' morally not a whit worse, against whom we have to issue post-office fraud orders; (and Mr. Long's writings are just as palpably fraudulent devices to obtain money as are the advertisements and the like against which we issue these fraud orders.)" Roosevelt pointed out that he had said that it was a "'mechanical' (I did not say 'mathematical') impossibility for a wolf to bite into the heart of a caribou as Mr. Long describes." He explained in detail, appealing to the authority of Merriam and Hornaday, why it was indeed mechanically impossible. (Actually, the phrase "mathematical impossibility" had appeared twice in the published interview. Roosevelt did not correct the phrase when he reviewed Clark's original manuscript, nor did he change it when the interview was reprinted as part of his published presidential papers.)[40]

As to the issue of psychology, "You are completely in error; the only question of psychology involved is the psychology of a clever, reckless, and deliberately untruthful man." Roosevelt pointed out that he and Burroughs disagreed on the question of animal reasoning. Furthermore, "It is not worth while to attack a man's theories when he has invented all the facts on which he bases them." He concluded by urging the *Outlook* not to support Long's sort of fraud. "In thus doing it seems to me," Roosevelt wrote, "that the *Outlook* is (of course entirely unintentionally) false to every principle of real morality."

Lawrence Abbott wrote his handwritten reply to the president from his home on July 6—his wife had just given birth to a son that afternoon. He confessed to being the author of the editorial note and expressed confidence in the president's and Burroughs's statements, except for Burroughs's views on animal reasoning. Roosevelt's letter and others had convinced him that Long was not scientifically competent. He did say, though, that his family enjoyed Long's books and, he felt, they had stimulated an affection for wildlife. He promised, though, that he would pay closer attention to his young daughter's nature study.[41]

The president sent back a hearty "Three cheers for Mrs. Abbott and the boy!" and extolled the virtues of women in childbirth. He tried again to justify his involvement in the controversy. "I condemn Long," he wrote, "simply because he is so impudent and so shameless an impostor, and has such real ability of its kind, that I felt he was in danger of discrediting nature study generally." He enclosed additional information that would assure Abbott of Long's trespasses. Abbott responded with thanks and the admission that Roosevelt was right and the *Outlook* wrong. A few days later the magazine published an article by Burroughs describing Roosevelt's great skills as a naturalist.[42]

While all this was going on, Theodore Roosevelt and John Burroughs were also occupied with another matter—passenger pigeons. The president thought he had seen some of the pigeons at Pine Knot in Virginia on May 18. The birds were very rare, although they had once numbered in the millions. ("They come in such multitudes," Burroughs had written thirty years before, "they people the whole air; they cover townships, and make the solitary places gay as with a festival.") It was an important sighting, because passenger pigeons had not been reported for nine years. Roosevelt, though, was cautious. He described his sighting to Burroughs and C. Hart Merriam, hoping for their confirmation. Initially Burroughs was skeptical, but later assured Roosevelt that he had seen correctly and reported that Dallas Lore Sharp had seen three of the birds the year before near Boston. A few weeks later Burroughs visited Sullivan County, New York, to investigate recent sightings by residents who were familiar with passenger pigeons. His interviews convinced him that they had, indeed, seen passenger pigeons. Roosevelt may well be the last naturalist of standing to report seeing this now extinct bird in the wild.[43]

In July the president shot a yellow-throated warbler and sent the prepared skin to the American Museum of Natural History. He did this reluctantly, but thought it was an unusual and important sighting. "The breeding season was past," he wrote to Burroughs, "and no damage came to the species from shooting the specimen; but I must say that I care less and less for the mere 'collecting' as I grow older." A week later he wrote to Burroughs to tell how accustomed the animals seemed to be to the presence of humans at his Oyster Bay home. "Really I have begun to feel a little like a nature faker myself," he confessed as he wrote of the events of the past two weeks. Describing how a chipmunk would cross the tennis court during a match, he quipped, "I suppose that Mr. Long would describe him as joining the game."[44]

Amidst all of these natural history activities, Theodore Roosevelt was also occupied with his duties as the head of state. For one thing, he was contending with diplomatic tension between the United States and Japan that threatened to break into war. This was fanned by anti-Japanese activity in California that broke into riots that June. There were even rumors, some coming via diplomatic channels, that the Japanese were planning to invade the Pacific Coast. That summer, while the nature fakers controversy raged and the president was helping to plot the next and final blow against William J. Long, he was also preparing to dissuade Japanese intentions with a wave of a very big stick—he sent the United States naval fleet on a world tour as an international display of power.[45]

Whacking William J. Long with the Big Stick

"Speak softly and carry a big stick" was one of Theodore Roosevelt's mottos. For four years he spoke privately against William J. Long and the other nature fakers, and when that proved fruitless he tried to strike a killing blow through the Clark interview. The blow, however, seemed to do little more than goad Long into a fight. Long's public letter to the president and interviews with the press attracted attention. His spunk in the face of what appeared to be a bullying president won him sympathy. The president's attack left many readers puzzled, because the literary quality of Long's books and articles and their genuine ability to stimulate an interest in and affection for wildlife seemed to be endorsements enough of their value. Long's outspoken and protracted defense of himself and his work testified to the strength of his indignation and his belief that he, not the president, occupied the moral high ground.

Long, however, did not know that Roosevelt had shared some of his views and debated them with John Burroughs. In fact, Roosevelt appreciated some of Long's writing. In a letter to Henry L. Stimson, United States Attorney for New York, the president wrote, "Long's book has come. That story about the quail is a really beautiful one." The story, which appeared in Long's *Fowls of the Air*, was indeed beautiful. It was a touching story of how the sight of bobwhite quails amidst the exotic birds at the Zoological Gardens in Antwerp evoked the New England landscape for a homesick American student, William J. Long. But another chapter in the book, about how mergansers teach their young to swim and fish, broke the spell. Roosevelt thought it was "comical to think of Long writing such truck about a wild duck when all he has got to do is to go to the nearest barn yard and watch a hen that has hatched ducklings take them to the nearest puddle and see how much 'teaching' she has got to do to get them to swim."[46]

In July 1907, Long wrote the preface for a new book, *Whose Home Is the Wilderness*, that again stated his belief in the individuality of each wild animal and its psychological kinship to humans. "Indeed," he wrote, "I find that any animal or bird becomes interesting the moment you lay aside your gun and your prejudices and watch with your heart as well as your eyes wide open; especially so when, after an hour's silent watching, the animal suddenly does some little significant thing that you never noticed before, and that reminds you that this shy little life is, after all, akin to your own." Repeating his criticism of Roosevelt, but not mentioning him by name, Long went on to write:

> Even among those who have had the opportunity of watching the rare wild creatures, two things still stand in the way of our larger knowledge, namely, our hunting and our prejudice. It is simply impossible for the man who chases through the woods with dogs and rifles, intent on killing his game, ever to understand an animal. As well expect the barbarian who puts a village to fire and slaughter to understand the peaceful spirit of the people whom he destroys in their terror and confusion.... And the man who goes to the woods with a preconceived idea that animals of the same species are all alike, that they are governed solely by instinct and show no individual wit or variation, merely binds a thick veil of prejudice over his eyes and blunders blindly along, missing every significant little thing which makes the animal interesting.[47]

From the outset, William J. Long seemed intent on engaging the president in a public debate. Roosevelt, though, remained silent, as John Burroughs and George Shiras advised. Nevertheless, a new attack on Long was in preparation. At first, Edward Clark thought of writing something on his own, and he also urged the president to act, but Edward Nelson of the U.S. Biological Survey stepped forward with a better idea. As soon as Long began to defend himself, Nelson approached Clark with the idea for a "symposium" of comments on the controversy made by the prominent field naturalists of the country. The naturalists, Nelson argued, would give public testimony to Roosevelt's capabilities as a naturalist and condemn Long. Clark approached *Everybody's Magazine* with the idea. J. O'Hare Cosgrave, editor of the magazine, agreed that it would put an end to Long and the other nature fakers. He scheduled publication for September.[48]

The president, too, liked the idea of the symposium and even helped out by soliciting George Shiras's participation. Immediately after Long's open letter to Roosevelt was published in May, Shiras had written to the president to express his feelings about the Connecticut author and to share damning information about wolves in Newfoundland. Roosevelt asked Shiras to write "five hundred words of terse appreciation of Mr. Long" for the *Everybody's* symposium. In the end, though, the magazine relied on extracts from Shiras's original letter.[49]

Nelson took charge of gathering short statements from the scientists, and by the end of June most of them had agreed to participate. (His efforts were a feather in his cap, a point that became clear when the president invited him for lunch after the article went to press.) With some prodding from Clark and Cosgrave, Nelson succeeded in gathering their written comments by the end of July. The scientists, unable to be brief, submitted statements averaging more than three times the requested five hundred words, and Clark was forced to edit them heavily. There was an additional problem—the scientists did not want John Burroughs to participate in the project. Some even threatened to withdraw their contributions if he was included. They felt that including a statement from Burroughs would undermine the article's impact. Clark resisted the suggestion but eventually gave in, and Burroughs's brief comments were rejected.[50]

Theodore Roosevelt also began making plans, against the advice of some of his friends, to publish a response under his own name. He hoped to have it published simultaneously in *Everybody's* and *Outing*, but after discussing the matter with Clark and J. O'Hare Cosgrave he decided, to their delight, to permit publication in *Everybody's* alone. He began work on the article late in June, but it was not until the end of July that, after submitting and withdrawing two versions, he settled on the final text. In the process, his original note grew into a full article that included extracts from Shiras's letter. Clark and Cosgrave decided to pair the scientists' symposium and the president's article to wield a devastating blow against the nature fakers.[51]

Meanwhile, Caspar Whitney of *Outing* was planning a blow of his own. At first he planned a short piece, saying a few words about the background and experience of each of the key players in the controversy. It grew, though, to five pages. Whitney had avoided writing seriously on the subject, but recent efforts to introduce Long's books into the schools convinced him to act. Roosevelt pressed him to include a substantial part of Shiras's letter, but after a good deal of thought Whitney declined, saying he feared it would duplicate what was coming out in *Everybody's*. Although Caspar Whitney was happy to receive Roosevelt's assistance, he lamented that the president did not choose his *Outing* as the vehicle for the "Nature Fakers" article. Roosevelt, a bit miffed, replied, "I thought I had already told you that the reason these statements of mine appeared in *Everybody's Magazine* was purely due to the accident of one reporter, Clark, being a naturalist and feeling as strong about Long and company as I did," and pointed out, "how many, many magazines and periodicals make complaints similar to yours. I hope you now understand the situation."[52]

In August, Roosevelt wrote to another of Lyman Abbott's sons, Ernest Abbott of the *Outlook*. He enclosed an advance copy of Whitney's article. Roosevelt continued to be distressed by the *Outlook*'s editorial position, pointing out that the Abbott family "ought not to lend the weight of names which carry so much respect to help a noxious impostor." He urged that the family read the article. Abbott, in turn, promised to speak with his father when he returned from Europe, but offered little hope, cautioning that the family was rarely of one mind.[53]

What Abbott did not mention and Roosevelt seemed not to know was that Lyman Abbott had a personal involvement with William J. Long. The elder Abbott was, like Long, an ordained Congregationalist minister, and his magazine had vigorously defended Long during the controversy with the North Cambridge Council in 1898. In addition, in 1899 Lyman Abbott participated in the ceremony installing Long as pastor of the First Congregational Church in Stamford, Conn.[54]

"ROOSEVELT WHACKS DR. LONG ONCE MORE," announced the *New York Times* when Clark's symposium and the president's article were published in the September *Everybody's Magazine*. Clark's article, "Real Naturalists on Nature Faking," began by saying that some naturalists of international reputation "have a word to say now about nature faking and nature fakers." First, though, he described Edward Nelson's efforts to gather the naturalists' statements, disassociating the president from the project. This was not entirely true, since Roosevelt had engineered Shiras's contribution and, as early as June 27, Cosgrave had solicited his recommendations on whether the article should be written, who should contribute, and how it should be structured. It did, though, counter Long's claim in July that the president had been soliciting contributions from scientists all around the nation. The remainder of the article consisted of the naturalists' comments, each accompanied by an introductory line or two by Clark.[55]

"Apparently there is no imaginable intimacy with wild beasts and birds that this gentleman has not struck up," William T. Hornaday wrote of Long. "To judge by [his books] only God himself could know the wild creatures as the Rev. William J. Long claims to know them, and only the

Omnipotent eye could see all the things that Mr. Long claims to have seen." He argued that a school board that allows Long's books in its schools "is recreant to its duty and deserves severe censure" and that acceptance of Long's views of animal life is a sure sign of "profound ignorance." J. A. Allen, curator of mammalogy and ornithology at the American Museum of Natural History, called Long's books "pernicious." In his own contribution, Edward Nelson urged that "all who know the truth and who care for the honest nature study or for literary honesty should raise their voices against such writings."

C. Hart Merriam suggested that Long was blessed with a "Creative Memory" and that with such a memory "it is quite sufficient to walk in the woods or fields until an animal is seen, or, if the animal is shy, until its track or other evidence of its presence is encountered. He may then hie homeward with the assurance that the Creative Memory will do the rest." Frederick A. Lucas, curator-in-chief of the Museums of Brooklyn Institute, decried those who claimed that the nature fakers' books were of value because they stimulated interest in nature. Barton W. Evermann of the U.S. Bureau of Fisheries pointed out that Long's fish stories were, indeed, fish stories.

Clark quoted George Shiras at length. Shiras, who had been elected to Congress in 1903, was a skilled naturalist and a pioneer in the use of flash photography on wildlife at night. He knew a good deal about the natural history of Newfoundland. His comments about William J. Long's white wolf story were damning. Beginning with Long's first sighting of the wolf in the midnight shadows, Shiras wrote, "So here we have the keen-eyed doctor, pen in hand, sitting expectantly on the deck of a schooner and telling his readers just how a wolf looked and acted at night, half a mile or more away on the mountain top, behind the fishing village." Furthermore, he pointed out, Newfoundland had been without wolves for many years and its 250,000 coastal residents had never seen even a track. Quoting Long's description of his method of tracking Wayeeses—"All over the Long Range of the Northern Peninsula I followed him, guided sometimes by rumor, a hunter's story or a postman's fright"—Shiras indicated that Newfoundland was larger than Ireland, and then noted cynically, "As letter-carriers, wolves, and rumors were then unknown in the interior of Newfoundland—the doctor's triple alliance was a strong one."[56]

Theodore Roosevelt's following article, "'Nature Fakers,'" was the coup de grace. (The *Times* described it as a fatal shot at small game.)[57] It also gave his opponents their definitive name. (Edward Clark was not the first to use "fakir" to describe these writers, nor was Roosevelt the first to use "faker." But Clark's article popularized the term *nature fakir* and, over the summer, popular usage understandably transformed it into *nature faker*.) The president began with a sort of honor roll, acknowledging the work of skilled, responsible nature writers: John Burroughs, John Muir, C. Hart Merriam, Frank Chapman, William Hornaday, George Shiras, Steward Edward White, Frederic Remington, Olive Thorne Miller, J. A. Allen, Ernest Ingersoll, Whitmer Stone, and William Cram. Then he attacked the "yellow journalists of the woods." "Like the White Queen in 'Through the Looking-Glass,' " he wrote, "these writers can easily believe three impossible things before breakfast; and they do not mind in the least if the impossibilities are mutually contradictory." He then sailed into the nature fakers' stories, focusing on those of William J. Long, "the most reckless and least responsible" of the lot (he did not mention Seton, Roberts, or London), and dismissed them as bearing "the same relation to real natural history that Barnum's famous artificial mermaid bore to real fish and real mammals."

Roosevelt had crafted a careful strategy. He avoided the quagmire of the nature fakers' animal psychology by writing, "There is no need of discussing their theories; the point is that their alleged 'facts' are not facts at all, but fancies." He also shifted the focus of attack (and responsibility) from the writers to their publishers and school boards, concluding:

> Men of this stamp will necessarily arise, from time to time, some in one walk of life, some in another. Our quarrel is not with these men, but with those who give them their chance. We who believe in the study of nature feel that a real knowledge and appreciation of wild things, of trees, flowers, birds, and of the grim and crafty creatures of the wilderness, give an added beauty and health to life. Therefore we abhor deliberate or reckless untruth in this study as much as in any other; and therefore we feel that a grave wrong is committed by all who, holding a position that entitles them to respect, yet condone and encourage such untruth.

Caspar Whitney's *Outing* editorial, a more humorous jab at the nature fakers, was also published in September. "The truth is," he wrote, "that I have refused to take and tried to keep out of the position of taking the fake stories or their creators seriously; it seems to me such a waste of time and sometimes of temper." He felt the nature faker was so vocal in his own defense because, since he had no standing among scientists, his salvation lay in mystifying the public and keeping up the controversy, "for well he knows that it is more lucrative to be damned than to be ignored in the nature fakir trade." Whitney believed that readers were more interested in reading fairy tales than facts and that it was the fairy tale qualities of the nature fakers' stories that appealed to such a wide audience.

Whitney commended the efforts of Burroughs and Roosevelt, and even had relatively kind words for Seton and Roberts. He had, however, few good words for William J. Long's natural history. Long's works, he felt, had value as fiction, but he deplored the idea that they would be used in schools as natural history readers: "What a commentary on the fitness of the educational boards!" He did, though, provide something of a defense of the integrity of the man. "Naturalists call Long by a short and no gentle term," he wrote, "I who have followed him rather closer than he would believe, and know him to be capable of trustworthy work, look upon him as a dreamer, as by way of being a psychological phenomenon. . . . Why the dreamer should mistake his visions for natural history fact is not to be explained I am sure by mere wish to deceive; there is some psychic reason for it beyond the grasp of most of us, which may one day be revealed." Having had his say, Caspar Whitney concluded that it was time to put an end to the whole thing, because "no man of real wild animal experience is going to keep up this fool controversy."[58]

John Burroughs was pleased with the *Everybody's* articles and Theodore Roosevelt was delighted with Whitney's editorial. Whitney, though, was unhappy when he saw that the president had omitted his name from the "honor role" of nature writers that began the "Nature Fakers" article. He felt slighted and wrote confidentially to Roosevelt, saying that a number of reporters had asked that the omission be explained. Roosevelt assured Whitney that it was simple forgetfulness on his part and he promised to correct the matter when the article was published as a part of his presidential papers, promptly sending the instruction to do so to his publisher.[59]

The Aftermath

Although the nature fakers had received a killing blow, the "fool controversy" died slowly. Reverend Theodore Wood, Vicar of Saint Mary Magdalene's Church in England, for example, leaped to Long's defense. "President Roosevelt may be an extremely able man," said Wood, "but the fact that he is President of the United States hardly qualifies him for delivering ex cathedra pronouncements on questions of natural history." He then proceeded to resurrect the ghost of woodcock surgery. Citing witnesses supporting Long's stories about woodcocks treating their own broken legs, he implied that this practice was common among European woodcocks. He did not have eyewitnesses, though, just people who had found feathers or grass covering an injury, "fixed by means of a gluelike substance."[60]

Editorializing in "The War of the Naturalists," the _New York Times_ favored the president's position. It did not reject Reverend Wood's information, but argued that

> A fact, to be true in the relation in which Dr. Long employs his facts, must be typical. The children who read his books may be led to infer from the account of the wounded woodcock that it was characteristic of this kind of gamebird, when shot, to mend its broken bones with splints. Facts might be adduced to show that the bones of living human beings are flexible like India rubber; that the muscles are rigid as granite; that bodies are "Siamesed," and that minds are controlled by "double personalities," and from a sober relation of these facts an inhabitant from Mars would be completely bewildered and deceived as to what are the real, typical facts of human life on this planet. In spite of British scientific quibblers, we think, the president is still on firm ground.

"Old Sportsman," a letter writer to the _Times_, seemed not to agree and reported finding a Wilson's snipe with a "mud splint" on its leg. Another writer, though, rejected the notion that a woodcock can splint its own leg and, as for Reverend Wood, wrote, "Oh, there are naturalists and naturalists, and sometimes one of the other class is dubbed eminent."[61]

An "old-time hunter," L. F. Brown, was given a full-page interview in the _Times_ three weeks later to vent his indignation at Roosevelt's attack on Long, calling Roosevelt's criticism "shallow and false" and the president "a posing glutton of the limelight." He disputed Shiras's claim that there were no wolves in Newfoundland, claiming that he had heard them just eight years before and that native guides told him of wolves that "became white in Winter." As did Long, he emphasized the individuality of wild animals and their intelligence, and he ridiculed those who did not:

> One or two gifted American women, and two or three men— Mr. Burroughs among them when younger, and not jealous and querulous—have written with considerable knowledge of birds and some beasts. But their writings have been "pot-boilers," and they have taken good care to stay with civilization in towns, as the President does except a very few days in a year. It is amusing to find some of these persons named by the president patronizingly, as he coolly assumes that "we who care for the wild creatures" really know their shy ways as they are unshot, unfenced or uncaged.[62]

Brown was displaying one of the most curious facets of Long's defense. He, Long, and others made a great effort to demonstrate that Theodore Roosevelt's status as a hunter rendered him incapable of appreciating the subtle minds and beauty of the woodfolk. Yet, they continually appealed to the authority of hunters, trappers, sportsmen, and their guides to support Long's views of animal life in the wild.

Ernest Thompson Seton had been traveling in the Canadian barrens for seven months and, mercifully, missed the whole flap. Perhaps he would also have been caught in the controversy if his essay "Natural History of the Ten Commandments" had been published a little earlier. (Burroughs felt that Seton's argument did not "hold water, at least not much of it.") As it was, *Century Magazine* did not publish the essay until Seton's return. The article argued that the biblical commandments were "fundamental laws of all creation," not just of human conduct. He argued, for example, that species that were promiscuous (had high reproductive rates, such as rabbits), or polygamous (such as elk) were inherently unhealthy and subject to disease and debilitation. In a sense, the article was an effort to identify rules of behavior that govern interactions among individuals of a species: an important enterprise led astray by religious anthropomorphizing.[63]

Jack London felt that, given the journalistic hysteria following Theodore Roosevelt's attacks, "the only thing for a rational man to do is to climb a tree and let the cataclysm go by." He did just that and waited a year before publishing his own defense. London was clearly and justifiably hurt by being labeled a nature faker. "Time and again, and many times, in my narratives, I wrote, speaking of my dog-heroes: 'He did not think these things; he merely did them,' etc.," he protested. "And I did this repeatedly, to the clogging of my narrative and in violation of my artistic canons; and I did it in order to hammer into the average human understanding that these dog-heroes of mine were not directed by abstract reason, but by instinct, sensation, and emotion, and by simple reasoning."

Turning to specifics, London argued that Roosevelt had built his case by claiming that one of London's books had a lynx kill a wolf, which was not true, and that he had two dogs best a wolf-dog in a fight, which simply amounted to little more than a difference of opinion over the relative merits of dogs and wolf-dogs. Then, turning to the president's friendship with Burroughs, which he termed an "unholy alliance," he pointed out that the two "are agreed that animals do not reason" and proceeded with a detailed critique of Burroughs on this account. The article featured caricatures of London on one page and of Roosevelt and Burroughs on the facing page. London's image extolled "reason," with a bookend-bust of

"Reason!"

Mr. London to his amanuensis: "Simple reflex action, compound reflex action, memory, habit, rudimentary reason, and abstract reason"

"Reason!" proclaims Jack London. From _Collier's Weekly_ (5 Sept. 1908).

Burroughs in the background propping up books entitled _Faking and Fakirs_ and _Studies in the Ego_. On the opposite page, his opponents proclaimed "instinct" as they stared at a bird—Roosevelt with a pistol in his belt and Burroughs with a bird's nest in his hat.[64]

True to form, Theodore Roosevelt was unable to let London's article stand unchallenged. He must have been especially upset, because London's article was published by _Collier's_ magazine and the _Collier's_ company was publishing his collected presidential addresses. He fired off a long letter to one of the magazine's editors, Mark Sullivan. Quoting chapter and verse from London's _White Fang_, Roosevelt demonstrated that London was inaccurate in his description of his own book and asserted that the errors

"Instinct!"

The President and Mr. Burroughs observing carefully the antics of tom-tits and snipe. Theodore and John together: "Instinct, sheer instinct!"

"Instinct!" assert Roosevelt and Burroughs. From *Collier's Weekly* (5 Sept. 1908).

were intentional. Furthermore, he pointed out that he and Burroughs did not agree on the issue of animal instinct. "As a matter of fact," Roosevelt wrote, "I believe that the higher mammals and birds have reasoning powers, which differ in degree rather than in kind from the lower reasoning powers of, for instance, the lower savages." He emphasized, though, that he did not want to enter into a public debate with London. Rather, his complaint was with *Collier's*, because they gave London a forum for his views.[65]

William J. Long was curiously silent during the debate following the president's second attack in the September 1907 *Everybody's*. In fact, he had vanished from the scene. A *Times* reporter journeyed to Stamford in hope of an interview and asked a cabman for directions to Long's house. At first, the man could not place the author, but then said, "Oh, you mean Long, that nature faker; right this way, sir." But the house was closed and a neighbor told the reporter that Long was up at Moosehead Lake, Maine. Rumor had it that the attacks had made Long ill. Perhaps he had suffered another breakdown?

In October, though, William J. Long emerged from two months in the Maine woods "refreshed and full of fight," claiming that there was no truth to the rumors. "All was so peaceful in the big woods from which I have just returned that I had forgotten all about Mr. Roosevelt's numerous controversies," he told a reporter, "but I read his last attack on the train coming down—a rather rude welcome back to civilization." He, too, took issue with Shiras about the absence of wolves in Newfoundland, but the president won the brunt of his ire. "In a word, the only fakir in the whole controversy, in my judgment, is the big fakir at Washington." He ridiculed

Ready for Roosevelt. By Louis M. Glackens. From *Puck*, 2 Oct. 1907. Courtesy of Theodore Roosevelt Collection, Harvard College Library.

Roosevelt's forthcoming bear hunt in the South, but suggested the recent attacks were not worth an answer.[66]

Roosevelt's autumn hunting trip in Louisiana, though, proved too tempting a target. Two weeks later Long called him a butcher and painted a ludicrous picture of the brave wilderness hunter. "He went into the canebrake," Long was quoted as saying, "according to accounts, with six or eight professional hunters, two surgeons, 60 odd dogs, unnumbered camp followers, camera men and a few dispatch bearers to carry out accounts of his heroism to a breathless world." Continuing his attack on the man, rather than on the issue, he said, "The funny thing is that presently he will be out with a magazine article, telling us about the habits of Louisiana bears and incidentally calling liar to some other man who had gone into the canebrake by a different route and seen more than he has." The president did kill a bear, although the total body count was much smaller than in years past. He was especially pleased by having sighted two ivory-billed woodpeckers in a cypress grove.[67]

That autumn Long did some hunting of his own. He wanted to prove that Roosevelt's criticism of his wolf story was wrong and went, he wrote, "straight to the big woods and, as soon as the law allowed, secured photographs and exact measurements of the first full-grown deer that crossed my trail." In other words, he shot and dissected a deer (probably more than one). After studying the placement of the heart in the deer's chest cavity ("the point of the heart, as the deer lay on his side, was barely five eights of an inch from the surface"), he concluded that a wolf could kill a deer with a bite to the heart. "The chest of a caribou is anatomically exactly like that of other deer; only the caribou fawn and yearling of 'Northern Trails' have smaller chests than the animals I measured." His findings, however, went unnoticed—the battle was over.[68]

For the most part, William J. Long was driven out of the nature writing business. In June 1907, at the height of the controversy, Ginn & Company issued *Wayeeses, the White Wolf*, a book version of his "Wayeeses the Strong One" story. In 1908 Ginn published a school edition of the book and a classroom collection of the other stories from *Northern Trails*. But these were the last they published of Long's nature books. His output of nature articles dropped to next to nothing. By the end of the year the Philadelphia public schools dropped his popular, much-loved nature books from its curriculum. This was neither the first nor last school department to discard William J. Long's studies of the woodfolk.[69]

* * *

Clarence Hawkes considered the nature fakers controversy "a veritable tempest in the teapot," but once it was over the blind nature writer wrote, "I now realized that if I ever make a bad break in regard to my natural history statements that I was doomed." He and many other writers began to check and recheck their stories to be sure they were accurate, as did their publishers. Dallas Lore Sharp's publisher, for example, "had an expert naturalist and woodsman hunting up and down every line of [his book *The Fall of the Year*] for errors of fact, false suggestions, wrong sentiments, and extraordinaries of every sort." In addition, much of the reading public became a bit more skeptical. Twenty-five years after the controversy ended, Frank Chapman wrote, "We still have nature fakers with us, but today there is far less chance that the product of their pens or cameras will pass editorial censorship or deceive the public than there was when the former were keener for copy and the latter knew less about nature."[70] John Burroughs and Theodore Roosevelt had won their war with the sham naturalists. The battle they had fought, though, involved far deeper issues than they ever imagined. The deeper conflict continues to rage.

5.
IN SEARCH OF AN EARTHLY EDEN

America was a land of growing industrial strength as it entered the twentieth century. Its muscles were machines. Entire drainage basins had already been managed to provide power to nineteenth-century mills, the steam engine had released even greater power and girdled the continent with railroad tracks, and electricity was reshaping industry once again. The United States and Europe were in the midst of enormous social, technological, and scientific changes. Consider, for example, that at the same time young John Burroughs worked in the United States Treasury and penned his early nature essays, Karl Marx was laboring in the library of the British Museum on *Das Kapital*; in 1899, the year after Seton published *Wild Animals I Have Known*, Joseph Conrad published *Heart of Darkness*. In 1903, the same year Roosevelt and Burroughs vacationed in Yellowstone, Marie and Pierre Curie won the Nobel Prize for their work with radioactivity; and the same year that Charles G. D. Roberts published the antics of Red Fox, 1905, Albert Einstein published his Special Theory of Relativity and his fateful formula, $E=mc^2$.

The new technological foundation of our society presented major new cultural problems. In 1899, the novelist Joseph Conrad, speaking through Stein, the butterfly collector in *Lord Jim*, put it this way:

Man is amazing, but he is not a masterpiece.... Perhaps the artist was a little mad. Eh? What do you think? Sometimes it seems to me that man is come where he is not wanted, where there is no place for him; for if not, why should he want all the place? Why should he run about here and there making a great noise about himself, talking about the stars, disturbing the blades of grass?

In 1910, John Burroughs, no enemy of science, used a religious metaphor to describe the problem. "We cannot vault into the saddle of the elemental forces and ride them and escape the danger of being ridden by them," he wrote. "We cannot have a civilization propelled by machinery without the iron of it in some form entering our souls."[1]

The debate about nature faking took place within the context of these and other large social issues involving the value of science and technology and our relationships with the natural world. Its obvious focus, aside from the question of fraud, was on such questions as: Are animals simply living machines? Do they share common mental processes with humans? Do they have value, rights, and a spiritual identity that exists outside of their utility to humans?

Animals as Things

In the great hall of dynamos at the Paris Exposition of 1900, historian Henry Adams confronted the psychological and spiritual impact of these societal changes and later described them in more directly religious and mythic terms.

As he grew accustomed to the great gallery of machines [Adams wrote of himself], he began to feel the forty-foot dynamos as a moral force, much as the early Christians felt the Cross. The planet itself seemed less impressive, in its old-fashioned, deliberate, annual or daily revolution, than this huge wheel, revolving within arm's length at some vertiginous speed, and barely murmuring—scarcely humming an audible warning to stand a hair's-breadth further for respect of power—while it would not wake the baby lying close against its frame. Before the end, one began to pray to it; inherited instinct taught the natural expression of man before silent and infinite force. Among the thousand symbols of ultimate energy, the dynamo was not so human as some, but it was the most expressive.[2]

Our technology, symbolized by the dynamo, had become a new religious force of enormous physical power and control that was unconcerned with the living, procreative forces of nature once worshipped as goddesses. "Every one, even among Puritans, knew that neither Diana of the Ephesians nor any of the Oriental goddesses was worshipped for her beauty. She was goddess because of her force; she was the animated dynamo; she was reproduction—the greatest and most mysterious of all energies; all she needed was to be fecund."[3] Adams had discerned that the major driving force of our time is at odds with the biological world that sustains us. We are without equally compelling, life affirming psychological or spiritual forces to tip the balance in favor of living in harmony with our environment.

The roots of the problem, though, go back much earlier than the nineteenth century, to the dominant Western intellectual and religious traditions that viewed humans as separate from the rest of nature. While humans are persons with souls and minds, the rest of nature is composed of objects, animate and inanimate, with which people can do as they wish. The Judeo-Christian God resides not within the natural world, but outside of it in a supernatural heaven. Animals in Europe did not fare well in all of this. Since they were without souls, many theologians argued, God did not require that they be given any special treatment. Some people argued

"Whatsoever Adam called every living creature, that was ye name thereof." By W. Tringham Sculp. From John Ray, *The Wisdom of God* (London: D. Williams, 1762).

against cruelty to animals, but not for the animals' sakes. Cruelty was wrong only when directed toward people. They feared, though, that the habit of cruelty to animals may also lead a person to act cruelly toward other people. This contrasted sharply with the views of traditional cultures, which recognized that plants, animals, and the rest of nature have spiritual identities that must be respected—thus, the split between natural and supernatural has little meaning. It also contrasted with other historical interpretations of the Judeo-Christian tradition.[4]

Charles G. D. Roberts recognized the problem this dominant religious tradition presented for animals. In 1902, he wrote that in the eyes of Christianity, "Man was the only thing of consequence on earth, and of man, not his body, but his soul." Thus, nature and its creatures were of no value except as they served humans, God's favorites.

> The way of nature was the way of death. In man alone was the seed of the divine. Of what concern could be the joy or pain of creatures of no soul, to-morrow returning to the dust? To strenuous spirits, their eyes fixed upon the fear of hell for ourselves, and the certainty of it for their neighbors, it smacked of sin to take thought of the feelings of such evanescent products of corruption. Hence it came that, in spite of the gentle understanding of such sweet saints as Francis of Assisi, Anthony of Padua, and Colomb of the Bees, the inarticulate kindred for a long time reaped small comfort from the Dispensation of Love.[5]

The interpretation of the Judeo-Christian texts that Roberts criticized was a part of the intellectual climate that led to the development of European science and its ability to break nature into component parts and to figure out how they work. This knowledge, combined with the technological drive to increasingly improve the human condition (at least the condition of the people who had the money and power necessary to wield the technology) drove the wheels of material progress—the intellectual power behind the dynamo. Nature, while it had no spiritual value, had great economic value as natural resources. Progress came to be measured as the increasing ability to dominate nature and shape its resources to satisfy human needs.

In the seventeenth century, as anatomists began to understand human and animal anatomy in terms of levers and pumps, they recognized the similarity between animals and machines. They also recognized the physical and biological similarities between humans and animals. How, though, to reconcile this with the certainty that humans were the Creator's chosen on earth? René Descartes resolved the question by arguing that human speech, thoughts, and feelings were products of the soul. Since animals do not have souls they, thus, do not either think or feel. If some animals surpassed humans in some physical skills, he argued, "it is nature which acts in them according to the disposition of their organs, just as a clock which is only composed of wheels and weights is able to tell the hours and measure the time more correctly than we can do with all our wisdom." Animals were simply machines, and instincts were innate patterns of behavior programmed by the Great Clockmaker to help them survive.[6]

Nearly three hundred years later, John Burroughs reflected these historical traditions when he wrote that animals are "rational without reason, and wise without understanding." He went on:

> Animal behavior ... is much more like the behavior of natural forces than is that of man: the animal goes with Nature, borne along by her currents, while the mind of man crosses and confronts Nature, thwarts her, uses her, or turns her back upon herself. During the vast aeons while the earth was peopled by the lower orders alone, Nature went her way. But when this new animal, man, appeared, in due time Nature began to go his way, to own him as master. Her steam and her currents did his work, her lightning carried his messages, her forces became his servants.[7]

Humans are in control, he argued. We dominate nature and reshape it to meet our own needs. Animals are a part of the machinery of nature. No wonder Burroughs felt that they cannot reason any more than can a rock or a tree.

Scientists, however, became dissatisfied with Descartes's mechanistic view of animals. They saw that animals respond to sensations from their environment and alter their behavior accordingly. Although they recognized that animals have innate, fixed instincts, they also noticed that animals learn from their experiences. In addition, scientists believed that behavior and reasoning could be explained in naturalistic terms, without appealing to God. Nevertheless they continued to believe that there was a significant difference between humans and animals—humans are capable of abstract reasoning and animals are not. Mind replaced soul as the distinguishing characteristic of humanity.[8]

Following the publication of Charles Darwin's *The Origin of Species* in 1859, it became acceptable to assume that the human mind evolved from animal origins. This made it easier to believe that within the animal world one can find a broad variety of behavior and mental abilities, ranging from

143

pure instinct to reasoning powers close to those of humans. John Burroughs seemed unable to accept this view of animal psychology, although he admired Darwin and recognized that animals are capable of learning from their experiences. Theodore Roosevelt, on the other hand, argued that various animals displayed a wide range of psychological abilities, including the ability to reason: for example, that a chimpanzee could reason, while a salamander might not.

However, regardless of Roosevelt's assessment of their psychological abilities, he still considered animals to be objects whose first role was to satisfy human needs. He railed against the destruction of wildlife by "game hogs," but this was because they killed more than their fair share and did it by unsporting methods. For example, in 1885 he wrote, "The extermination of the buffalo has been a veritable tragedy of the animal world." He went on to describe it as "without parallel in historic times." Nevertheless, he supported the buffalo's extinction in the cause of "progress" and the Euro-American subjugation of the continent's natives.

> While the slaughter of the buffalo has been in places needless and brutal, and while it is to be greatly regretted that the species is likely to become extinct, and while, moreover, from a purely selfish standpoint many, including myself, would rather see it continue to exist as the chief feature in the unchanged life of the Western wilderness; yet, on the other hand, it must be remembered that its continued existence in any numbers was absolutely incompatible with anything but a very sparse settlement of the country; and that its destruction was the condition precedent upon the advance of white civilization in the West, and was a positive boon to the more thrifty and industrious frontiersmen. Where the buffalo were plenty, they ate up all the grass that could have supported cattle. . . . From the standpoint of humanity at large, the extermination of the buffalo has been a blessing.[9]

It may seem ironic to recall that Roosevelt is remembered as one of the fathers of conservation in the United States. These views fit, however, within his acceptance of animals as useful objects. In 1907, just before the nature fakers controversy reached its crescendo, Gifford Pinchot and his staff developed the concept of resource conservation and began to construct its underlying theory. In their view, forests, rivers, and rangeland were natural resources that required scientific management to insure that they would be in perpetual supply. This was a wise and essential program in the face of escalating resource exploitation, and it received Theodore

Roosevelt's enthusiastic support. The philosophy of conservation underscored the role and responsibility that people have as stewards of nature.[10] On the other hand, it was also another manifestation of the philosophy of nature as a thing existing solely to satisfy human needs. Resource conservation embodied the view that humans are intimately linked with the natural world. The link, though, was of an economic nature, forged by human dependence upon its resources, including wildlife. Moral considerations only involved people, in their sharing of these resources. Although people were physically linked with nature, there were no moral or spiritual ties.

The "spaceship earth"[11] metaphor, which became so important to environmentalists in the 1970s, provides a powerful image of a finite, self-contained earth that must recycle its resources and limit its population if those who dwell on it are to survive. It also presents an image of a human community embraced within a unifying environment and responsibility. Nevertheless, it too is a machine image that implies that someone, presumably human, is in control, and wise control is defined solely in terms of the welfare of its human passengers. As with the philosophy of conservation, our moral obligations are to our fellow humans and there are no moral or spiritual ties to the rest of the machinery of the spaceship or to the natural world.

Henry Adams's dynamo of physical power over nature provides a useful metaphor for the driving forces of American society. The conservationists devised an essential means of protecting the resources that feed the flames powering this dynamo, but nature was still fuel for the flames. Are there other equally powerful metaphors that can fill the void left by the goddesses who once linked humanity with the organic, procreative, and eternally growing, renewing powers of the natural world? In addition to our economic link with nature, are there also moral and spiritual links? More specific to the nature fakers controversy: Are there ways of understanding animals as something more than things, something more than simply living machines?

Animals as Human

The nature lovers explored these questions and proposed two answers. One answer was that we are linked with nature by bonds of beauty—by our ability to find aesthetic value in the world around us. The other, more sophisticated answer was that animals are very much like people.

In 1902, one nature study textbook pointed out that "After the necessities of life are secured, man has instinctively turned toward the beautiful to complete his satisfaction in nature. . . . Nature study should thus fill and surround our homes and schoolhouses with the most beautiful things attainable and instill the spirit of creating and preserving the natural beauties of roadside and field and forest rather than that of ruthless destruction."[12] Nature writers drew upon this theme again and again. They described and praised nature's beauty and urged their readers to protect it. Mountains, rivers, forests, wildflowers, and wildlife all were of aesthetic value. And the experience of nature's beauty, the writers often claimed, touched something deep within nature lovers and renewed their lease on life. Roosevelt and many other conservationists also found extraordinary beauty in nature. Their delight in this beauty was a strong motivation to study and protect wildlife.

The danger, though, was that people might protect the beautiful parts of nature and forget about the rest. In addition, a thing of beauty may remain just that, a "thing," abstracted from its full, living context. John Burroughs was aware of the problem and, nearly thirty years before the nature fakers controversy, pointed out that "Nature does nothing merely for beauty; beauty follows as the inevitable result; and the final impression of health and finish which her works make upon the mind is owing as much to these things which are not technically called beautiful as to those which are." Nature is organic, growing, and all part of one whole. "The beauty of nature includes all that is called beautiful, as its flower; and all that is not called beautiful, as its stalk and roots."[13]

Charles G. D. Roberts recognized another non-utilitarian link between people and wildlife. He pointed out that with the weakening of old religious and intellectual dogmas people were beginning to recognize their ancient kinship with the earth's creatures. In a statement complimentary to animals, but reflecting the racism of his time, he wrote that "As far, at least, as the mental intelligence is concerned, the gulf dividing the lowest of the human species from the highest of the animals has in these latter days been reduced to a very narrow psychological fissure."[14] Bonds of kinship are much stronger than those based on an appreciation of beauty alone.

Roberts's concept of kinship was rooted in an evolutionary understanding of nature. The popular notion of Darwinism recognized, much to the distress of some people, that humans are related to animals. Now we were beginning to see the flip-side of that coin: Animals have human qualities. In the nineteenth century, animal welfare advocates taught that, contrary to Descartes's philosophy, animals can feel pain and that humans have an obligation to prevent their suffering. Now, the writers of "realistic" wild animal stories were saying that humans were not the only creatures sharing the phenomenon of mind. Animals, too, have minds and mental processes similar to our own. The debate over our obligations to animals shifted from the question of whether animals suffer pain to include the question of whether animals can reason. It was an easily polarized debate, because animal psychology at the end of the nineteenth century offered instinct and reason as the only options for explaining the mental life of animals.[15] This debate was a main root of the nature fakers controversy, and a major reason that the controversy became so heated. Conventional wisdom only offered two very different alternative views of animal mentality.

The danger in attributing reason to animals is that it becomes still easier to project human traits upon animals without justification in fact. The tendency to anthropomorphize animals was not new, but many nature lovers often seemed to do it to extremes. This was certainly the case with the nature fakers, but their critics were also guilty. William T. Hornaday, for example, wrote that

> Of all quadrupeds, deer are the greatest fools, wolves are the meanest, apes the most cunning, bears the most consistent and open-minded, and elephants the most intellectual.
>
> Of birds, the parrots and cockatoos are the most philosophic, the cranes are the most domineering, the darters are the most treacherous, the gallinaceous birds have the least common-sense, and the swimming birds are by far the quickest to recognize protection, and accept it.

Even Theodore Roosevelt fell into this trap. In his book *The Wilderness Hunter*, he judged the elk bull to be "a very unamiable beast, who behaves with brutal ferocity to the weak, and shows abject terror of the strong. According to his powers, he is guilty of rape, robbery, and even murder." Roosevelt saw these as morally inferior traits and shot accordingly. "I never felt the least compunction at shooting a bull," he wrote, "but I hated to shoot a cow, even when forced by necessity. Maternity must always appeal to one."[16]

Despite the anthropomorphic pitfalls, the notion that animals can reason had a positive ethical impact: It forged a new moral link between people and nature based on a moral kinship with animals. Our shared psychology entailed a shared morality and, thus, our moral obligations to animals are similar to our obligations to other people. "Since, then, the animals are creatures with wants and feeling differing in degree only from our own, they surely have their rights," wrote Ernest Thompson Seton. "This fact, now beginning to be recognized by the Caucasian world, was first proclaimed by Moses and was emphasized by the Buddhist over two thousand years ago."[17] Seton and many of the animal story writers went still farther, proposing that animals not only have rights but also follow their own standards of morality and social conduct. Their animal heroes displayed marital fidelity, courage, and a sense of fair play and were conscientious parents who educated their young.

Seton and Long even argued that human morality and animal morality shared a common origin. In "The Natural History of the Ten Commandments," Seton argued that the biblical commandments "are fundamental laws of all creation" that govern both human and animal behavior. Long argued that animals are inherently more moral than humans. In the voice of Peter Rabbit, he explained, "your vices are pure human inventions, man having apparently used his reason in developing moral vices that the wild animals would not tolerate for an instant." In this respect, calling a person an animal was a compliment. "Morality," Peter Rabbit went on to say, "is the inborn sense of harmony with a law which you did not make, but which you recognize both by instinct and practice to be right and good."[18]

These views were not simply products of the authors' private fantasies. Seton, Long, and many other authors had observed animals in the wild and learned that their behavior could be explained in terms of social rules. While the popular notion of wolves, for example, was that they were bloodthirsty creatures that treated each other with cruel savagery, Seton and Long recognized that wolves do not kill unnecessarily, that they worked in cooperative social units characterized by little aggressive behavior, and that they share the fruits of the hunt with their fellows. Seton, especially, made a lifelong study of animal behavior, which he carefully documented with photographs, sketches, and field notes. The best of the realistic animal story writers, and Seton in particular, provided models of a new approach to the study of animals: the study of animal behavior in the wild. They convinced thousands of amateur naturalists to set aside their shotguns, butterfly nets, and egg collections and to study, instead, living animals. In the process, they popularized an emerging new science based on this study that is now known as ethology.[19]

Nature lovers often condemned the more traditional approaches to natural history based on collecting specimens, measuring and naming them, and describing their variations. This became their model of science (a narrow view, at best), whose value they derided. Seton understood these methods, but William J. Long was among the quickest to reject this approach to knowledge, which he regarded as the "questionable slaughter of untold innocents in the acquisition of its superficial knowledge."[20] In spite of the bogus proposition that these research methods produced nothing of value, many of the scientists who employed them were also careful observers of wildlife behavior. Even Long's chief nemesis, the hunter and naturalist Theodore Roosevelt, was an extraordinary student of animal behavior.

The nature lovers' real complaint was that the traditional methods of natural history research killed animals. This was compounded by their confusing the toll taken in the course of legitimate research with the vast, wasteful destruction of wildlife caused by countless nature hobbyists trying to build private collections. Even so, the death rate was declining. In fact, the shotgun was on its way out as an essential tool of the bird watcher. Although there continued to be disagreement among experts over how much confidence could be placed in a bird sighting if the specimen was not

Animal Psychology. By Charles Copeland. From William J. Long, *Brier-Patch Philosophy* (Boston: Ginn, 1906).

in hand (a reasonable concern, given the poor quality of the optics and field guides that were available at the time), in the first decades of the twentieth century opera glasses and field glasses became the bird watcher's preferred tool. The die was cast in 1934 when Roger Tory Peterson's *A Field Guide to the Birds* provided an accessible and reliable guide to bird identification using a method that Ernest Thompson Seton had illustrated and popularized thirty years before.[21] This opened the field to women and countless others who found the glass preferable to the gun.

Hunters were also under attack. Many nature writers, wild animal story writers in particular, were outspoken in their opposition to hunting and trapping. J. P. Mowbray, for example, wrote of watching a favorite woodchuck as it "looked at dogs and men, trying, in one momentary glance of wonder, before he was torn to pieces, to comprehend the inexplicable injustice and cruelty of it." Clarence Hawkes wrote of the thoughtless destruction of birds by boys with slingshots. Animal stories were especially effective, because their readers developed an empathetic love of the animal characters only to witness their death at human hands. Charles G. D. Roberts's Red Fox, for example, saw his father die in an effort to lead the hounds away from his family, was hunted by farmers, became the quarry in a British-style fox hunt, and found fellow woodland creatures caught in traps and snares. Roberts and William J. Long described animals that chewed off their feet to get free of traps. Long described a muskrat who "waddled through the grass like a bear or a monkey, for he had no fore feet to rest on," because they "had been twice caught in man's abominable inventions."[22]

Writers such as Seton, Roberts, and Long placed humans as only one of the moral species within a larger moral universe. Indeed, they often went farther and represented humans as an evil force within the universe. (Seton wrote, for example, "No animal will give up its whole life to seeking revenge; that evil kind of mind is found in man alone. The brute creation seeks for peace.") These authors and their colleagues presented the public with a life-centered rather than a utilitarian, human-centered view of nature and paved the way for the more self-consciously ecological writers and ethicists who followed them.[23]

One of the things that set Long most apart from his fellow nature writers was his belief that wild animals do not feel the pain of the predator's claws, the hunter's bullet, or the trapper's snare. Long believed that the life of wild animals is a "gladsome life," well provided by nature with food and the other amenities they require to live, as well as with the ability to enjoy the game of survival. "All his life the animal plays the game," Long wrote, "and if you watch a fox playing ahead of the dogs, you may conclude that the element of danger probably adds considerable to the animal's joy of living." Such a beneficent nature, he believed, cannot allow its creatures to suffer. He wrote, "Three fourths, at least, of all our [human] pain is mental; is born of an overwrought nervous organization, or imagination," which wild animals lack. When they are sick, they go to sleep until they are well. When wounded, "They sink into a dozy, dreamy slumber, as free from pain or care as an opium smoker," and sleep until they heal or die.[24]

This may help to explain Long's relationship with his hunting dogs. A harsh disciplinarian, in one book he illustrated that his dogs' responses were displays of emotion, rather than of physical pain, by describing how they responded to his lash. "No matter how hard the lash fell," Long wrote of one dog, "he never winced; he seemed made of stone."[25]

How, then, could he argue against hunting, if animals feel no pain? Long did not rely on the prevention of suffering to justify kindness and condemn hunting cruelty. He recognized that hunting was an essential part of life, for many animals must hunt and kill other animals in order to survive. Long was himself a hunter and fisherman (and poacher), but he took only what he needed for food. However, he argued that hunting for sport is out of harmony with the ways of nature and, thus, wrong. There is no animal, he argued, "that naturally or instinctively goes out, as you do, and hunts for sport or pleasure. An animal hunts only for food, and only when he is hungry. When his hunger is satisfied he ceases to hunt, and naturally and instinctively lets all other animals severely alone." Also, firearms and traps are not a part of the natural game of survival and unfairly tip the odds in favor of the hunter. In response to those who suggested that sport hunting was a natural response to an inherited hunting instinct, Long's Peter Rabbit argued:

> As a matter of fact, only a very small minority of you men have what you call a sporting instinct. Women, I am told, are more numerous than men; they have also stronger instincts. If hunting were an instinct, then you would naturally expect to find it strongest in women, especially as the female animal generally has to hunt more than the male in order to support herself and her little ones. But your women have no instinct to hunt; indeed, with a few rare exceptions, they seem to have a strong feeling or instinct against it, on account of the needless cruelty and suffering involved.[26]

In the eyes of Long, Seton, and many nature lovers, wild animals were not things. Indeed, their animal heroes sometimes seemed to be moral beacons for humans. Long and Seton, in particular, looked to nature and wild animals as sources of moral guidance. They needed no argument to justify protecting nature; it was the hunter and civilization that required an excuse. In short, Long and Seton tipped conventional ethics on its head. In their view, it was nature, not civilization, that was moral, and it was to nature that we must look for ethical guidance. They played similar tricks with religion. They believed animals had a spiritual identity and this belief was the bedrock on which their moral philosophies stood.

Animals as Divine

"Each thing that grows here seems to be adapted to the needs of other living things, and all for us," said one of William H. Boardman's characters in *The Lovers of the Woods*. "The Earth was made for man, and there is a God."[27] This statement may have typified the views of resource conservationists. However, while it is ecological in tone, this human-centered theology did not satisfy many nature lovers, who preferred, instead, a religion centered on nature. They were in the process of discovering a new, biological goddess to replace the mythic images of the ancient goddesses that succumbed to the dynamo—Mother Nature herself. And along with Mother Nature came her children—the center of the nature fakers controversy—the animals.

With the weakening of the predominant interpretation of the biblical relationship between humans and nature and with the rise of science, the image of a god in a supernatural heaven apart from the natural world also began to weaken. This did not mean the end of religion, but the recognition that nature itself has a spiritual value and identity. One approach was to acknowledge that God is located outside of nature, but that all creatures shared a spiritual relationship with the deity similar to that of humans. Another view placed the deity within and expressed through nature. In practice, the nature lovers often muddled the two, leaving only the certainty that nature, including wildlife, was in some way divine.

In many cases the nature lovers' spiritual images of nature were rooted in a shallow, self-centered, Victorian sentimentalism that made a mockery of whatever legitimate spiritual experiences and insights they had regarding their relationship with nature. In the words of a contemporary critic, "The senses may indeed be inlets of spirituality. But in the typical nature-lover of the present day one observes a great deal of sensuousness and a negligible degree of spirituality." James Russell Lowell had put it more directly: "I look upon a great deal of the modern sentimentalism about nature as a mark of disease." But the same critic of nature lovers who quoted this statement by Lowell went on to write:

> When Christianity came in, great Pan died, we are told, and all the classic divinities fled away. But in the course of a few centuries they all came back again, with new names, to be sure, and under a more sinister aspect. De Quincey has beautifully described the trouble which the priests had to keep them within bounds in that forest of Domrémy where Joan of Arc dwelt. Then came the Protestant Reformation and a rationalizing spirit, and the wilderness finally got cleared again of witches and fairies; but Wordsworth has been accused of pantheism, and [the British nature writer] Richard Jefferies came near being a worshipper of nature, in the Pagan sense. Perhaps, after all, the instinct of the human race is not wholly wrong in this matter; perhaps there is something besides carbon in the wilderness.[28]

Many people felt that there was "something besides carbon in the wilderness" and they struggled to put their feelings into words. "Some people do not well know that God is out-of-doors," wrote William A. Quayle in his syrupy *In God's Out-of-Doors*. "I marvel at them. He is everywhere. ... He made the out-of-doors and loves it, and haunts it, as Jesus did the mountain and the sea." Quayle's approach turned Christianity into a nature religion in a manner akin to natural theology. He called upon his readers to admire nature as it revealed the wonderful works of God.[29]

While Quayle's praise of nature was overtly religious, many nature writers also praised nature and natural beauty. Their tone was reminiscent of the natural theologists' efforts to praise God through the study of the creation. The baton had passed from the scientists to the nature writers. In an increasingly secular age, though, God often seemed to be left out of the equation and what remained was a deep sense of wonder at and appreciation of the workings of nature and its beauties. Perhaps it is more accurate to say that although speaking of God was out of fashion, there was a spirituality implicit in all of nature and no need to mention a separate deity. This has remained an important facet of nature writing throughout the twentieth century.[30]

The more overtly pantheistic sentiments of some nature lovers were expressed, perhaps, through their taste for garden-ornament busts of the great god Pan. Some writers also used outright pantheistic images and personified Mother Nature. Hamilton Wright Mabie, for example, wrote prose as saccharin as Quayle's, extolling the virtues of a personified Nature. In pages decorated with images of nymphs, satyrs, and shepherds, he proclaimed that "there is a something behind the glory of summer, and they only have entered into real communion with Nature who have learned to separate her from all her miracles of power and beauty; who have come to understand that she lives apart from the singing of birds, the blossoming of flowers, and the waving of branches heavy with leaves." The great secret Mabie learned from Nature, from the murmuring of "things which lie at the roots of instinct rather than within the recollection of thought," was that he was "no alien in this secluded world [of Nature]; my citizenship is here no less than in that other world to which I shall return, but to which I shall never wholly belong."[31]

John Muir described such mystical experiences with greater clarity: "You cannot feel yourself out of doors; plain, sky, and mountains ray beauty which you feel. You bathe in these spirit-beams, turning round and round, as if warming at a camp-fire. Presently you lose consciousness of your own separate existence: you blend with the landscape, and become part and parcel of nature." For Muir, nature was not just natural resources waiting

Goddesses of Nature Personified: "To-morrow the blossoms will begin to sift down from the snowy branches." By Charles Louis Hinton. From Hamilton Wright Mabie, *Under the Trees* (New York: Dodd, Mead, 1902).

to be extracted, manufactured, marketed, and consumed. It was beautiful and divine and existed on a grander scale than he, yet he was also a part of it. This realization was one of the motivating forces behind the wilderness preservation movement that Muir came to symbolize. Euro-Americans had come a long way in the less than two centuries since William Bradford described America as a "hideous and desolate wilderness."[32]

Muir and many others were touched by the transcendental philosophy preached by Ralph Waldo Emerson: that the experience of nature was a doorway to spiritual Truth. In 1836 Emerson wrote, "Standing on the bare ground—my head bathed by blithe air and uplifted into infinite space— all mean egotism vanishes. I become a transparent eyeball; I am nothing; I am part or parcel of God." Muir idolized Emerson and when the philosopher visited Yosemite the naturalist hoped to take him into the wilderness to experience its transcendental wonders. But Emerson's traveling companions were protective of the old man, warning that "Mr. Emerson might take cold; and you know, Mr. Muir, that would be a dreadful thing." Muir was heartsick when they parted, for he felt "that Emerson of all men would be the quickest to see the mountains and sing them. . . . After sundown I built a great fire, and as usual had it all to myself. And though lonesome for the first time in these forests, I quickly took heart again,—the trees had not gone to Boston, nor the birds; and as I sat by the fire, Emerson was still with me in spirit, though I never again saw him in the flesh."[33] While Emerson philosophized about the spiritual values of nature, Muir lived them.

John Burroughs was also something of a transcendentalist and considered Emerson to be his "spiritual father." Nevertheless, his writings are an extraordinarily detailed, although unsystematic, record of a man's struggle to accommodate his pantheistic vision of nature with his faith in a scientific understanding of his world. Burroughs was "a vitalist with a mystical limp" who sensed through his own observations of nature a vital life force doing its creative work through organic evolution. Yet, he also felt the "cosmic chill" of a universe largely alien to and unmindful of humans, which gave his philosophical musings an existential flavor. "Our own earth must have been millions of years without man," he wrote, "and will again be millions without him. He is the insect of a summer hour. The scheme of the universe is too big for us to grasp—so big it is no scheme at all. . . . Any God we can conceive of is inadequate. The universe is no more a temple than it is a brothel or a library. The Cosmos knows no God—it is *super deus*." Burroughs felt a religious awe in the presence of nature, but rejected theological efforts to systematize reverence:

What mankind will finally clothe themselves with to protect them from the chill of the great void, or whether or not they will clothe themselves at all, but become toughened and indifferent, is more than I can pretend to say. For my own part, the longer I live the less I feel the need of any sort of theological belief, and the more I am content to let the unseen powers go their own way with me and mine without question or distrust. They brought me here, and I have found it well to be here; in due time they will take me hence, and I have no doubt that will be well for me too.[34]

The views of most nature lovers were simpler and much more comforting. Whatever the theological variations, their approach could be summed up by Ray Stannard Baker (under his *nom de plume*, David Grayson) in his conversation with a botanist whom he came upon studying wildflowers in his field:

"I have been a botanist for fifty-four years. When I was a boy I believed implicitly in God. I prayed to him, having a vision of him—a person—before my eyes. As I grew older I concluded that there was no God. I dismissed him from the universe. I believed only in what I could see, or hear, or feel. I talked about Nature and Reality."

He paused, the smile still lighting his face, evidently recalling to himself the old days. I did not interrupt him. Finally he turned to me and said abruptly,

"And now—it seems to me—there is nothing but God."[35]

The indigenous peoples of North America provided a model of living in a close physical and spiritual relationship with nature and its wildlife. It is a spiritual relationship so close that the distinction between natural and supernatural loses its meaning. Henry Thoreau and John Muir shared this perception, as did many of the nature lovers.[36] Ernest Thompson Seton had a deep respect for the ways of Native Americans and their understanding of nature and became one of the best known popular apostles of their way of life. While most Euro-Americans revered the pioneers who brought civilization to the wilderness, Seton despised them as despoilers and believed that the European culture they spread was a corrupting influence. He also revolted against traditional Christianity.

The turning point in Seton's religious views came in 1893, when he was working in New Mexico and attended a religious service with the cowboys. When the minister preached, "All we were born in iniquity, and in SIN did our mothers conceive us," a Texan jumped up, pulled out his pistol and shouted, "Damn your soul, my mother didn't conceive me in no such way. My mother was a good woman.... Get down on your knees now, and take it all back, or I'll blow you full of holes."

"What kind of religion is it," Seton wondered, "that puts the stamp of sin on every God-appointed natural human emotion and relationship?" Over the years he adopted something of a Native American–style pantheism that was also informed by his knowledge of natural history.[37]

Many of the nature writers singled out as nature fakers viewed animals not only as in some way human, but also as beings with a spiritual character. No wonder they and many other literary naturalists were disturbed by the suggestion that animals are simply creatures of instinct, akin to machines. William J. Long was particularly articulate and sophisticated in his statements of his theology of nature and wildlife. His interpretations of animal psychology were grounded in his theology.

Like Seton, Long's religious beliefs also changed as he matured. While a teenager he rejected his family's Catholicism and eventually became a Congregationalist minister. His religion was quite universalist in orientation, though, and grew to encompass all of nature. Even the first human, he wrote, "came to feel the presence of some one else moving in the solitudes, some one who spoke in flowers and trees and stars, and in life that continually renews itself, instead of in canoes or wigwams, which were the man's own mode of expression." When someone once suggested to Long that his views sounded pantheistic, the author replied, "I suppose so, but to me all nature is alive and responsive. Even trees seem half conscious." He also offered that he did not "like to wear rubbers which are non-conductors, between me and mother earth."[38] His daughter recalled a ritual that he performed whenever they found a woodland spring. Long pulled out his collapsible cup (silver, with a gold lining) and filled it with water. Before drinking, however, he always poured the first cupful on the ground to thank the gods who put the spring there.

At its root, Long's belief in the ability of animals to reason was built on a theological foundation. He believed all mental processes were natural expressions of the mind of God and that the laws of mind were universal laws of the universe. "So if, as your scientists claim, there be any unity in the force or the God that thinks these laws of the universe and the brier patch, then the laws of mind are probably also constant. Any truth, therefore, which you discover about your own mind—which constitutes your psychology—must apply to any mind in the universe wherever you find it, whether in heaven or hell, in the brier patch or in the professor's easy-chair."[39] Thus, animal psychology and human psychology were one and the same. The difference between the two were, in Long's view, questions of degree rather than of kind.

Long's philosophy bore a similarity to that of Alfred Russell Wallace, co-author with Darwin of the theory of evolution by natural selection. Wallace began to interpret human mental powers in spiritual terms when he converted to spiritualism after attending a séance in 1865. He believed that organic evolution was not a sufficient explanation for the human mind and our higher ideals. Their origins, Wallace argued, lay in the intervention of a higher, spiritual intelligence.[40] Long extended this view to the whole animal world.

Charles G. D. Roberts felt that the development of sympathetic love for and understanding of animals among Euro-Americans was a matter of "spiritual significance." However, he believed this was the limit of human appreciation of wildlife. "There would seem to be no further evolution possible," he wrote, "unless based upon a hypothesis that animals have souls. As souls are apt to elude exact observation, to forecast any such

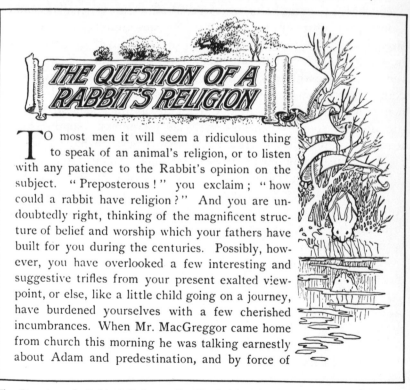

THE QUESTION OF A RABBIT'S RELIGION

TO most men it will seem a ridiculous thing to speak of an animal's religion, or to listen with any patience to the Rabbit's opinion on the subject. " Preposterous ! " you exclaim ; " how could a rabbit have religion ? " And you are un-doubtedly right, thinking of the magnificent struc-ture of belief and worship which your fathers have built for you during the centuries. Possibly, how-ever, you have overlooked a few interesting and suggestive trifles from your present exalted view-point, or else, like a little child going on a journey, have burdened yourselves with a few cherished incumbrances. When Mr. MacGreggor came home from church this morning he was talking earnestly about Adam and predestination, and by force of

The Question of a Rabbit's Religion. By Charles Copeland. From William J. Long, _Brier-Patch Philosophy_ (Boston: Ginn, 1906).

development would seem to be at best merely fanciful."[41]

William J. Long was not so timid—he believed animals were capable of religion and, perhaps, even immortality. "You forget that religion had a boyhood," Long wrote, "that instead of being rational and theological, and therefore full of doubts, it was at one time natural and spontaneous and gladly sure of itself, as only boyhood knows how to be." In the voice of Peter Rabbit he argued that religion

> is part intuition and part reason, intuition at its purest and reason at its highest point, both at work upon the final questions of life. Now the Rabbit has intuition, that is, inborn knowledge independent of his senses, as you admit when you speak of his instinct; he has also, as we have seen, some good claim to elemental reasoning. Apparently, then, there is no intrinsic impossibility in the idea of his possessing at least a rudimentary religion, since he has some small measure of the two powers, of reason and intuition, out of which your own religion first sprang.

Long believed both that animals sense the presence of God, or a "greater Life," and that they have an "idea of a common kinship, or brotherhood, in view of the great common life"—at least they demonstrate more brotherhood than do humans. Animals were even capable of a sort of prayer. "So far as a prayer can be without words," he wrote, "the animal's whole life and effort is a prayer for more life, and for the good of life as he knows it." His theories about animal mind and religion were linked by his view of animal immortality. "If you are just brain, if there is nothing in your sense of duty but albumen, and nothing in your love but phosphates, then you scatter to the elements and are lost; but if you are mind, then, so far as we can know or reason, no fire can burn or water drown or any death affect you in the least."[42] Thus, if one acknowledged that animals have minds, one must also grant the possibility of animal immortality.

Long believed in animal immortality. Although he couched his conclusion with the tentative words of a scholar proposing a theory for examination, we can be sure of Long's belief. In the voice of his alter ego, Peter Rabbit, he wrote:

> So far, then, as the animal seems to you to possess a rudimentary mind, you may reasonably claim for him some small chance for immortality. Every animal, as well as every man, reproduces in himself from birth to death the whole history of his race; and the history of any race seems to be an upward striving, through pain

and loss, to more and more perfect things. Where the process began, where mind emerged from matter, or first clothed itself in matter, the Rabbit does not know, but leaves the question cheerfully to One who was probably present with the morning stars, and whose action has been reasonable and constant ever since. It seems, however, that the process, once begun and long continued, can never end rationally until "the desire of every living thing" for more life shall be accomplished. . . . Death to the animal is but a sleep, and the only thought in his head when he lies down for the last time is Nature's whisper that he will waken as usual when the right time comes. Now Nature deceives nobody, nor does she long tolerate any deception. It would be most irrational, even for a rabbit, to suppose that Nature has told him truth every hour of his long life, only to whisper a falsehood at the last moment.[43]

John Burroughs also pondered the question of eternal life. In his last years, he thought a great deal about such matters. He, too, envisioned a kind of immortality, but it stood in sharp contrast with Long's notions. It was ecologically bonded with the earth rather than with a supernatural afterworld. In Burroughs's view, mind and body are phenomena of energy and matter, both quite natural, thus his immortality lies in the immortality of his physical components—matter and energy.

I shall not be imprisoned in that grave where you are to bury my body. I shall be diffused in great Nature, in the soil, in the air, in all the living and flowing currents of the world, though I may never again in my entirety be embodied in a single human being. My elements and my forces go back into the original sources out of which they came, and these sources are perennial in this vast, wonderful, divine cosmos.[44]

William J. Long, unlike Burroughs, believed in a loving God. Ten years earlier he had become embroiled in a theological controversy with the Cambridge Council because he refused to compromise in his belief that a loving God would never condemn souls to eternal damnation. Later, in 1908, Long addressed the Boston Teachers Club at the city's Symphony Hall. Fresh from his battle with Theodore Roosevelt, he still proclaimed the truthfulness of his stories and his vision of nature. "When I say that there is no animal psychology," he proclaimed, "I mean that the law which applies to your own mind applies to any mind. When you speak of human nature, what do you mean? You mean love."[45] He believed that all life reflected this love, that it was based on cooperation rather than competition, and that a loving God would not permit animals to suffer or exist outside of divine grace.

Both Long and Seton believed that nature was a source, if not the source, of moral and spiritual values and that the veneer of civilization often distorted and destroyed these values. Both believed that Native Americans and children were closer to nature in their views, more natural, and, thus, more in tune with these values. Long and Seton may have differed in some elements of their theology, but their greatest difference lay in the value each placed on science. Seton understood and practiced the methods of science in his effort to better understand the natural world. In a sense, Long was a *nature* theologian, but not a *natural* theologian. He rejected science as a source of knowledge that could be useful in his effort to paint a meaningful picture of our place in nature and in the moral and spiritual universe. In the process, he left himself wide open to attack as a nature faker.

Worlds in Conflict

The nature fakers controversy was far more than a clash over the accuracy of animal stories or the question of whether animals can reason. At the turn of the century, America was in the midst of a cultural transition regarding the relationship between people and nature. This transition is still in process. The nature fakers controversy was one aspect of this shift, a clash between fundamentally different understandings of the human relationship with nature. It helps to reflect upon such a conflict in terms of the different worldviews, ethos, and religious beliefs involved.[46] Every culture can be described in these terms, and individuals reflect these aspects of their culture. *Worldview* refers to rational concepts of how the world is structured—how its parts, nature and humans, relate with each other. *Ethos* refers to moral and aesthetic beliefs and styles. *Religion* and *myth* function to bring worldview and ethos into harmony in ways that are psychologically acceptable and meaningful. They explain how the world came to be structured this way and why its moral principles are what they are. Each principal player in the nature fakers controversy (Long, Seton, Roosevelt, and Burroughs) differed from the others, but it is possible to discern a pattern of differences between the opposing sides.

Worldview. All except Long accepted the Darwinian view of evolution by natural selection, believing that humans are joined together with all other living things by their common biological and evolutionary history. Seton, Long, and Burroughs believed that they shared some sort of a direct spiritual relationship with the rest of nature. Roosevelt, on the other hand, seemed to hold the more traditional Christian view that animals and the rest of nature did not have spiritual identities. Seton, Long, and Roosevelt all believed that animals are capable of reason, in varying degrees; Burroughs did not.

Ethos. Each found great beauty in nature, which they valued enormously and wanted to preserve. With the exception of Long, each found that science was a valuable tool for discovering the beauty revealed in the complex patterns of nature. Both Seton and Long recognized that nature was a source of moral wisdom that could guide human affairs. Indeed, they considered human civilization a morally corrupting influence. Roosevelt's moral relationship with nature originated out of the obligation to use its resources wisely and conserve them for future generations. His moral responsibility was to other people, not to nature. Both he and Burroughs believed nature itself was morally neutral.

Religion. There were strongly pantheistic elements to the religious views of Seton, Long, and Burroughs. Both Seton's and Long's spiritual universes were flavored with their Christian origins, especially Long's, although both rejected the Calvinistic image of a wrathful God. Long went still farther and envisioned nature as the benevolent expression of a God who cares for each living creature. Burroughs could not accept this view. In his view, nature cared only for life and humans had no greater claim to that phenomenon than did any other species. Throughout his life, Burroughs felt a homesickness or nostalgia that he described as "almost a disease." This may have been his emotional response to the "cosmic chill" he experienced in the face of an uncaring universe. He did not have a philosophy or religion strong enough to brace himself before such a cosmos.[47] Although Theodore Roosevelt appears not to have been particularly religious, he was raised a Christian and his views seem not to have deviated from those traditional channels.

Thus, we find that Seton and Long stood apart from Burroughs and Roosevelt in finding moral wisdom through the study of nature. William J. Long stood apart from them all in rejecting science and the Darwinian view of the world it supported. These differences become particularly clear when we look at the way these men dealt with death.

Dealing with Death

"Nature does not care whether the hunter slay the beast or the beast the hunter," John Burroughs wrote, "she will make good compost of them both, and her ends are prospered whichever succeeds."[48] In other words, nature does not play favorites. However, although nature may be indifferent, humans are not. Writers and their readers seemed to care about the fates of the animal heroes in their nature stories. Many also proselytized against hunting and trapping. All had to deal with death, but not all handled it in the same way.

Ernest Thompson Seton's stories were often based on that common denominator of animal life—death. "The life of a wild animal," he wrote, "*always has a tragic end.*"[49] By this he meant that animals always die, and rarely do so in their sleep. This was the fate of so many of his animal heroes. The very fact that Seton's animals usually died attested to the truthfulness of his stories: This was simply the way of nature. (It was different, of course, when animals died by human hands.) He and other animal story writers were caught up in the popular view of Darwinian nature: a place of gnawing hunger, "kill or be killed" conflict, and survival of the fittest.

Charles G. D. Roberts, for example, told of a cow and bull calf that found themselves in the wilderness. At first the wild animals stayed away, because of the cowbell's clanging. Later, when the bell was silenced, the bull saw the reality of nature that the noise had kept at a distance:

> But now he saw an occasional slim and snaky mink at its fishing; or a red fox stealing down upon the duck asleep in the lily patch; or a weasel craftily trailing one of the brown hares which had of a sudden grown so numerous. . . . Suddenly a soundless gray shadow shot from a thicket and dropped upon the rabbit. There was a squeak, a feeble scuffle; and then a big lynx, setting the claws of one paw into the prey, turned with a snarl and eyed venomously the still, dark form under the maple.

Nature was a place of death—death pruning out the unfit. "The wild kindred are seldom blind, and very seldom stupid," Roberts wrote elsewhere, "because those members of the fellowship who are possessed of such defects sooner or later go to feed their fellows."[50]

Jack London's fiction also embodied this view of nature. "Nature was not kindly to the flesh," he wrote in "The Law of Life," a tale about an aged Eskimo left by his family to die, as was the way of his people. Nature, he wrote:

> had no concern for that concrete thing called the individual. Her interest lay in the species, the race. . . . The rise of the sap, the bursting greenness of the willow bud, the fall of the yellow leaf— in this alone was told the whole history. But one task did Nature set the individual. Did he not perform it, he died. Did he perform it, it was all the same, he died. Nature did not care; there were

plenty who were obedient, and it was only the obedience in this matter, not the obedient, which lived and lived always.... To life she set one task, gave one law. To perpetuate was the task of life, its law was death.[51]

It was rare to find a wild animal that died of old age in nature stories. Most were eaten, shot, or came to misfortune long before age could take its toll. Even Seton's aging bear Wahb chose a sort of suicide over death by old age. Crippled and in pain, he walked into the poisonous gases of Death Gulch. "The odor that he once had hated was attractive now.... His body craved it. For it seemed to numb his pain and it promised sleep, as it did that day when first he saw the place." As he walked into his death he felt, "The Angel of the Wild Things was standing there, beckoning, in the little vale."[52]

Nevertheless, in the face of perpetual death, the young carried on and life prevailed. Charles G. D. Roberts's stories often revealed the cyclical nature of life and death. "The body of the dead snake," he wrote, "was soon a centre of teeming, hungry, busy life [insects], toiling to remove all traces of what had happened." He also used poetic narrative to resolve the tension between life and death: "When all was still once more on Ringwaak, presently descended again the enchantment of the mystic light. And under its transforming touch even the torn bodies lying before the bright face of the rock lost their hideousness, becoming remote, and unsubstantial and visionary."[53] Death (except by the gun and other technologies of civilization) was a part of nature. Herbivores eat plants and carnivores eat meat. The individual may die, but life continues.

John Burroughs, too, was captivated by Darwinism, which appeared again and again in his essays. " 'Bought by the blood of Christ' is the hyperbole of the Church," he wrote in his journal, "but every child that is born today is bought by the blood of countless ages of barbarism, or countless lives of beings; and this not figuratively, but literally. Out of an ocean of darkness and savagery is distilled this drop of human blood, with all its possibilities." These possibilities, which were won after "a million years of gross selfishness," included "a benevolent throb!"[54] His view of nature, though, was more bleak than that of the animal story writers. Where Burroughs found benevolence only in the human heart, other writers found it in the heart of nature.

Many nature writers viewed nature as more than simply savagery, competition for survival, and a struggle to live. Indeed, much of their writing can be viewed as a revolt against this vision of nature. In Darwin's view, plants and animals struggle for life because more young are produced than can survive and reproduce. Those that have the ability to succeed, that survive and reproduce, pass their survival traits on to their offspring. Thus, there is a natural selection of those traits most fit for survival. Just what these traits might be will vary according with the species and their environment. The fittest plant might be one that grows quickly and captures sunlight better than others, or one that produces the most seeds or seeds that can be carried farthest on the wind to grow in new areas. Fitness for animals might be associated with a solitary individual's abilities to stalk and kill, or with timidity and the ability to hide from predators, or with the ability to cooperate with other individuals in hunting or rearing young.

The popular view of evolution emphasized the killing. But there was more than death going on in the woods; animals were also involved in cooperative social behavior. In 1902, Petr Kropotkin, a Russian aristocrat turned anarchist, published *Mutual Aid*, which emphasized cooperation rather than competition as an evolutionary force. He pointed out:

> As soon as we study animals—not in laboratories and museums only, but in the forests and the prairie, in the steppe and the mountains—we at once perceive that though there is an immense amount of warfare and extermination going on amidst various species, and especially amidst various classes of animals, there is, at the same time, as much, or perhaps even more, of mutual support, mutual aid, and mutual defence amidst animals belonging to the same species, or at least, to the same society.

Kropotkin was not arguing against natural selection. He was arguing for a broader view of what was being selected. He made an important point, and nearly fifty years later ecologist Marston Bates argued that "this competition, this 'struggle,' is a superficial thing, superimposed on an essential mutual dependence—a cooperation that has become so all-pervasive, so completely integrated, that it is difficult to untwine and follow out the separate strands." Evolutionary biologists have even found genetic arguments supporting some kinds of altruistic behavior.[55] Although it is likely that few nature writers read Kropotkin, many seemed to agree with his views.

William J. Long, though, did not. He did not believe there was a struggle for existence at all. Life in nature was a "gladsome life" without suffering and although there was death, there was no knowledge of death. In effect, the Garden of Eden did not exist somewhere in our mythic past: It was right here on earth, now. It was nature.

An Earthly Eden

In *School of the Woods*, Long told of seeing an eagle "spread his wings wide and stiff" and slant gently downward to the earth. "Just within the fringe of the forest I found him, resting peacefully for the first time on mother earth, his head lying across the moss-cushioned root of an old cedar, his wings outstretched among the cool green ferns—dead." This was his image of how animals die: peacefully, gently, and without pain. Long believed that "Nature knows no tragedies," because she cares for her own. "A partridge falls under the owl's swoop. That is bad for the partridge,—who is, however, almost invariably one of the weak or foolish ones who have not learned to be obedient with his brethren,—but there are two young owls up in the treetop yonder, who will rejoice and be glad at the good dinner brought home to them by a careful and loving mother." This passage described the process of natural selection, but Long found no struggle. Although some fell prey to other animals, their death was swift and painless. Death by starvation and freezing was also without pain.

In Long's view, most animals die of illness or old age. Since animals have no knowledge of death, they also have no fear of death, nor do they suffer. They do, though, sense that something is wrong, and each goes off into hiding and waits for nature to take its course. People rarely see this happen, because it is a private, secluded event. Long, though, had seen a dead wood warbler: "He had fallen asleep there, in peace, by the spring that he had known and loved all his life, and whose waters welled up to his lips and held his image in their heart to the last moment." This was how most animals die—"The shadows lengthen; the twilight deepens; his eyes grow drowsy; he falls asleep. And his last conscious thought, since he knows no death, is that he will waken in the morning when the light calls him."[56]

Although Long seemed to believe that he was arguing against Darwinism, he was really arguing (along with Seton and others) against the popular view of nature as a stage for savage cruelty. He did not understand Darwinism. Long's view of the struggle for life was as a personal struggle or conflict *experienced* by individual animals as they fought each other for survival. He seemed to feel that he could disprove Darwinism by demonstrating that animals neither suffer nor experience a struggle. However, Darwin had expressed a view similar to Long's. The concluding sentence of the chapter on the struggle for existence in *The Origin of Species* reads: "When we reflect on this struggle, we may console ourselves with the full belief, that the war of nature is not incessant, that no fear is felt, that death is generally prompt, and that the vigorous, the healthy, and the happy survive and multiply."[57]

Some nature writers might have argued with parts of Long's theory about animal suffering; many would have disagreed about how many animals have the opportunity to die of old age. But Long was not alone in believing that animals could be injured and experience no pain. Charles G. D. Roberts, for example, wrote about a moose that felt a blow, but no pain, when it was shot. "He had no pain, no realization that anything had gone wrong with him. But his eyes took on suddenly a harassed, anxious look, and he felt himself growing tired. He must rest a little before continuing his flight." Even Dallas Lore Sharp de-emphasized the notion of struggle. "Struggle and death go on," he wrote, "but, except where man interferes, a very even balance is maintained, peace prevails over fear, joy lasts longer than pain, and life continues to multiply and replenish the earth." The notion that nature is not cruel and that animals do not experience a struggle, of which Long was the most eloquent proponent, gained increasing support among nature writers as the twentieth century progressed.[58]

Many nature lovers seemed to view nature as an earthly Eden. Long provided the most articulate literary exploration of this terrain. Although there is death, its creatures are not aware of it. They feel no pain and experience no struggle, and there is the promise of immortality. All are watched over by God as expressed through beneficent Mother Nature. If this is not enough, the lives of her creatures are joyful and gladsome. He wrote, "Nature above and below tingles with the joy of mere living—, a joy that bubbles over, like a spring, so that all who will, even the race of men who have lost or forgotten their birthright, may come back and drink of its abundance and be satisfied." Nature, he argued, "is perfect and complete."[59]

Playing further with this religious imagery—if there is an Eden, is there sin and are there sinners in nature? Of course there are. We are the sinners. A quick reading of writers such as Long and Seton suggests that our sin is that of being human, that humans are a destructive element out of harmony with nature and, thus, have no place in it. On reading closer, though, we find that Native Americans and children are kin to nature, at least before civilization gets to them. The real sin is civilization—a new environmental version of original sin. We bit the apple of scientific and technological knowledge and became aliens within a world of nature. We were not cast out of Eden, but ran away in our pursuit of civilization and technology. But the nature lovers offered a way to salvation: Put aside your gun and traps, turn your back on civilization, open your heart, and return to the bosom of nature.

Science and Sentiment

The nature fakers controversy was, on one level, a literary expression of a larger conflict within the nature study movement. It was a debate over whether the goal of nature study was to educate students in the sciences or to teach an appreciation of and sense of harmony with nature.[60] This was an unfortunate and false dichotomy, because it is essential that we join both approaches in our efforts to understand our environment. A sense of harmony with nature that is based on an inadequate or false understanding of the natural world may feel good, but it is useless as a guide to ecological harmony. William J. Long and other nature fakers fell into this trap.

Long was confident in his beliefs. His willingness to direct his readers to Mauran Furbish to confirm his tale about how osprey school their young in fishing underscores his confidence. Nevertheless, the great difference between what Furbish told Long and what Long believed he heard demonstrated his lack of attention to the accuracy of his own reports and those of his informants. He was not interested so much in the scientific value of his work as in its ability to promote in his readers an appreciation of and feelings of kinship with nature and wildlife. His nature stories were strongly shaped by his theological views. However, Long claimed repeatedly that his stories were true. This obligated him to be sure of his facts, but he rejected the tools that enabled him to accomplish this.

He was not, though, ignorant of science. While a student at the Bridgewater Normal School, Long took courses in astronomy, botany, advanced botany, chemistry, geology, physics, advanced physics, physiology, and zoology.[61] It is likely, though, that he was taught by rote and required to memorize a body of scientific information rather than to learn the methods of inquiry and discovery that are the heart of science. Long seemed unsympathetic to the value of scientific methods, which derive new understandings of nature by reasoning inductively from specific observations to more general principles. He was much more comfortable with the deductive methods of traditional philosophy, beginning with grand principles and working from them to specifics. His notions of animal psychology, for example, were more rooted in his fundamental belief that "any law which you find in your own mind must apply to any mind in the universe, wherever you find it"[62] than in close observation of the behavior of animals in the wild.

To defend himself, Long constructed a distorted, half-true image of science and proceeded to demolish it. He represented nature study as "appreciation" and science as mere "description." "Certainly your scientists are searching for truth, but curiously confine themselves to material things, as if there were no difference between a house and a home, and as if the only possible interest in a house was to be found in its cellar," he wrote in the voice of Peter Rabbit, "and so, to a rabbit who thinks, they bear the same relation to philosophers that a tailor bears to a teacher." Elsewhere, he wrote, "the difference between Nature and Science is the difference between a man who loves animals, and so understands them, and the man who studies Zoology; it is the difference between the woman who cherishes her old-fashioned flower-garden and the professor who lectures on Botany in a college class-room."[63]

William T. Hornaday disagreed. In 1904 he argued: "Men of science who study the minds of animals do not idealize their subjects, or ascribe to them super-human intelligence; nor are they always on the alert to ascribe to every simple action some astounding intelligence and far-fetched motive. In the Study of animal intelligence, the legitimate Truth is sufficiently wonderful to satisfy all save those who crave the sensational, regardless of facts."[64] Long's position was unsound, even if we grant that he was operating as a philosopher and nature-lover rather than as a scientist. He believed that his stories and his philosophy of nature and wildlife applied to the real world outside of his readers' back doors. This means that he had to be accurate in his descriptions of that world, regardless of where his meditations eventually took him. He often was not accurate and, in this respect, many of the scientists' criticisms of his stories and books were right on target.

In all fairness to Long and other well-meaning nature fakers, the state of knowledge about the behavior of wildlife was very poor in his day. Even the cautious John Burroughs believed much of animal behavior—for example, the coordinated movements of animal herds and flocks—could be explained only by animal telepathy, a sort of "community mind." Scientists still debate about the nature of animal intelligence and whether animals are self-conscious or can use deception to get their own way. For that matter, it is difficult to figure out what is going on in the minds of humans. Recent research even suggests that the courtroom testimony of expert psychologists and psychiatrists is less reliable than statistics are in predicting a person's future behavior.[65]

As another example, in 1920 the *Auk*, official journal of the American Ornithological Union, published a paper entitled "The Occult Senses in Birds" that argued that animals have as yet unexplainable sensory abilities. These unknown senses account for the ability of birds to navigate during migration (homing sense), of vultures to find carrion (food-finding sense), and of insects to locate mates over great distances. The Smithsonian Institution judged the paper good enough to reprint it in its annual report.[66] The nature writers were treading on new ground—and even though scientists criticized their explanations for many animal behaviors, the scientists themselves sometimes did not have anything better to offer.

In W. F. Ganong's view, the root of the problem of truthfulness in animal stories lay in the difference between the objectives of science and literature. "The charm of the study to the man of science," he wrote, "is the triumph of demonstrating the truth." On the other hand, the new rash of nature writers valued nature primarily as fodder for their literary mill. "To [them] the truth is not of first importance, and imagination is allowed to improve upon nature whenever she can thereby be made more available for literary uses." However, the enormous popularity of William J. Long's and Charles G. D. Roberts's stories did not rest on their literary charm. Their success, according to Ganong, depended on the fact that "they tell about animals, not as they are, but as people like to think they are."[67]

Which brings us to a delightful short story, "The Nature Faker," published in *Collier's Weekly* in 1910, three years after Roosevelt's killing blow against the nature fakers.[68] The story, which reveals an important aspect of the controversy, tells of poor Herrick, a gentleman "with much money and no sense of humor" who was rejected by his true love. "But, as Herrick truly loved Miss Catherweight, he could not worship any other woman, and became a lover of Nature. Nature, he assured his men friends, does not disappoint you." So he went off to Connecticut, bought an abandoned farm (a parody of Ernest Thompson Seton's Connecticut home, Wyndygoul)[69] and converted it into a wilderness garden.

> It consisted of two hundred acres of dense forest and hills and ridges of rock. It was filled with mysterious caves, deep chasms, tiny gurgling streams, nestling springs, and wild laurel. . . . Around the preserve was a high fence stout enough to keep poachers on the outside and to persuade the wild animals that inhabited it to linger on the inside. . . . Every day, in sunshine or in rain, entering through a private gate, Herrick would explore this holy of holies. . . . In time he grew to think he knew and understood the inhabitants of this wild place of which he was the overlord. He looked upon them not as tenants, but as his guests. And when they fled from him in terror to caves and hollow tree-trunks, he wished he might call them back and explain he was their friend, that it was due to him they lived in peace. He was glad they were happy. He was glad it was through him that, undisturbed, they could live the simple life.

But Herrick's friend lured him into the corruption of New York City for an evening at a music hall. There he had the misfortune to witness a trained bear act. The bears dressed in costumes, engaged in a boxing match, and danced to "The Merry Widow Waltz." " 'That,' exclaimed

Brunn and Clara dancing heavily, while Hey pretended to conduct the music of the orchestra

"That," exclaimed Herrick when he saw the dancing bears, "is a degrading spectacle." From Richard Harding Davis, "The Nature Faker," *Collier's Weekly* (10 Dec. 1910).

Herrick hotly, 'is a degrading spectacle.' "

Kelly exclaimed with exasperation: "Confound the bears!" he cried. "If you must spoil my supper weeping over animals, weep over cart-horses. They work. Those bears are loafers. They're as well fed as pet canaries. They're aristocrats."

"But it's not a free life!" protested Herrick. "It's not the life they love."

"It's a darned sight better," declared Kelly, "than sleeping in a damp wood, eating raw blackberries—"

"The more you say," retorted Herrick, "the more you show you know nothing whatsoever of nature's children and their habits."

"And all you know of them," returned Kelly, "is that a cat has nine lives and a barking dog won't bite. You're a nature faker."

Herrick bought the bears at a premium price and, despite his friends' claims that the bears loved the dancing life, released them in his game preserve where they could return to their natural ways in the breast of nature. He followed them into the woods to reassure himself that the bears would adapt themselves to the old ways of their kind. His efforts were rewarded: "They drank from the running streams, for honey they explored the hollow tree trunks, they sharpened their claws on moss-grown rocks, and among the fallen oak leaves scratched violently for acorns."

One evening, Herrick's friends gathered on his terrace after a fine dinner. Their host was less interested in the lovely piano music drifting through the windows than in scolding his doubting guests. " 'No one shall molest them, no one shall force them through degrading tricks. Hereafter [the bears] can choose their life, and their own home among the rocks, and the—' Herrick's words were frozen on his tongue," for he suddenly saw a shocking sight. The bears were on the opposite side of the terrace, waltzing. "From their happy expression, it was evident they not only were greatly enjoying themselves, but that they felt they were affording immeasurable delight to others."

Misguided Herrick was called a nature faker, but was he telling false stories about bears or was he attributing them with special powers of reason and intelligence? No. What he did was assume that the bears fit within his own romantic vision of how bears should live. Herrick was a nature sentimentalist. He was more interested in his own sentiments about bears than in the intrusive reality of the bears themselves. The fictional Herrick reflected the feelings of many people around the nation who enjoyed the nature fakers' stories because, as Ganong pointed out, "they tell about animals, not as they are, but as people like to think they are." John Burroughs agreed with Ganong. "The tendency to sentimentalize nature has, in our time, largely taken the place of the old tendency to demonize and spiritize it," he wrote. "It is anthropomorphism in another form, less fraught with evil to us, but equally in the way of a clear understanding of the life about us."[70]

Many nature books of the time carried an extraordinary freight of Victorian sentiment and gushing, syrupy prose that left many of their authors open to serious criticism. Dallas Lore Sharp put it this way: "Raptures run through nature books as regularly as barbs the length of wire fences." One literary critic of the day wrote that if Thoreau "returned incognito to twentieth century Concord," he would hear

of "the Godful woods," of "the forest-cathedral" of "tree-thoughts," of "Nature's old love-song" (I quote from one or two of the Nature

Books of the past year); he would have been told that the meadowlark surpasses any opera, that the orchid of the fields is, like man, fashioned from the earth, but is "a fairer and lovelier product," that birds are the best of friends, for they bring no "misunderstandings and disappointments" and never grow old and they sometimes have "so much to express, so much tempera-ment"—at least if you assume "the viewpoint of the bird." . . . "This hypethral temple," I read in one of the recent books, ". . . is the only temple on earth where there is no cant, no twaddle, no hypocrisy, and no croaking about our sins." What is this if it is not cant and twaddle?[71]

Indeed it was, but for all their cant and twaddle the nature writers and nature lovers were articulating a relationship with nature that was new to the dominant European-American culture. These sentiments flew in the face of historical, economic, technological, and intellectual traditions. They challenged the notions that animals live solely by instinct, that nature is cruel, and that wild animals (especially carnivores) are vicious beasts intent upon destruction. They gave voice, though sometimes in a faltering and poorly conceived manner, to a new relationship between humans and nature. The popularity of their writing attests to the fact that they were not alone in their views. They reflected as well as shaped the views of a growing segment of the population. Many authors did not find an effective means of expressing this new view of nature, and their writing often seemed to be, and sometimes was, extraordinarily shallow.

Long was among the most articulate and philosophically sophisticated of these writers. He pointed to a different vision of nature—and Burroughs and Roosevelt bit off his finger. Perhaps Long deserved it, but it was certainly unfortunate. It is tempting to wonder what might have happened if Long had come under the influence of an inspired teacher of science. What if he had found a teacher who, like Louis Agassiz, told students to take their text from nature, not books, yet inspired scientific inquiry in the outdoors? But he did not, and his theory of nature was terribly flawed. He studied history, philosophy, and theology on advanced levels. He spent months and years in sympathetic rapport with the wilderness. He honed his intellectual and psychological tools to craft a theory of moral and theological sophistication. In the end, though, he lacked the understand-ing of scientific inquiry necessary to articulate a valid description of the natural world. Although William J. Long was not a conscious fraud, his biology and natural history were biased by his expectations. He was a lousy observer.

New Visions

There were greater depths just beyond his reach. Long and the others were part of a major social revolution—a revolution that is still under way. They were exploring the ethical, emotional, and religious aspects of a new vision of our relationship with nature, a landscape that scientists were not well equipped to travel. But the nature lovers and nature fakers had great difficulty linking their new vision of nature and wildlife with the real animals in a real, evolving ecological setting. To explore these depths, they needed also to use the tools of science.

The Darwinian revolution, however, was not simply a revolution in biological theory. It was, and continues to be, a revolution in the way we think about ourselves: our relationship with the living world around us, our sources of moral guidance, and our religious foundations. Darwin did not

Charles Darwin in 1881. Photo by Elliott & Fry. From Francis Darwin, ed., *Charles Darwin* (London: John Murray, 1908).

begin this process. There were other theories of organic evolution before he proposed the mechanism of natural selection. And the revolution did not end with the nineteenth century—it is still in progress. It took nearly 250 years for organic evolution to become an accepted biological theory, spanning 180 years before the publication of Darwin's *Origin of Species* and roughly 70 years afterward. And it is taking still longer for non-scientists to accept the theory.[72]

Accepting evolution involved much more than simply accepting a particular theory as true. What, for convenience, is called the Darwinian revolution actually involved changing a whole constellation of beliefs. First, the accepted view of the earth's age had to expand enormously, moving from theories of a relatively young earth (about six thousand years old) to one of great antiquity. Only then would we have the span of time necessary for evolutionary change to take place. We also had to recognize that our world is a changing world and learn to view change as something that is happening continuously, not solely as the result of sudden catastrophic events. Third, we had to recognize that evolution does not progress in a line of increasing perfection from the lowest to the "more evolved" highest (us). Instead, evolution had to be seen as change in adaptive response to environmental circumstances, without necessarily producing improvement in an absolute sense.

Other beliefs needed to change that were not simply scientific in nature. These related to religious, philosophical, and other aspects of our cultural worldview. For example, we had to accept the evolutionary process as something that worked on its own without the necessity of a god residing outside of nature who continually tinkered with the creation. We also had to break out of the essentialist view of the world. This philosophy, first put forth by Plato, proposes that the world of our experience is an expression of fundamental, discrete, and immutable forms, or essences, that underlie it. In biological terms, the view of species as distinct and immutable forms is incompatible with evolution as the changing genetic composition of a population or organisms. Finally, we had to do away with our anthropocentric view of the world as something that exists for our benefit or that must conform to values defined in terms of human morality—a task we have yet to accomplish.

It is not surprising that it took so long for the scientific community to accept the evolutionary view. And it is not surprising that the public in general is having still greater difficulty. Although the Darwinian revolution may have taken place in the biological sciences, it is still in progress in the world of the non-biologist. After all, the Copernican revolution still has not completely altered our worldview: We still speak of the sun rising and setting, as if it were revolving around us. It is much more useful to an astronomer to use the sun as the central reference point in our solar system than it is to use the earth. In our everyday lives, however, it is simpler to place the earth at the center of our psychological universe, because most of us are not trying to navigate from one planet to another. The same cannot be said, however, about our narrowly anthropocentric worldview. We are trying to move about within our ecological environment, and anthropocentrism is not necessarily our best point of reference for this task.

The Darwinian revolution, then, is more than a revolution in the scientific worldview. It is a vast cultural revolution impacting ethos and religion as well. We are still trying to adjust culturally to this new vision. The key players in the nature fakers controversy were each involved in this process. Despite their differences and faults, they were piecing together a new vision of our relationships with nature. Each had pieces of the puzzle, but none put it all together. Theodore Roosevelt understood the natural history, political process, and resource management issues. John Burroughs understood the natural history and evolutionary theory and their philosophical and religious implications. Seton and Long and Burroughs pointed out that we have moral obligations to nature, as well as to other people. Seton, Long, and Burroughs each tried to craft a religion of nature.

The term *nature faker* suggests a conscious effort at fraud on the part of the faker. Long was not a fraud. He was, though, careless in his interpretations of animal behavior, because he rejected the methods of science as tools useful to his quest. If few of the fakers were frauds, what is a nature faker? Perhaps the term is best applied to people whose sentiments about nature blind them to the real living animal in the wild—people whose deeply held personal beliefs lead them to spin fanciful visions of nature. Animals go on being animals despite what we think of them. What we think of them, though, affects our ability to live together within this natural world.

6.
THEIR PATHS DIVERGE

The paths of many writers and naturalists intersected during the nature fakers controversy, but when this "storm in the forest" passed and the dust settled each went his own way. Despite all the noise and bluster, few changed their positions. Many authors, publishers, and school committees did pay closer attention to issues of accuracy, but little else changed. Long was defeated, but not converted. John Burroughs had sharpened the focus of his attack, but he seemed largely weary of the whole thing. President Roosevelt held his strategically placed ground. Jack London was secure in his own views. The question of whether animals can reason was not resolved. Science education and nature appreciation often remained poles apart.

Charles G. D. Roberts, never a major participant in the controversy, had larger literary matters on his mind. Although animal stories were an important part of his writings, Roberts had established his reputation as an early poet of the Canadian Confederation and turned his pen to novels, stories, and books about Canada and its history. He received many honors for his diverse literary accomplishments, including a knighthood from King George in 1935. Roberts is now remembered as the "father of Canadian literature."[1]

The debate did shake Ernest Thompson Seton. As a result of the controversy, many people, such as novelist Zane Grey, ultimately regarded him as a fake. Seton, however, had a sound natural history background, and he set out to prove his scientific abilities to the world. In November 1907, several days after returning to Wyndygoul from his trip to the barrens, Seton wrote Burroughs that he agreed that some of the animal stories may have gone too far. He informed the elder naturalist that he was preparing a work that he could stand by. Seton's *Life Histories of North American Animals* (1909) was based on his extensive field observations and wide reading of the scientific literature. He later expanded it into his four-volume *Lives of Game Animals*. In 1927, ironically, it won him the John Burroughs Memorial Association's second Burroughs Medal for outstanding nature writing.[2] The books became classics in American mammalogy. Seton continued, though, to constrain wild animals within human morality and to give credence to the more outlandish accounts of the strategies of foxes to lose pursuing hounds.

Following the controversy, Seton increasingly devoted his time to youth groups and Native Americanism. His Woodcraft Indians organization was slowly spreading throughout the nation. This work attracted the attention of Robert S. S. Baden-Powell, a British hero of the Boer War, who was creating his own group, the Boy Scouts.[3] Baden-Powell's program was based on the model of military scouts, complete with a hierarchical structure of authority and uniforms similar to those of the South African Constabulary. Seton shared his ideas and writings with Baden-Powell, who borrowed and plagiarized them to introduce woodcraft into the Boy Scouts. However, the two men had very different conceptions of boys. Seton romanticized childhood and believed that civilization distorts the innate goodness of children. Baden-Powell believed the disciplined authority of adults was necessary to make children grow into responsible, patriotic adults. For Seton, woodcraft and Native American ways were essential elements at the core of scouting. Baden-Powell, who was building a paramilitary organization, viewed them more as play elements useful to capture the children's attention.

Seton became chief scout of the Boy Scouts of America in 1910, the year it was founded, and wrote its first handbook. He was never comfortable, though, with the organization. The Boy Scouts quickly dwarfed his Woodcraft Indians, in large part because of its centralized, businesslike management. Seton was particularly distressed as World War I neared and the Scouts geared up to prepare boys for patriotic military service. Theodore Roosevelt, an exuberant patriot, warned the Scouts that they had pacifists in their midst who resisted training the boys to bear arms.[4] Many viewed Seton as a pacifist, and in 1915 the Boy Scouts finally ousted the Canadian-born naturalist on the grounds that he was not an American citizen.

Seton's interest in Native Americans continued to grow. He eventually moved to New Mexico, built Seton Village, and wrote and lectured on Native American cultures. In 1932 he established his College of Indian Wisdom, a summer institute to train youth leaders and others in Native American ways. The first summer he had twenty-five students; enrollment had grown to two hundred (plus fifty experts on staff) by 1940, its final year of operation. By the time he passed away in 1946, Seton had made major contributions toward improving Euro-American understanding of this continent's indigenous peoples.[5]

In Quiet Retirement—1910. By John T. McCutcheon. From *Collier's Weekly* (5 Sept. 1908).

Theodore Roosevelt left office in 1909. He was fifty-two years old and ready for adventure. That spring he set off on a year-long expedition through Africa under the sponsorship of the Smithsonian Institution. In 1912, unhappy with the performance of Howard Taft, the man he had picked to succeed him as president, Roosevelt ran for re-election and lost. In 1913 he was off on another expedition. This time, his party journeyed down a recently discovered and unexplored river, the Rio da Duvida, or River of Doubt. They discovered that the river, now named the Roosevelt, was a thousand-mile-long branch of the Amazon. The two-months'-long river journey was terribly difficult, as they lost canoes, food, and a companion in the rapids. Roosevelt nearly died, suffering from malaria, dysentery, and a festering wound sustained when he rescued two of his party from the river. He never completely recovered his health. Nevertheless, he continued an active political, literary, and scientific life until his death in January 1919.[6]

John Burroughs. From John Burroughs, *Leaf and Tendril*, Riverby Ed. (Boston: Houghton Mifflin, 1908).

"Heard of Roosevelt's death last night," John Burroughs wrote in his journal, "and have had a lump in my throat ever since." The elder naturalist, now eighty-one years old, was surprised by how deeply he was touched by his friend's death. Two weeks later, he made a tearful visit to the grave. "A pall seems to settle upon the very sky," he later wrote. "The world is bleaker and colder for his absence from it. We shall not look upon his like again."[7]

In the eighty-four years that spanned his birth to his death in 1921, John Burroughs witnessed the transformation of America. He was eyewitness to the Civil War, lived through World War I, saw the telegraph succeeded by telephone and radio, and saw the nation transformed by railroads and, later, by the automobile. In 1912, much to his surprise, he received a letter from Henry Ford, who claimed to be an admirer of his books. As an expression of his admiration (and with a touch of hero worship), Ford presented Burroughs with one of his cars. Burroughs was proud of the Model T and enjoyed driving about the countryside, often to the distress of his family and friends. When parking his car after one drive, for example, he got "rattled" and ran it through the side of the barn with "a great splintering and rattling of boards and timbers." His most memorable auto trips were in the company of his new friends, Ford, Thomas Edison, and Harvey Firestone, during their lavish camping trips through the Adirondacks and the Great Smoky Mountains.[8]

While his nemeses moved on with their lives, William J. Long was left to pick up the pieces of his own. He had given up his public battle with Theodore Roosevelt several months after the president's final blow in *Everybody's Magazine*, but his silence did not signify defeat. Although Ginn & Company did not publish any new nature books by Long, it continued to promote his old ones, which remained in print for decades. His first book, *Ways of Wood Folk*, first published in 1899, did not go out of print until 1938. His next book, *Wilderness Ways*, remained in print for nearly fifty years.[9] Long also plotted a quiet vindication. He set out to prove his skills as a naturalist, much as Seton set about proving his own. Over the next few years, Long produced a series of carefully conducted natural history studies.

In 1908 he published "Stories from the Trail," a detailed description of one of his hikes through the snow, the tracks and other evidence of wildlife that he saw, and the conclusions he drew from them. Illustrated by photographs and a drawing of fox track patterns, it was a successful effort to demonstrate his skills as a field naturalist. Two more essays, published at one-year intervals, added to his argument that wolves were peaceful, cooperative creatures rather than ravenous beasts. These studies probably grew out of field studies he did for the Canadian government. One wonders, though, whether Theodore Roosevelt saw his account of the wolf that killed a deer with a bite to the kidneys: "With one terrific snap the buck's back was broken, and he lay helpless on the ice."[10]

Despite these essays, William J. Long's nature writing dwindled to a trickle. He appeared, for all practical purposes, to be out of the nature writing business. Long became a literary historian.[11] His next book, *English Literature*, was published in 1909. One reviewer called it "highly commendable" and another described it as "an effort to vitalize the subject by relating it to the life of the author and of his age as well as to the mind and the imagination of the pupil." Four years later, he published a second textbook, *American Literature*. This was quite a change from his stories of the woodfolk, but it was not a radical change in his interests. After all, Long was a European-trained historian and philosopher. The books were great successes, both in the United States and abroad, and were followed by other books on history and literature, as well as a classroom edition of *Alice's Adventures in Wonderland*, which he edited and annotated.[12]

His work, though, did not go without criticism. In 1925 a historian published a "corrective" to Long's view of English history. He claimed that parts of Long's *English Literature* fell "very short of being accurate summaries of historical events and social conditions." Despite the criticism, Long's books continued to be popular. *American Literature* remained in print until 1952; a new, enlarged edition of *English Literature* was published in 1945 and remained in print until 1972, twenty years after Long's death.[13]

He did not, though, give up his interest in nature and the outdoors. Long continued to spend months in the wilds of Maine or Canada each year, camping and staying at hunting camps. His wife followed her husband to the woods, but more out of duty than preference. His daughter Frances, who recalled that she was raised to be a "combination of Elizabeth Barrett Browning and Pocahontas," remembered these trips with affection. She cherished the magic, joy, and surprises that her father created for his children: teaching them to fish and canoe, making ice cream appear mysteriously on the ridge pole of the tent, and the shared ritual of watching the sunset in silence. Long sometimes jokingly teased the children by accusing them of laughing during the ritual—it was not laughter, but a loon calling on the lake. Once, when his son was ill, he rafted a cow out to their camp to provide fresh milk. The family often stayed until ice began to form on the lake.[14]

Long's house on Norton Hill in Stamford, with its library and formal study, was neat as a pin and displayed the orderliness one might expect of a scholar. The family spoke pure, proper English; each morning his son presented himself by saying, "Good morning, Father. My duty to you, sir." However, Long did not do his writing in this ordered universe. His working study was in the center of town. As one visitor described it:

> Here he revels in a delicious confusion and disarrangement. Newspapers, letters, books, photographs, notebooks, souvenirs of days in the big woods, are everywhere, not even excepting the floor. In fact, the floor seems to have taken up all the odds and ends of over-turned wastepaper baskets. One feels as if wending his way through a forest of broken trunks, quantities of leaves, and crumbling debris of all sorts. To make more realistic the impression that one is in the path of a tornado is the rumble of trolley cars, the toots of automobiles, the clatter of horseshoes and iron tires on the pavement, and the calls of drivers and peddlers.

This was his preferred working environment. "It brings me closer to humanity, to the men and women who daily bear the burdens of the world," he told his visitor. "Far from disturbing me, the sound of their coming and going is a stimulus to good, honest work." Here he plotted a satirical revenge against Theodore Roosevelt.[15]

Long was not one to forget a wrong and he could not resist the temptation to poke fun at Roosevelt. In 1912, Roosevelt was making his last bid for the presidency under the banner of his Bull Moose party. Long's article "The Bull Moose as a Political Totem" used Roosevelt's own writings to describe the political virtues of the moose. After describing the uncouth natural history of the moose and its apt choice as a political symbol, Long ended:

> In appearance the bull moose is an awkward and most ungainly brute, a relic of some earlier and more barbarous age, when strange marsh beasts wandered up and down the earth, meeting wild and hairy men. As our esteemed authority says, he is "strange and uncouth in look as some monster surviving over from the Pliocene." Among modern, more highly developed animals and men he is wholly out of place. He never learns wisdom, but comes to the same false calls and follows the old, primordial trails.... And when you think of it seriously, the professional politician, who lives all his life on the public domain, agitating, destroying, but never creating or doing any constructive work, is also a relic and a survival of barbarism.

Long also questioned Roosevelt's claim that moose can gallop. "I will not say that a moose never galloped," he wrote, "I only declare firmly that the man who saw him gallop was not sober."[16]

In 1919 Long published *How Animals Talk*, his first new nature book in more than a decade. It was, perhaps, no coincidence that Theodore Roosevelt, his most powerful critic, had died that January. Over the next four years his new publisher, Harper & Brothers, marketed two additional books and reprinted *Brier-Patch Philosophy*. The books revealed a much more cautious and thoughtful, although no less imaginative, Long. (Commenting on his views about animal telepathy, a reviewer wrote, "We marvel that the author has found time to observe so much in so many climes and forget to analyze his more revolutionary statements.")[17]

Long held the manuscript of his last nature book, *Mother Nature: A Study of Animal Life and Death*, for twelve years, until he had complete confidence in its conclusions. Published in 1923, it was Long's crowning statement of his philosophy that nature was a place without struggle, fear, or pain. Although the substance of his ideas had not changed, he now wrote for adult readers and tried to win them to his side by carefully constructed arguments and descriptions of animal behavior. He even moderated his views about animal reasoning. "As for the wild creatures one meets," he wrote, "it is doubtless hard to read their motives aright, since they follow their instinct where we stumble among reasons; but we have still enough of the animal in our nature to interpret their mood or feeling from their actions, their voices, their expressions."[18]

He continued to defend wolves, based on his field studies of the animals and his continuing, deeply held belief in the "gladsome life" of nature. In December 1922, the *New York Times* reported that wolves had devoured three Canadians. A few weeks later, Long protested to the *Times*. He had investigated the story and found that it was not true. "I write this in justice to the wolf and to Ontario. The one is a very intelligent wild beast; the other is a delightful place where I have slept in the Winter woods with less danger than in my own bed."[19]

Controversy seemed to follow the Reverend Dr. Long. Although he did not have a church, Long remained a minister in full standing and officiated at his daughters' weddings. The Connecticut Attorney General, however, felt that clergymen without a church could not legally perform marriages. He made this ruling just a few days after Long married his daughter Lois to New Yorker cartoonist Peter Arno. The attorney general's ruling, Long proclaimed, "has violated a principle which is a hundred years older than Blackstone, and which has been valid in Connecticut ever since the Rev. Thomas Hooker led his brave little flock down through the wilderness to found the Hartford colony." The marriage survived the ruling, and Long's daughters joked about the matter.[20]

Long began publishing his books anonymously after 1929. He published at least two more books and several magazine articles under another, but unknown, name. It is not clear why he did this. Perhaps he lost credibility following the 1925 criticism of his historical accuracy. According to Glenn W. Moon, with whom Long was the anonymous co-author of *Story of Our Land and People* (1938), their publisher wanted this high school textbook to appear under the name of a professional educator.[21] Moon was a history teacher at Stamford High School.

A few years after his wife's death in 1936, William J. Long moved from his Norton Hill home to the Davenport Hotel in Stamford, where he spent his remaining years. He was an active participant in the town meeting and politics and continued his annual pilgrimages to the northern woods. Long's special quest was for trout and salmon. He often fished the Hartland salmon pool on the St. John River and in other parts of New Brunswick. Lawrence Sweet, his fishing guide in his final years, remembered Long as the finest sportsman he had accompanied in the woods. Long would arrive in mid-June, fish through the summer, and leave in September after a meal of deer liver.

He continued his fishing trips until 1952, when he was eighty-six years old. He had been ill and was sick most of the time at the camp. Finally Sweet's brother, Raymond, took Long to the hospital. This was his last fishing trip. William J. Long died of liver cancer in Stamford, Connecticut, on December 9, 1952.[22]

Before he died, however, Long had the pleasure of seeing Theodore Roosevelt's behind-the-scenes scheming against him revealed to the world. That summer, while he was in Canada, Harvard University Press published the fifth volume of Elting E. Morison's *The Letters of Theodore Roosevelt*, which included the president's private correspondence in the nature fakers controversy. In response, the *Boston Globe* published an article about the controversy that was sympathetic to Long. The writer reported, with some exaggeration, that although Long "never got President Theodore Roosevelt to apologize, he did make a big dent in T. R.'s conscience" about his hunting. Her assessment of Long may have been influenced by Henry P. Roberts, the *Globe*'s composing room foreman, who had been one of Long's pupils many years before at Nantucket High School.[23]

The last of his nature writings that William J. Long saw in print appeared in *Sports Afield* and *Nature Magazine* in the late 1940s and early 1950s. In 1947, a year after Ernest Thompson Seton's death, *Sports Afield* ran a three-part series of articles, "The Incomparable Mr. Seton." Its discussion of the nature fakers controversy presented a terribly confused version of Long's story about the woodcock that put a cast on its broken leg and of the story's role in the controversy. Long quickly responded with his own article, "The Woodcock, Again," which set the record straight. One reader wrote to the magazine to commend Long's observations as "closer to the truth than either Seton or Burroughs and, certainly, Roosevelt." *Sports Afield*'s editor invited Long to submit more articles, leading to a series of wildlife articles. A respected naturalist and author, Wayne Hanley, described Long's *Sports Afield* articles as "credible" and felt that they "restored some of his earlier success."[24]

Following his death, though, Lois Long Fox found unpublished manuscripts in her father's safe and was determined to see them in print. Some, including Long's account of his youthful delight at fox hunting and a description of how porcupines "throw" their quills, appeared as a series of essays in *Sports Illustrated*. The magazine described Long as "one of the great American naturalists of the 20th century." Fox then edited these and others into two books, *The Spirit of the Wild* and *Wings of the Forest*—the first volumes of William J. Long's nature writing to appear in thirty-three years.[25]

The nature fakers controversy is now a dim memory, recalled mostly by historians. The reputations of Ernest Thompson Seton, Charles G. D. Roberts, and Jack London survived the battle. William J. Long, however, is remembered as a sham—when he is remembered at all. His defenders have been few and their defenses guarded. A year after Long's death, for example, Alan Devoe wrote a review of a new anthology of Ernest Thompson Seton's articles. Devoe, a naturalist and editor of the *Saturday Review*, was a former Woodcraft Indian and an admirer of Seton. He also knew Long, whom he considered a friend and counselor. Devoe probably had Long as well as Seton in mind when he described John Burroughs's original *Atlantic Monthly* article, "Sham Natural History," as "one of the nastiest in the history of responsible critical journalism" and Roosevelt's "war-hoops" as cruel. A few years earlier, Devoe had called the controversy "a painful and disedifying business." Although he did not defend Long by name, he expressed views about animals' experience of death and their mental processes that were similar to Long's. He also argued that a woodcock may indeed dip its broken leg in mud, which later hardens into a cast. He drew the line, however, at consciously fabricated splints.[26]

Two years later, *New York Times* reviewer J. Donald Adams also defended Long. "At this distance from the heat of the fray," he wrote, "it seems admissible that Dr. Long occasionally gave rein to improbabilities," but he was not a fraud. Long, he pointed out, had a sound knowledge of the north woods. He proposed that Long also had a knowledge of the Rocky Mountain region equal to Theodore Roosevelt's. Long and Roosevelt, he argued, were simply "men of a different cast of mind."[27]

The authors who were called nature fakers probably had a much greater impact upon the public's perception of wildlife than did the more scientific writers. If they sometimes failed to present an accurate picture of nature, they often presented an antidote to the prevailing vision of nature as a stage for savage conflict among bloodthirsty beasts. Their readers grew to care about the welfare of their wild animal heroes and to recognize a kinship between wildlife and humans. Their books, now sitting on the shelves of used bookstores, are tattered and worn by years of reading and re-reading.

One indication of their impact is found in the response to a 1986 survey conducted by Reading Is Fundamental (RIF). RIF contacted a number of prominent people throughout the United States, asking them to name their "all-time favorite children's book," as well as two others "too good for kids to miss." Nearly fifty people provided well over two hundred recommendations. Only three of the books, though, could be called nature books or books about wildlife—and each author had been attacked as a nature faker. Jack London's *Call of the Wild* was the favorite of journalist and author Jim Trelease and of the bishop of Washington, John T. Walker. It was a "too good to miss" for surgeon Michael DeBakey. Folk singer Pete Seeger's favorite was Ernest Thompson Seton's *Rolf of the Woods*. Finally, President Ronald Reagan's all-time childhood favorite was *Northern Trails* by William J. Long. "This was a book about nature," the president wrote, "and it began my lifelong love of the outdoors."[28]

* * *

By 1913, John Burroughs was weary of the controversy. "Whether the dog, the cat, and the cockroach reason or not, shall trouble me (and them) no more," he wrote and meditated upon a chipmunk that scampered about his cabin.

> Does the pretty little rodent reason about all this? Ah! my reader, ask some one else! As for me, I will content myself with his companionship as he runs along my study table, pokes his nose into the arch made by my hand, under which the kernels lie, and even climbs to the crown of my head. He sets me to thinking, and I, if I do not set him to thinking, at least aid him in adding to his

winter supplies. We are both learning something; day unto day uttereth knowledge, and even a chipmunk shares a little of the wisdom that pervades the universe.[29]

Burroughs, Roosevelt, Seton, Long, and all the others set the nation to thinking—thinking about the real as well as the mythical animals; about our moral responsibilities to wildlife; and about the larger philosophical and religious perspectives that unite us all, be we human or not, within this living planet we share. We are still in the midst of muddling our way toward a vision of nature and wildlife that embraces both a deep love of living things and an informed understanding of the ecological systems that support them. If we are wrestling with similar issues today, it is not surprising that nature lovers did not have all of the answers nearly a century ago.

AFTERWORD: THE FAKERS TODAY

As years passed, the nature fakers controversy began to fade from memory. Even the term *nature fakers* began to change in meaning, losing its connection with the literary controversy and becoming a general term for natural history misinformation and old wives' tales. The term was used by the National Park Service rangers responsible for enforcing park rules to poke fun at the rangers who taught natural history to park visitors, calling them "pansy pickers, bug sniffers, and nature fakers." In the title of a manual for nature educators published in 1988, *The Nature Fakir's Handbook*, the original meaning has been completely lost: The author and editors believed that the term referred to Hindu nature mystics.[1]

Although talk of nature fakers has all but vanished, the issues at the root of the controversy remain. Whenever the public really cares about something, there are people eager to turn the situation to their own advantage. The bogus book salesman in 1907 who took orders for nature books that went unfilled represented one extreme. Joseph Knowles represented another. In 1913, with reporters and photographers as his witnesses, he removed his clothes and disappeared into the forest of northern Maine. He was to spend the next two months alone in the wilderness. He would, he claimed, begin naked and provide whatever food, clothing, and shelter he needed with his own bare hands and ingenuity. The public was captivated by nature and woodcraft and eagerly followed Knowles's exploits, which he reported in messages (written with burnt sticks on birch bark) that he left for the press. Two months later he emerged, in good health and clothed in animal skins; thousands of people turned out to give him a hero's welcome when he returned to Boston. Knowles's book about his experience sold 300,000 copies. It turns out, though, that he was a fraud. He had spent his time in a cabin fabricating his story and the evidence that convinced an easily deceived public.[2]

Responsible publishers have learned to check their authors' facts and credentials and, one hopes, today we enjoy a much more credible selection of nature books.[3] However, the problem of fakers will always be with us. The promise of turning a good profit can tempt an author or publisher to set standards aside and produce a popular yet bogus book. For example, Lynn V. Andrews's books, including _Medicine Woman_, exploit the public's interest in returning to nature, native peoples, the occult, and feminism. Her personal accounts of being indoctrinated into a society of aboriginal "medicine women" have sold well. Cree Indians, however, claim her descriptions of their ceremonies are fanciful, a Mohawk newspaper described her as a "plastic" medicine woman, and Australian Aborigines cannot recall her visit. Although her books claim to be fact, they appear to be fiction.[4]

In 1987, the editor-in-chief of _Publishers Weekly_ asked, "Are some publishers metamorphosing into snake-oil salesmen?" and pointed out that publishers face a special responsibility when a book steps beyond being merely entertaining and purports to instruct. He wrote, "We're not calling for impossible virtue in a world notably short of it—simply suggesting that publishers should see themselves as important and influential citizens who should behave accordingly in the books they choose to publish." Although his views echoed those of Theodore Roosevelt eighty years before, John F. Baker was not commenting on nature faking. He was referring to the recent spate of books on pseudo-science, the occult, alien abductions, and the like. Beech Tree Books, for example, published Whitley Strieber's account of his abduction by aliens from outer space under the title _Communion: A True Story_. Similarly, Random House marketed Budd Hopkins's book about the same incident, _Intruders_, with a full-page advertisement in the _New York Times Review of Books_, featuring a letter from the publisher attesting to its truthfulness.[5] The issue of faking remains with us, although the material being faked may have changed.

The nature fakers' problem, though, was less one of fraud and more one of sentimentalism, philosophical bias, and an inability or unwillingness to use the tools of science as a source of information about nature and wildlife. In some cases, the fakers' views have been gaining broad acceptance. Wolves and other predators, for example, are now more readily accepted as necessary participants in nature's processes rather than viewed as rapacious, bloodthirsty destroyers. The view that we have moral obligations to nature is also gaining acceptance, although it still encounters a great deal of resistance, especially from those who stand to profit from the exploitation of natural resources. Laws requiring environmental impact statements for large construction projects and those designed to protect endangered species and wilderness areas are based, in part, on this concept. There is even a widely discussed theory, first published in *Southern California Law Review*, that grants natural objects legal rights, including the right to sue in court.[6] What was once a radical idea is now becoming a part of our social, political, and legal institutions.

Sadly, many people reject the notion that humans are an integral part of and dependent upon the natural world—especially when they can turn a quick profit by doing harm to the environment. This is not surprising for an economic system in which a long-term investment spans merely a few years, while ecological processes span decades and centuries. Perhaps *this* can be called nature faking, since it is a product of desires (economic desires in this case) that are unmindful of nature's processes.

The root issues that underlay the nature fakers controversy remain with us. We continue to debate our role in nature and our moral obligations to animals. The tension between science and sentiment has not gone away, and we continue to allow our biases and expectations to distort our understanding of nature. However, the new controversies that provide arenas for these issues rarely involve literary fraud, and they are in many ways far more important then the naturalists' literary debate.

Protestant fundamentalists, for example, are responsible for one of the most recent and most carefully planned efforts at nature faking, which goes under the name of "scientific" creationism. They have persistently opposed the concept of organic evolution. Their efforts to suppress the understanding that humans evolved from other animals or even that the earth is more than six thousand years old began early in this century. Between 1921 and 1929 alone, thirty-seven measures were introduced in state legislatures to prevent the teaching of evolution. With the failure of their efforts to prevent the teaching of evolution, such as in the 1925 "Monkey Trial" of Thomas Scopes, the fundamentalists shifted tactics. Most recently, they tried to require that their own religious views, based on the creation myth in the book of Genesis, be taught in public school classrooms.

Their strategy is to disguise their religious views as science and pass laws requiring that they be given equal time with evolution in science classes. A 1981 Arkansas law required that both be taught as scientific models and provided a definition of the new "science":

> "Creation-science" means the scientific evidences for creation and inferences from those scientific evidences. Creation-science includes the scientific evidences and related inferences that indicate: (1) Sudden creation of the universe, energy, and life from nothing; (2) The insufficiency of mutation and natural selection in bringing about development of all living kinds from a single organism; (3) Changes only within fixed limits of originally created kinds of plants and animals; (4) Separate ancestry for man and apes; (5) Explanation of the earth's geology by catastrophism, including the occurrence of worldwide flood; and (6) A relatively recent inception of the earth and living kinds.[7]

The next year a United States District Court judge determined that the law actually required the teaching of a religion in the public schools and ordered the state not to implement it.

Although the fundamentalists claim they are only interested in teaching creationism as an alternative scientific model, it is clear that they are interested only in teaching the fundamentalist Christian version of creation. There is, though, a multitude of creation myths. Some embody much more of a biological concept than does that of Christianity. Would the fundamentalists, for example, be satisfied with the Hindu creation story described in "The Upanishads"?[8] In the beginning there was only God, who could feel no pleasure or delight. So God split into a man and a woman; they made love and she gave birth to humans. She turned into a cow and ran away. He turned into a bull, caught her, and cattle came into the world. She turned into other animals, and he accordingly caught and impregnated her each time. Eventually all of the earth's creatures were created out of God. Thus, God is the creation: Each creature is a face of God, and sex is, in effect, God playing hide and seek with Itself.

The scientific view of nature does not support a literal, fundamentalist interpretation of the Bible, and Protestant fundamentalist theology can not adapt to it. So many stick their heads in the sand and reject this worldview. Their approach is much like William J. Long's: They reinvent the world to fit their beliefs without letting reality intrude. Unlike Long, these new nature fakers devised a strategic fraud (misrepresenting their religious views as science) to promote legislation to coerce the teaching of their theology in the public schools. Fortunately, most Christians do not have such an impoverished and inflexible understanding of Christianity, and many churches and theologians are now nurturing the life-centered perspectives that exist within their religion.

With the rebirth of the environmental movement in the late 1960s and early 1970s, there was also a new flowering of nature sentimentalism and romanticism. Many people felt good about nature, but did not have sufficient understanding of natural history and ecology to expand beyond simply an emotional attachment to wilderness and wildlife. The television character outdoorsman Grizzly Adams was a prime product of this approach. A friend and protector of wildlife, he extolled the virtues of living in harmony with nature. But this one-sided view of nature and how people fit within it had built-in contradictions. As a *TV Guide* reviewer pointed out, Adams could say that he would not harm a living thing while offering a bowl of stew to a lost child. Although the show could get "a bit woodsier-than-thou," he wrote, it is useful to reflect on the meaning of that bowl of stew. Once in a while, "Grizzly Adams konks one of his little furry friends with an ax, skins the critter and tosses it in a pot with a mess of spuds. That, too, is nature."[9] It was, though, a side of Adams's fictional life close to nature that the show chose to ignore.

The media, especially television, play an important educational role as they feed the public's hunger for nature and wildlife. Coffee-table books of wilderness photographs and countless televised nature programs have nurtured a deep love and affection for nature among millions of readers and viewers. This has helped generate record-high memberships in environmental organizations such as the Audubon societies, the Sierra Club, and the National Wildlife Federation. It has also generated tremendous support for environmental protection legislation. On the other hand, the media tend to be very selective. The viewer is a passive consumer of packaged, vicarious experiences of nature. Viewers see mostly birds and mammals—particularly those that are novel, large, colorful, and spectacular. The less pleasant aspects of nature are often missing, such as the lice, fleas, ticks, worms, and other parasites (equally a part of nature) that infest the noble predators and beautiful birds. Wildlife seems to be everywhere, and there is always action to follow. The viewer is not aware of the days and weeks that the filmmaker waited to capture a single scene, because the tedium has been edited out of the show. As a result, people are often disappointed when they finally do get a chance to visit a wild place—nothing seems to be happening.[10]

Efforts by the media to examine and warn of the serious environmental damage caused by pollution, habitat destruction, and other human impacts have also helped to mobilize broad public support for environmental protection. However, the emphasis on the harm done by people promotes the view that humans (except for a few environmental heroes) and civilization are an evil force in the landscape. Contrasted against a sanitized, Edenic vision of an unchanging, balanced world of nature—a world of only lovely animals—this presents a polarized image of good versus evil, nature versus humanity. But the world of nature, which includes humanity, is a world of death as well as life, change as well as stability, parasites and maggots as well as gazelles and bald eagles. The polarized vision of Edenic nature against evil humans creates as many problems as it helps to solve.

Tinkering with the Works

The same is true of the view that humans must work to right every perceived "wrong" in nature. In October 1988, for example, three gray whales were found trapped by arctic ice. The plight of the trapped whales became the focus of international attention as rescuers from the United States and the Soviet Union worked together to free the whales from the ice and return them to the open sea. It became a major educational event that captured the attention of millions of people around the world. Environmentalists used it to inform the public about the problems of this and other whale species. Many critics, however, argued that the whole effort was a waste of millions of dollars to save only a few animals and that the money spent on the rescue effort could have been used much more effectively in other ways to protect whales.

There are additional grounds for criticism. What were the attitudes toward nature underlying the rescue effort? The tremendous worldwide expression of public concern about the welfare of these animals and the multinational efforts to save them reaffirmed one of the best qualities in humans—the ability to care about the welfare of other species. The event, though, tacitly displayed two other attitudes, first, that _humans are in control._ Whatever the problem, we can and should intervene and use the powers of science and technology to set things right. The rescue effort reflected the very attitude toward nature that created our environmental crisis. And what was the whales' problem? They were dying. This points to the second tacit attitude: _There is no place for death in nature. Prevent it when you can._ However, in an ecological world there can be no life without death, and efforts to eradicate death from nature are also efforts to eradicate life.

Religious fundamentalists are not the only people who have difficulty dealing with change. The same is true of some environmentalists and animal welfare advocates. Their efforts to preserve, conserve, and protect wildlife are often efforts to maintain the status quo without regard for the larger ecological context. However, they inevitably run up against questions of what is and is not worth protecting; when are preservation efforts working against normal ecological change; and when do efforts to prevent the death of animals represent a rejection of death as a necessary component of living systems? Throughout, there is also the question of how we are to think of and value wild animals, if not as pets or furry little people. We are still trying to thread our ways through these questions—as were the nature lovers, nature fakers, and their critics nearly a century ago.

Wild animals are not pets. Domesticated animals are species that have often lived with humans for thousands of years. Their genetic traits have been selected to function within this relationship. Adult dogs and cats continue to have juvenile characteristics, even though they are sexually mature. They have been bred to display the big eyes and puppy-like or kitten-like facial features and care-soliciting behavior that endear them to their owners. Pets, farm animals, and other animals under human care are dependent on us, and our first obligation is to care for them well.

Our obligation to pets is not a useful guide to understanding our obligation to wild animals. Wild animals live lives independent of humans. They are genetically adapted for life within the wild. Our first obligation to wild animals is to leave them alone, unless there are compelling arguments to the contrary. This is easy to say, but in practice things can become very complex. As we humans alter our environments, we also alter the environments of wildlife. There is growing agreement that we must protect their ecosystems (as well as our own) using methods such as land protection, planning the pace and pattern of development, and controlling commercial exploitation and hunting. To what extent, though, should we intervene in the lives of individual wild animals?

No one wants to eradicate life or, when they think about it, death from nature. The question, then, is: When is it appropriate to intervene, and when is it not? We as a culture are still trying to find an answer, are still in the process of articulating our obligations to other species. Whatever the answer, it does not lie alone in a responsibility to protect the lives of individual wild animals. Humans are rarity in nature. We produce relatively few young that have a prolonged childhood, and we give them tender, loving care. Family members, friends, and associates are important to us as individuals. We freely protect the lives of other people, even at great cost to ourselves. (We are also learning how very important it is to control our rate of reproduction to prevent the horrifying suffering that can come with overpopulation.) This is part of the survival strategy of our species. The vast majority of other species, however, do not employ this strategy.

In very few of the hundreds of thousands of animal species are the young nurtured for any length of time, nor do individuals form lasting

195

bonds with each other. Many species produce young in vast numbers, which insures that a few will survive and reproduce in the face of high mortality; all become the fodder that sustains other organisms. This is their survival strategy, and there is no need to value and care for individuals. Tapeworms, for example, are little more than an array of reproductive organs and, fortunately, very few of each worm's millions of eggs grow to wormhood. Rabbits are able to produce another generation of rabbits in the face of high mortality by reproducing "like rabbits." Predation is one factor that can help to keep a population healthy, by controlling population size and, in the process, weeding out the weak and sick. In a sense, death is a species' way of "learning," because it culls the less adaptive hereditary traits out of the pool of genetic information.[11] Death and life are opposite sides of the same coin.

Often, though, people find this "unpleasant" side of nature repulsive. In a time when nature is often conceived as an earthly Eden, it is no wonder that we block its ugly face from our minds. Some have looked full in the face of nature and questioned why beauty and abominations co-exist. Thomas Huxley and John Burroughs called nature indifferent to its creatures' suffering. Pondering the existence of parasites, Annie Dillard concluded that "The creator is no puritan." Others, however, have found evil in the garden. One scholar finds "gross immorality" in the pervasiveness of pain, death, and selfishness in the biological world.[12] It is no wonder that some people are morally committed to undo the "wrongs" against wildlife that are committed both by humans and by nature itself.

Nature writer Bradford Torrey tried to thread his way through this problem over a century ago. "The whole earth is one field of war," he wrote. "Every creature's place upon it is coveted by some other creature.... The import of this apparent wastefulness and cruelty of Nature, her seeming indifference to the welfare of the individual, is a question on which it is not pleasant, and, as I think, not profitable, to dwell." He went on to conclude, "We see but parts of her ways, and it must be unsafe to criticise the working of a single wheel here or there, when we have absolutely no means of knowing how each fits into the grand design, and, for that matter, can only guess at the grand design itself."[13]

Despite himself, though, Torrey was moved to attempt to rescue a young bird from the mouth of a snake.[14] Emotionally, he favored some animals over others and stepped in to help the ones he preferred. Now, a century later, we have a much better understanding of the ecological workings of nature than did Torrey. Nevertheless, we still often impose our own values—values at odds with ecological and evolutionary processes—upon wildlife. Many people are emotionally and morally unable to leave a wild animal alone and "let nature take its course" if they believe the life of an animal they like is endangered. Their reasons may be noble, but this is not necessarily an effective way to achieve many wildlife protection goals.

In recent years, a growing number of wildlife rehabilitation centers have appeared across the nation to serve the needs of thousands of people who "rescue" the injured and "orphaned" wildlife they have found. They bring more birds than snakes and more squirrels than rats to be treated, but they care deeply about the animals they do select to "save." They may feel good about themselves and their effort to help, but are these samaritans really helping the animals? They often are not. The "orphans" they pick up, for example, often are not orphans at all but have, with all good intentions, been kidnapped from their parents by these caring people.[15] In addition, many of the "cured" animals die shortly after being released, especially if those providing medical care are not also sensitive to the behavior, natural history, and ecological needs of the animal.

Wildlife rehabilitation is of little or no ecological benefit and it rarely has any impact upon the survival of a species. For these reasons, many ecologically based environmental organizations are reducing or discontinuing their wildlife rehabilitation programs and using their limited resources in ways that have a more significant and lasting impact. One philosopher has argued that giving medical treatment to wild animals is the moral equivalent of drinking a piña colada: "you don't need it, the money you spend doing it could do far more good elsewhere, but you owe yourself something in life. Yet, while it is not *wrong* to do it, it is also not right—not efficient, not even wise."[16] In other words, if it makes you feel good, then you might as well do it, if you can do it properly. If done improperly, wildlife rehabilitation can amount to little more than torture, despite the best intentions.

Wildlife rehabilitation may, with some exceptions, be a waste of time as a tool to protect wildlife populations. It can, though, benefit individual animals, if done selectively and with great skill. People value individual animals and the public wants these services. Individual animals are tangible, and their real or imagined suffering strikes a responsive human chord. People do not want to see them (especially mammals and birds) in distress. In protecting these animals they are also protecting and proclaiming something wonderful and precious in themselves—the ability to love and care about species other than their own. But species and ecosystems are more abstract and less tangible than individual animals. It is much more difficult for people to care about such abstractions than it is to care about a warm ball of fuzz or feathers quivering in their hands. The best of the wildlife rehabilitation centers know this and use their clients' interests in injured animals to motivate them to learn about ecology and environmental issues.

On the other hand, wildlife rehabilitation can also perpetuate the sentimental image of animals as furry little people and the notion that death has no place in nature. However well intended, it can also further support the destructive belief that humans can and should exercise control over nature. Wildlife rehabilitation programs that do not make an effort to overcome these distortions and place what they do within a larger ecological context perpetuate a distorted view of wildlife and our role in nature.

A Bullet for Bambi

Caring about the welfare of individual wild animals is not enough if one wants to preserve, conserve, and protect wildlife—no more than giving money to a panhandler will eliminate poverty from the world. It may be of value, but only in a limited sense. Even the efforts of humane societies have limited value when they lack an ecological perspective. There is a danger of doing more harm than good, even to individual animals, as shown by the events surrounding efforts to protect deer.

Deer have played an important role in American history. Recently, this history has been largely one of conflicts over whether or not deer should be hunted. For centuries, deer have been exploited as an important source of food and for sport. Deer have also been admired for their great beauty. Their graceful form and "doe-eyed" countenance attracts a great deal of affection. Felix Salten probably did more than anyone else to stimulate this affection when he published his famous 1928 novel, _Bambi_. The novel and Walt Disney's film adaptation have touched the hearts of millions of people. An extraordinarily sentimental and anthropomorphic portrayal of deer, _Bambi_ accomplished for these animals what _Black Beauty_ did for horses. John Galsworthy praised Salten, noting, "He feels nature deeply, and he loves animals."[17] But it takes knowledge as well as feeling and love to protect deer. They are not domestic animals, and efforts to protect them without understanding the larger ecological story of their lives in the wild are often doomed to failure.

This was the lesson learned from the tragic destruction of the mule deer herd in Arizona's Kaibab National Forest. In an effort to protect the herd and ensure good hunting, 6,214 predators (mountain lions, wolves, coyotes, and bobcats) were destroyed between 1906 and 1923. The herd grew from 4,000 deer in 1906 to 100,000 in 1925. But by 1927, more than half the deer died of starvation and disease. Predators had helped to keep the herd healthy and within a reasonable size. Without predators, the forces left to control the population were starvation (as the enormous herd overbrowsed and destroyed the vegetation), disease, and hunting.[18] Recent deer hunting debates, however, suggest that animal rights advocates have not learned this lesson. The Angel Island controversy is a case in point.

Black-tailed deer were introduced to Angel Island in 1915 when it was occupied by the army.[19] Located in San Francisco Bay, this island, only one square mile in size, became a state park in 1955. Hunting was banned, and the deer population began increasing. By 1966 the herd had grown to an estimated three hundred starving deer, and California's Department of Fish and Game stepped in to reduce its size by shooting fifty deer. The hunt prompted a public outcry and, as the issue was debated, starvation solved the problem anyway. In the absence of hunting and predation, the only natural population controls were disease and, after the island's vegetation had been browsed away, starvation. After starvation reduced the herd's size, the island's vegetation recovered. By 1976 the herd had grown again, to 225. This time humane officers for the San Francisco Society for the Prevention of Cruelty to Animals (SF/SPCA) reported that "the suffering on the island was the worst he had ever seen in all his years of investigating cruelty cases." The SF/SPCA received permission to feed the deer while the state worked out a long-term solution. Supported by thousands of dollars of private donations, they set out nearly fifteen tons of feed and medicated pellets during the first feeding season. By then, though, starvation had dropped the size of the herd by one hundred deer. In 1978, an environmental impact study recommended relocating the deer to the mainland, but by summer 1981 the effort had not begun. In the meantime, the SF/SPCA kept feeding and, since the deer were not starving, the herd kept growing.

The Department of Fish and Game wanted to keep the herd from growing to a size that exceeded the carrying capacity of the island and, thus, keep both the herd and the island's vegetation healthy. Both wildlife managers and animal welfare advocates wanted to help the deer, but Fish and Game viewed this in an ecological context and saw the solution in controlling the herd size. Their priority was protecting both the herd and the island's vegetation, and they did not find a problem with shooting individual deer. Animal welfare advocates focused on the plight of individual animals and the need to prevent their suffering and death. They were shocked by a proposal to try natural population control by introducing a predator, the coyote, onto the island. Some said that they would prefer a quick death by shooting to the less humane method of predation. The SF/SPCA's position was that "The question is not what is the most humane method of killing the deer, but rather, how to eliminate the overpopulation problem effectively, and humanely, *without death*" (emphasis added). They were also upset to learn that the state wanted to amend the environmental impact report to include shooting as an option for wildlife management.

In 1981, after the SF/SPCA filed a lawsuit that led to an out-of-court settlement, the state began efforts to relocate the deer. The herd numbered at least 275 deer. Through a collaborative effort, the Department of Fish and Game and SF/SPCA relocated 203 deer to the Cow Mountain Recreation Area. A year later, only 15 percent of the relocated deer were still alive, a very low rate compared with the 72 percent survival rate of black-tailed deer native to that location. The SF/SPCA contested these figures, but they stopped advocating relocation as a solution to the problems on Angel Island.

By 1984 the deer population was back above two hundred and projected to hit more than three hundred in 1985. Fish and Game saw shooting or starvation as the only options for the deer, but the SF/SPCA did not agree. They proposed to sterilize the deer with chemical steroids. "We did so," they informed their members, "out of a deep conviction that the Angel Island deer are innocent animals that deserve to be managed by what is humane and right—not just what is cheapest and most expedient." Experimenting with a variety of baits, they lured the animals into trap enclosures, sedated them, and surgically implanted pellets containing the sterilant. They encountered problems, though. They could not capture enough of the herd, although some individuals were trapped repeatedly. After a total of two hundred and five captures, they were able to sterilize a total of only thirty individual does. This had only a limited impact on population growth.

The SF/SPCA wanted to find a solution "without death" that would allow the deer to "live in peace on Angel Island," but was not successful despite a determined effort. Without fanfare, park personnel began to selectively shoot the deer.

This was not an isolated conflict. Similar battles between wildlife managers and animal welfare advocates have arisen repeatedly. The controversy surrounding the white-tailed deer herd on the Crane Memorial Reservation in Ipswich, Mass., was particularly heated.[20] It underscored the unfortunate confusion of the issue of how best to protect the welfare of the deer and the debate over whether or not deer should be hunted. Although these are very different problems, they often overlap, and as the issues become confused the deer may suffer. The Crane Memorial Reservation is owned by the Trustees of Reservations, an old and respected land conservation organization. The reservation's deer herd had grown to the point that the reservation's vegetation was severely damaged by overbrowsing and, as a consequence, animals were starving. In 1983 the state's Division of Fisheries and Wildlife proposed to conduct a public hunt to control the size of the herd. This sparked strong opposition.

Animal welfare groups are traditionally suspicious of state and federal wildlife agencies because such organizations are supported by hunting fees and exist in large part to support sport hunting. They are also suspicious of the agencies' wildlife management programs. "Animal welfare organizations," according to the Humane Society of the United States, "have charged that wildlife management programs are little more than an excuse to subsidize sport hunting with public funds." The proposal to use a public hunt, rather than a privately hired sharpshooter, to cull the Crane Memorial Reservation herd was a tactical blunder. It demonstrated mixed motives and confused the ecologically pressing problem of managing the herd size with the separate and emotionally charged issues surrounding sport hunting.

The state called off the hunt after animal rights activists threatened to place their own bodies between the hunters and the deer. The controversy, however, was rekindled each autumn over the next few years instead of becoming a complex and acrimonious debate pursued in public hearings and the media. Differences of opinion emerged between the older, more traditional animal welfare organizations and the radical animal rights groups. The older organizations were able to enter into a dialogue with the Trustees and the Division of Fisheries and Wildlife. The animal rights activists, though, were more ideologically driven and refused to compromise. Environmental groups that might have voiced support of the Trustees kept a low profile, in part for fear of attracting the wrath of the animal rights groups. The issue was made still more complex by the presence of Lyme disease, a debilitating and potentially fatal infection transmitted by deer ticks. By the end of 1984, at least fifteen to twenty of the residents living along a road entering the reservation and five of the twenty-seven Trustees employees working on the Crane properties had contracted the disease. Over a period of eight years, the disease struck one-third of the residents along the road.

Animal advocates proposed relocating or sterilizing the deer, but with no success. Some seemed more interested in stopping the shooting than in keeping individual deer alive or in preventing the herd's starvation. "I'd rather see them starve to death than shot," announced one opponent to the hunt. "There's no physical pain involved in starvation," another later explained. "Nature's population controls are not cruel and starvation and disease do not cause pain." The advocates also seemed unconcerned with the impact of overbrowsing on the reservation's vegetation. In any event, they were unable to offer a viable solution to a very real problem. A decision was finally reached in January 1985. "Amidst several shouts of 'you're damning your souls,'" reported the *Boston Globe*, the Fisheries and Wildlife board voted unanimously to institute a controlled hunt. One animal rights advocate asserted, "It's collusion by the hunting lobby, and I find it horrible." Later, after five minutes of deliberation, a judge refused to issue a restraining order and a select group of hunters began their work.

* * *

The motion picture *The Bear* was released in 1989 with a splash of media hype. It was widely praised. Advertisements quoted *Parenting Magazine* as calling it "One of the most perfect films imaginable for parents to see with their children." Cleveland Amory, president of the Fund for Animals, praised it as "the best film ever made" about grizzly bears. It was a touching film that carried a powerful anti-hunting message. One reviewer endorsed it as neither anthropomorphic nor overly sentimental. Nevertheless, the basic premise of *The Bear* was the absurd notion that an adult male grizzly will adopt a bear cub. A film critic called it "a nature fake" and condemned its anthropomorphism. "It's saying that we shouldn't kill bears," she wrote, "because they're so much like us—after it fakes the evidence that they are."[21] However compelling and well meant the effort, how much hope is there for protecting real bears in the wild if we must rely on fantastical bears to motivate public concern?

Animal welfare advocates helped pioneer the way to a new public attitude toward domestic animals. Many nature writers, including the nature fakers, helped to expand this concern to include wild animals. They did this by writing sympathetic accounts about the lives of individual animals—accounts that motivated their readers to care about what happens to wildlife. Often, though, these writers accomplished this by presenting their animal heroes as furry or feathery little people. Readers cared for the animals as they would care for other people, or at least as they would for their own pets. In the end, though, the writers were trapped by their own genre. To develop human interest in their animal heroes, the authors had to present their animals in human terms, caught in plots that human readers could directly relate to. But their protagonists were not human.[22]

In 1926, one of the great nature educators, William (Cap'n Bill) Vinal, summarized the impact of the nature fakers in this way:

> The majority of children never will get true animal tales.... These writers tell about animals, not as they are but as their readers like

to think they are. I well remember my bitter disappointment in the learning powers of two pet rabbits after having read about rabbit intelligence as "observed" by [Seton and Long]. The average first grade reader is the initiator of the appetite which enjoys nature faking, the colored supplement of the Sunday newspaper, and shall we add, ante-nuptial love stories—situations remote from real life.[23]

Now, in the late twentieth century, we face similar forces that continue to foster anthropomorphic, sentimental, death-denying, and distorted or partial understandings of the natural world.

People who care about the welfare of individual wild animals must base their work on a sound understanding of the animals they wish to help. However, our notions of what is best for wild animals are often shaped by our experiences with the animals we know. Most often, these are our pets and domesticated animals. But this is an inadequate guide to action. We need to view wildlife in terms of "real life." We need to allow wild animals to be just that—animals living in an ecological environment. Not pets. Not furry or leathery little people. Just animals whose needs we must understand, respect, and accommodate—not objects upon which we project our own assumptions and emotional needs.

Animal rights advocates' values may be of use in clarifying our responsibilities to animals extracted from their ecological context. Their agenda, though, can sometimes be woefully inadequate as a guide to help us define our relationship with creatures that live largely independent of us and within a complex ecological environment. We now face the challenge of expanding our theories of animal rights to include the larger ecological context within which wild animals live.

In a sense, the new ecological view of nature is as much at odds with the status quo as was that of the animal welfare perspective a century ago. Ecologists and environmentalists tend to focus on the large-scale context (e.g., populations and ecosystems) within which the lives of individual animals are set. They are interested in protecting all forms of life. On the other hand, animal welfare and animal rights activists tend to focus very selectively on individual animals, especially mammals and birds. One rarely, if ever, hears them expressing concern about the earthworms, beetles (which comprise one-fifth of animal species), springtails, or hundreds of thousands of other animals in the world.[24] They express little or no interest in the welfare of the multitudes of plants, including fungi and bacteria, that are essential to the survival of individual animals. This makes it very difficult for them to deal effectively with wildlife issues, because their very conception of wildlife is impoverished.

Nevertheless, if there are elements of nature faking in some animal rights advocates' portrayal of wildlife, we must be cautious in our response to them. The animal rights movement is very diverse, as are the positions held by its members. Also, it is sobering to recall that the original nature fakers' views have sometimes proven correct, even though they went against accepted views of their time. As they focus their attention on the more abstract populations and ecosystems phenomena of nature, ecologists, wildlife managers, and environmentalists can easily lose sight of individual animals and our responsibilities to them. It is the animal welfare and animal rights advocates who are reminding us of this, and their messages must not be rejected out of hand. Although the new ecological worldview is relatively clear, we are still muddling our way into a new world of values and spirituality. The animal rights advocates play an important role in this process.[25]

We are still in the process of shaping a new relationship between people and nature. We have learned that the mythic power of Henry Adams's life-denying dynamo is creating a world that is hostile to humans, as well as to the rest of nature. He realized that we must find life-affirming contemporary versions of the goddesses of old. The nature lovers turned to Mother Nature and her children, wild animals. Environmentalists appeal to a grand ecological design, far greater than ourselves, that nurtures us, yet will strike us down if we violate its laws. Whatever new mythic power emerges to form the new foundation of our culture, it must embrace both understanding and emotion, science and sentiment. It must also help us to delight in and respect the multitude of other lives with which we share the earth, while affirming death as life's natural and welcome system. We built the dynamo. We are now assisting at the birth of what will follow.

BIBLIOGRAPHY OF WILLIAM J. LONG

The following bibliography of William J. Long's book-length publications is not complete. It includes only the first printing of each edition published in the United States, although foreign editions and translations were also published. It lists only one of his anonymous books, although there are likely to be others. The dates that his books went out of print, when known (courtesy of Ginn & Co.), are indicated in parentheses. The Wood Folk Series books are school editions. Most of their contents also appear in Long's other books. The bibliography is arranged in chronological order to show the progress of his career as a writer.

William J. Long. *The Making of Zimri Bunker: A Story of Nantucket in the Early Days*. Boston: L. C. Page & Co., 1899.

———. *Ways of Wood Folk*. Boston: Ginn & Co., 1899. Wood Folk Series, Book 1. (1938)

———. *Wilderness Ways*. Boston: Ginn & Co., 1900. Wood Folk Series, Book 2. (1949)

———. *Beasts of the Field*. Boston: Ginn & Co., 1901.

———. *Fowls of the Air*. Boston: Ginn & Co., 1901.

———. *Secrets of the Woods*. Boston: Ginn & Co., 1901. Wood Folk Series, Book 3. (1945)

———. *School of the Woods: Some Life Studies of Animal Instincts and Animal Training*. Boston: Ginn & Co., 1902.

———. *Wood Folk at School*. Boston: Ginn & Co., 1903. Wood Folk Series, Book 4. Essays selected from *School of the Woods*. (1936)

———. *Following the Deer*. Boston: Ginn & Co., 1903.

———. *A Little Brother to the Bear, and other Animal Studies*. Boston: Ginn & Co., 1903. Holiday edition.

———. *A Little Brother to the Bear, and other Animal Studies*. Boston: Ginn & Co., 1904. Wood Folk Series, Book 5. School edition of the 1903 book. (1940)

————. *Northern Trails: Some Studies of Animal Life in the Far North.* Boston: Ginn & Co., 1905.

————. *Brier-Patch Philosophy, by "Peter Rabbit."* Boston: Ginn & Co., 1906.

————. *Whose Home Is the Wilderness: Some Studies of Wild Animal Life.* Boston: Ginn & Co., 1907.

————. *Wayeeses, the White Wolf.* Boston: Ginn & Co., 1907. Holiday edition. Reprint of the "Wayeeses" section from *Northern Trails*.

————. *Northern Trails, Book I.* Boston: Ginn & Co., 1908. Published later in 1908 as *Wayeeses, The White Wolf.* Wood Folk Series, Book 6. School edition, with interesting new preface, of the 1907 Wayeeses book. (1935)

————. *Northern Trails, Book II.* Boston: Ginn & Co., 1908. Published later in 1908 as *Stories from Northern Trails.* Wood Folk Series, Book 7. Reprint of stories from *Northern Trails.* (1930)

————. *English Literature: Its History and its Significance for the Life of the English-Speaking World.* Boston: Ginn & Co., 1909. (1946)

————. *American Literature: A Study of the Men and the Books that in the Earlier and Later Times Reflect the American Spirit.* Boston: Ginn & Co., 1913. (1952)

————, ed. Lewis Carroll. *Alice's Adventures in Wonderland.* Boston: Ginn & Co., 1917.

————. *Outlines of American Literature: An Introduction to the Chief Writers of America, to the Books they Wrote, and to the Times in which they Lived.* Boston: Ginn & Co., 1917. (1949)

————. *Outlines of English Literature: An Introduction to the Chief Writers of England, to the Books they Wrote, and to the Times in which they Lived.* Boston: Ginn & Co., 1917. (1936)

————. *Outlines of English and American Literature: An Introduction to the Chief Writers of England and America, to the Books they Wrote, and to the Times in which they Lived.* Boston: Ginn & Co., 1917. (1948)

————. *How Animals Talk, and Other Pleasant Studies of Birds and Beasts.* New York: Harper & Brothers, 1919.

————. *Wood-Folk Comedies: The Play of Wild-Animal Life on a Natural Stage.* New York: Harper & Brothers, 1920.

————. *Mother Nature: A Study of Animal Life and Death.* New York: Harper & Brothers, 1923.

————. *Brier-Patch Philosophy, by "Peter Rabbit."* New York: Harper & Brothers, [1923]. Reprint of 1906 edition with a "Foreword to the New Edition."

————. *America: A History of Our Country.* Boston: Ginn & Co., 1923. (1954)

————. *Outlines of American Literature, with Readings.* Boston: Ginn & Co., 1925. (1951)

————. *Outlines of English Literature, with Readings.* Boston: Ginn & Co., 1925. (1946)

Mary L. Wheeler and William J. Long. *Readings in American Literature to Accompany Long's "Outlines of American Literature."* Boston: Ginn & Co., 1925.

Mary L. Wheeler and William J. Long. *Readings in English Literature to Accompany Long's "Outlines of English Literature."* Boston: Ginn & Co., 1925.

Elizabeth C. Coddington and William J. Long. *Our Country: A First Book of American History.* Boston: Ginn & Co., 1929. (1954)

[William J. Long and] Glenn W. Moon. *Story of Our Land and People.* New York: H. Holt, 1938.

William J. Long. *English Literature: Its History and its Significance for the Life of the*

English-Speaking World. Enlarged Edition. Boston: Ginn & Co., 1945. (1972)

————. *The Spirit of the Wild.* Garden City, New York: Doubleday, 1956. A posthumous collection of previously unpublished material edited by his daughter, Lois Long Fox.

————. *Wings of the Forest.* Garden City, New York: Doubleday, 1957. A posthumous collection of previously unpublished material edited by his daughter, Lois Long Fox.

ENDNOTES

Bowditch. "Real and Sham Natural History, Etc." and "Roosevelt on the Nature Fakirs, Etc." (cited as *Bowditch I* and *Bowditch II*, respectively). Bound scrapbooks prepared by Harold Bowditch, Houghton Library, Harvard University, Cambridge, MA.

HL. Houghton Library, Harvard University, Cambridge, MA. The library includes the extensive Theodore Roosevelt Collection as well as early correspondence from the files of the Houghton Mifflin Company and the *Atlantic Monthly.*

JB. John Burroughs.

LC. Theodore Roosevelt Papers, Library of Congress, Washington, DC.

TR. Theodore Roosevelt.

Woodbridge Interviews. Interviews with William J. Long's daughter, Frances Long Woodbridge, 11–13 August 1979, St. Louis, MO.

Preface

1. Bradford Torrey, *A Rambler's Lease* (Boston: Houghton Mifflin, 1889), pp. 71–72, 104–5.

Chapter One. The Rise of the Nature Lovers

1. John Burroughs, *Camping & Tramping with Roosevelt* (Boston: Houghton Mifflin, 1906), pp. 66–67; TR to C. Hart Merriam, 22 April 1903, LC.

2. *World* (8 March 1903), newspaper clipping, LC; Burroughs, *Camping & Tramping*, pp. 6–7; Elizabeth Burroughs Kelley, *John Burroughs: Naturalist* (New York: Exposition Press, 1959), p. 175; Burroughs, *Camping & Tramping*, pp. 66–67. Roosevelt's account of the trip appears in his *Outdoor Pastimes of an American Hunter* (New York: Charles Scribner's Sons, 1905), pp. 287–317.

3. Theodore Roosevelt, *The Wilderness Hunter*, Homeward Bound ed. (New York: Review of Reviews Co., 1910), pp. 274–75; Burroughs, *Camping & Tramping*, pp. 79–81.

4. " 'Nature Lovers,' " *New York Times Saturday Review of Books* (9 May 1903), p. 320.

5. Burroughs, *Camping & Tramping*, p. 11; Clara Barrus, *Life and Letters of John Burroughs*, 2 vols. (Boston: Houghton Mifflin, 1925), 2:62. For excellent examinations of public interest in living simply and close to nature during this period, see Peter J. Schmitt, *Back to Nature: The Arcadian Myth in Urban America* (New York: Oxford University Press, 1969); David E. Shi, *The Simple Life: Plain Living and High Thinking in American Culture* (New York: Oxford University Press, 1985), pp. 175–214.

6. Unless otherwise noted, biographical material on John Burroughs is derived from Barrus, *Life and Letters*.

7. John Burroughs, *Winter Sunshine*, Riverby ed. (Boston: Houghton Mifflin, 1904), pp. 10, 5–7.

8. "It is very simple," Burroughs wrote of the hermit thrush's song, "and I can hardly tell the secret of its charm. 'O spheral, spheral!' he seems to say; 'O holy, holy, O clear away, clear away! O clear up, clear up!' interspersed with the finest trills and the most delicate preludes" (John Burroughs, *Wake Robin*, Riverby ed. [Boston: Houghton Mifflin, 1904], p. 52).

9. Quotes in Barrus, *Life and Letters*, 1:145–47.

10. "Winter Sunshine," *Nation* (27 January 1876), p. 66. For a bibliography of Burroughs's work see Perry D. Westbrook, *John Burroughs* (New York: Twayne, 1974), pp. 138–40.

11. Fra Elbertus [Elbert Hubbard], *Old John Burroughs* (East Aurora, NY: Roycroft Shop, 1901), pp. 16–17.

12. Linnie Marsh Wolfe, *Son of the Wilderness: The Life of John Muir* (New York: Alfred A. Knopf, 1945), p. 321; Burroughs, *Camping & Tramping*, pp. 63–64.

    Burroughs's attachment to the familiar and comfortable stands in sharp contrast with the approach to nature of his friend John Muir. Burroughs and "John O' Mountains" became lasting friends when traveling together as fellow members of the Harriman expedition to Alaska in 1899. Muir was an outgoing, verbally dominating naturalist and explorer who reveled in his raw experience of wilderness forests, mountains, and glaciers. (Once he clung for hours atop a Douglas fir tree in the midst of a wind storm, swinging through an arc of twenty to thirty degrees, to enjoy the weather. "I kept my lofty perch for hours," he wrote, "frequently closing my eyes to enjoy the music by itself, or to feast quietly on the delicious fragrance that was streaming past.") Exploring the Alaskan coast from the luxury of Harriman's ship was plenty of adventure for Burroughs. At one point he got off the ship, intending to wait in the relative comfort of the town of Unalaska while the rest of the party steamed across the stormy Bering Straits to Siberia. Muir, though, caught him in the act and absconded with his luggage, leaving Burroughs no choice but to remain with the expedition (John Muir, *The Mountains of California* [New York: Century Co., 1894], pp. 251–57; William H. Goetzmann and Kay Sloan, *Looking Far North: The Harriman Expedition to Alaska, 1899* [New York: Viking Press, 1982], pp. 131–32; Barrus, *Life and Letters*, 1:381).

13. Robert Whitmore Bradford, "Journey into Nature: American Nature Writing, 1733–1860" (Ph.D. diss., Syracuse University, 1957); Roderick Nash, *Wilderness and the American Mind*, 3rd ed. (New Haven, CT: Yale University Press, 1982), pp. 75–77; Bradford, "Journey into Nature," pp. 392–415.

14. "The Publishing of *Walden*," in Philip Van Doren Stern, ed., *The Annotated*

Walden (New York: Clarkson N. Potter, 1970), pp. 38–41. See Nash, *Wilderness and the American Mind.*

15. Philip Marshall Hicks, "The Development of the Natural History Essay in American Literature" (Ph.D. diss., University of Pennsylvania, 1924), pp. 124–58.
16. Burroughs, *Wake Robin,* pp. xv–xvi.
17. Paul Russell Cutright, *Theodore Roosevelt: The Making of a Conservationist* (Urbana: University of Illinois Press, 1985), pp. 151–52.
18. Except where noted, this biographical sketch is derived from Morris West's *The Rise of Theodore Roosevelt* (New York: Coward, McCann & Geoghegan, 1979).
19. David McCullough, *Mornings on Horseback* (New York: Simon & Schuster, 1981), pp. 316ff.
20. Roosevelt, *Wilderness Hunter,* pp. 16, 19.
21. Paul Russell Cutright, *Theodore Roosevelt: The Naturalist* (New York: Harper & Brothers, 1956), pp. 80–85; Cutright (1985), pp. 192–95.
22. Roosevelt, *Wilderness Hunter,* p. 270.
23. Ibid., pp. 269–70.
24. West, *Rise of Theodore Roosevelt,* pp. 382–85.
25. Peter Bull, *The Teddy Bear Book* (New York: Random House, 1970), pp. 22–41; Daniel J. Gelo, "The Bear," in Angus K. Gillespie and Jay Mechling, eds., *American Wildlife in Symbol and Story* (Knoxville: University of Tennessee Press, 1987), pp. 149–51.
26. John Muir, *The Story of My Boyhood and Youth* (Boston: Houghton Mifflin, 1913), p. 1. Unless otherwise noted, this biographical sketch is derived from Stephen Fox, *John Muir and His Legacy: The American Conservation Movement* (Boston: Little, Brown & Co., 1981). See also Michael P. Cohen, *The Pathless Way: John Muir and American Wilderness* (Madison: University of Wisconsin Press, 1984).
27. Charles E. Fay, "Mountain Climbing as an Organized Sport," *Outlook* 71 (7 June 1902), pp. 377–84; TR to John Muir, 14 March 1903, LC; Fox, *John Muir and His Legacy,* pp. 125–26.
28. John F. Sears, *Sacred Places: American Tourist Attractions in the Nineteenth Century* (New York: Oxford University Press, 1989). Public efforts to correct the outrageous commercial exploitation and abuse that grew around Niagara Falls provided a model for similar efforts to protect the national parks.
29. Hans Huth, *Nature and the American: Three Centuries of Changing Attitudes* (1957; reprint ed., Lincoln: University of Nebraska Press, 1972), pp. 105–28; Kenneth I. Helphand, "The Bicycle Kodak," *Environmental Review* 4, no. 3 (1981), pp. 24–33.
30. *The White Mountain Guide Book,* 11th ed. (Concord, NH: Edson C. Eastman, 1873), pp. 41–42, 45–46, xii.
31. David E. Shi, *The Simple Life: Plain Living and High Thinking in American Culture* (New York: Oxford University Press, 1985), pp. 176–77; Huth, *Nature and the American,* pp. 63–69; Cynthia Zaitzevsky, *Frederick Law Olmsted and the Boston Park System* (Cambridge, MA: Belknap Press, 1982), pp. 97–99; Marilyn Thornton Williams, "The Municipal Bath Movement in the United States, 1890–1915" (Ph.D. diss., New York University, 1972).
32. Stanley M. Ulanoff, "The Origins and Development of Organized Camping in the United States 1861–1961" (Ph.D. diss., New York University, 1968), pp. 18–33; William M. Hammerman, ed., *Fifty Years of Resident Outdoor Education: 1930–1980* (Martinsville, IN: American Camping Association, 1980), pp. xv–xviii; Ernest B. Balch, quoted in *A Handbook of Summer Camps: 1925* (Boston: Porter Sargent, 1925), p. 29; Peter J. Schmitt, *Back to Nature: The Arcadian Myth in Urban America* (New York: Oxford University Press, 1969), p. 97. See also Ernest B. Balch, "The

First Camp—Camp Chocorua, 1881," in *A Handbook of Summer Camps: 1925*, pp. 35–45; Schmitt, *Back to Nature*, pp. 96–105. List of early "pioneer camps" in *A Handbook of Summer Camps: 1926* (Boston: Porter Sargent, 1926), pp. 29–31.

33. List of early "pioneer camps" in *A Handbook of Summer Camps: 1926*, pp. 29–31. "Where Girls Pass the Weeks of Summer in Camp," *Boston Sunday Herald* (16 August 1903), p. 32.

34. "Miss Diana in the Adirondacks," *Harper's Weekly* 27 (25 August 1883), p. 535.

35. Grace Gallatin Seton-Thompson, *A Woman Tenderfoot* (New York: Doubleday, Page & Co., 1900), p. 19; Martha Coman, "The Art of Camping: A Woman's View," *Outlook* 71 (7 June 1902), pp. 373–74.

36. "Appropriate Costumes for Girls to Wear When Camping Out," *Boston Sunday Herald* (19 July 1903); Coman, "Art of Camping," p. 376.

37. George P. Marsh, *Man and Nature; or, Physical Geography as Modified by Human Action* (New York: Charles Scribner, 1864), p. 36.

38. Frank Graham, Jr., *The Adirondack Park: A Political History* (New York: Alfred A. Knopf, 1978), pp. 70–71; Gifford Pinchot, *Breaking New Ground* (New York: Harcourt, Brace & Co., 1947); Paul Russell Cutright, *Theodore Roosevelt: The Making of a Conservationist* (Urbana: University of Illinois Press, 1985), pp. 200–202. See also Roderick Nash, *Wilderness and the American Mind*, 3rd ed. (New Haven, CT: Yale University Press, 1982); Samuel P. Hays, *Conservation and the Gospel of Efficiency* (Cambridge: Harvard University Press, 1959); Peter Matthiessen, *Wildlife in America*, rev. ed. (New York: Viking, 1987).

39. Francis Darwin, *The Life and Letters of Charles Darwin*, 2 vols. (New York: D. Appleton & Co., 1888), 1:368; Albert Schweitzer, *Out of My Life & Thought: An Autobiography* (New York: Henry Holt & Co., 1933), pp. 185–90.

   This does not mean no one felt sympathy for animals before the nineteenth century. The Quaker John Woolman (1720–1772), for example, recalled how he was "seized with horror" when, as a child, he killed a robin and orphaned her nestlings (*The Journal of John Woolman*, Harvard Classics 50 vols. [New York: P. F. Collier & Son, 1909], 1:178).

40. See James Turner, *Reckoning with the Beast: Animals, Pain and Humanity in the Victorian Mind* (Baltimore, MD: Johns Hopkins University Press, 1980); Gerald Carson, *Men, Beasts and Gods: A History of Cruelty and Kindness to Animals* (New York: Charles Scribner's Sons, 1972), quotation on p. 77.

41. A[nna] Sewell, *Black Beauty: His Grooms and Companions* (1877; reprint ed., Boston: American Humane Education Society, n.d. [1890]).

42. Turner, *Reckoning with the Beast*, pp. 122–37. See also Thomas Gilbert Pearson, *Adventures in Bird Protection* (New York: D. Appleton-Century Co., 1937); Robin W. Doughty, *Feather Fashions and Bird Preservation: A Study in Nature Protection* (Berkeley and Los Angeles: University of California Press, 1975); Floyd Malvern Murdoch, "For the Birds: Backgrounds of the Anglo-American Bird Treaty of 1916" (Ph.D. diss., American University, 1975).

43. Celia Thaxter, "Woman's Heartlessness," *Audubon Magazine* 1 (February 1887), p. 14.

44. Paul Brooks, *Speaking for Nature: How Literary Naturalists from Henry Thoreau to Rachel Carson Have Shaped America* (Boston: Houghton Mifflin, 1980), p. 174.

45. Doughty, *Feather Fashions*, pp. 97–104; Murdoch, "For the Birds," pp. 123–65; Stephen Fox, *John Muir and His Legacy: The American Conservation Movement* (Boston: Little, Brown & Co., 1981), pp. 151–54ff; photocopy of membership certificate provided by Massachusetts Audubon Society.

46. G. O. Shields, Introduction to Neltje Blanchan, *Birds That Hunt and Are Hunted*,

Nature Library (New York: Doubleday, Page & Co., 1904), p. viii; Fox, *John Muir and His Legacy*, p. 149.

47. Chester A. Reed, *North American Birds Eggs* (New York: Doubleday, Page & Co., 1904), pp. i–ii; A. Radclyffe Dugmore, *Bird Homes*, Nature Library (New York: Doubleday, Page & Co., 1904), p. 3.

48. *Audubon Magazine* 1 (February 1887), inside front cover; Florence Merriam Bailey, *Handbook of Birds of the Western United States* (Boston: Houghton Mifflin, 1902), p. xxvii.

49. W. J. Holland, *The Butterfly Book*, Nature Library (Doubleday, Page & Co., 1904), p. v; Gene Stratton Porter, *A Girl of the Limberlost* (New York: Doubleday, Page & Co., 1909); Brooks, *Speaking for Nature*, pp. 179–80.

50. William Paley, *Natural Theology, or Evidences of the Existence and Attributes of the Deity, Collected from the Appearances of Nature* (1802; reprint ed., Hallowell, England: E. Goodale, 1819), pp. 7–15; John Ray, *The Wisdom of God Manifested in the Works of the Creation*, 12th ed. (London: Rivington, Ward & Richardson, 1759), p. 180; Ernst Mayr, *The Growth of Biological Thought: Diversity, Evolution, and Inheritance* (Cambridge: Harvard University Press, 1982), pp. 103–5.

51. *The Natural History of Insects*, Harper's Family Library, no. 8 (New York: J. & J. Harper, 1831), p. 81; F. W. P. Greenwood, *Sacred Philosophy of the Seasons; Illustrating the Perfections of God in the Phenomena of the Year*, 4 vols. (Boston: Marsh, Capen Lyon & Webb, 1839), 1:5.

52. Lynn Barber, *The Heyday of Natural History, 1820–1870* (New York: Doubleday & Co., 1980), pp. 13–26; David Elliston Allen, *The Victorian Fern Craze: A History of Pteridomania* (London: Hutchinson & Co., 1969); Frances Lichten, *Decorative Art of Victoria's Era* (New York: Charles Scribner's Sons, 1950), pp. 153–66, quotation on p. 160.

53. Clifton F. Hodge, *Nature Study and Life* (Boston: Ginn & Co., 1902), pp. 1–31, quotation on p. 12. The following discussion of the nature study movement is based largely on Richard R. Olmsted, "The Nature-Study Movement in American Education" (Ed.D. diss., Indiana University, 1967); Peter J. Schmitt, *Back to Nature: The Arcadian Myth in Urban America* (New York: Oxford University Press, 1969), pp. 77–95; and Tyree G. Minton, "The History of the Nature-Study Movement and Its Role in the Development of Environmental Education" (Ed.D. diss., University of Massachusetts, 1980).

54. Frederick L. Holtz, *Nature-Study: A Manual for Teachers and Students* (New York: Charles Scribner's Sons, 1908), p. 53; Anna Botsford Comstock, Introduction to Frank Overton and Mary E. Hill, *Nature Study: A Pupil's Text-Book* (New York: American Book Co., 1905), p. 3.

55. Holtz, *Nature-Study*, p. 20; Hodge, *Nature Study and Life*, p. 30.

56. Elizabeth Cary Agassiz, ed., *Louis Agassiz: His Life and Correspondence*, 2 vols. (Boston: Houghton Mifflin, 1885), 2:765–76; Edward Lurie, *Louis Agassiz: A Life in Science* (1960; reprint ed., Baltimore, MD: Johns Hopkins University Press, 1988), pp. 379–81; "The Prayer of Agassiz," in Hyatt H. Waggoner, ed., *The Poetical Works of Whittier* (Boston: Houghton Mifflin, 1975), p. 450; David Starr Jordan, *Science Sketches* (Chicago: A. C. McClurg & Co., 1888), quoted in Olmsted, "Nature-Study Movement," p. 27.

57. Harlan H. Ballard, "History of the Agassiz Association," *Swiss Cross* 1 (January 1887), pp. 4–7; Arthur Newton Pack and E. Laurence Palmer, eds., *The Nature Almanac: A Handbook of Nature Education* (Washington, DC: American Nature Association, 1927), pp. 39–40.

58. Clara Barrus, *Life & Letters of John Burroughs*, 2 vols. (Boston: Houghton Mifflin,

1925), 1:285; Mary E. Burt, ed., *Burroughs' Birds and Bees; Sharp Eyes and Other Papers* (Boston: Houghton Mifflin, n.d.), pp. 3–6, front flyleaf adv.; Mary E. Burt, ed., *Little Nature Studies for Little People* (Boston: Ginn & Co., 1895), p. 3; sales figures clipped to JB to Houghton Mifflin, 20 August 1907, HL; advertisement in back of Mary E. Murtfeldt and Clarence Moores Weed, *Stories of Insect Life, Second Series: Summer and Autumn* (Boston: Ginn & Co., 1899); Francis W. Halsey, "The Rise of the Nature Writers," *American Monthly Review of Reviews* 26 (1902), p. 571.

59. Olive Thorne Miller, *The First Book of Birds* (Boston: Houghton Mifflin, 1899), pp. iii–iv.

60. Charles W. Eliot, "The New Definition of the Cultivated Man," quoted in Edward F. Bigelow, *The Spirit of Nature Study* (New York: A. S. Barnes, 1907), pp. 96–97.

61. Sara A. Hubbard, "A Group of Nature Books," *Dial* 31 (1 July 1901), p. 14.

62. Neltje Blanchan, *Nature's Garden*, Nature Library (New York: Doubleday, Page & Co., 1904), p. v.

63. Stern, *Annotated Walden*, p. 483; Barrus, *Life and Letters*, 1:254; William Frederic Badè, *The Life and Letters of John Muir*, 2 vols. (Boston: Houghton Mifflin, 1924), 2:268.

64. Halsey, "Rise of the Nature Writers," pp. 567–71; "Nature Writers Whose Works Are Popular," *Boston Sunday Herald* magazine (5 August 1903), pp. 5, 7; Paul Brooks, *Speaking for Nature: How Literary Naturalists from Henry Thoreau to Rachel Carson Have Shaped America* (Boston: Houghton Mifflin, 1980), pp. 165–80.

65. Charles M. Skinner, *Nature in a City Yard* (New York: Century Co., 1897); Charles C. Abbott, *Notes of the Night* (New York: Century Co., 1896), pp. 1–78; Hamilton Wright Mabie, *Under the Trees* (New York: Dodd, Mead & Co., 1902), pp. 13, 48. See, for example, William Hamilton Gibson, *Eye Spy* (New York: Harper & Brothers, 1897); earlier books were even more lavishly illustrated.

66. For the background of the animal story see: "The Animal Story," in Charles G. D. Roberts, *The Kindred of the Wild: A Book of Animal Life* (Boston: L. C. Page & Co., 1902), pp. 15–29; "The Animal Story," *Edinburgh Review* 214 (July 1911), pp. 94–118; Michel Poirier, "The Animal Story in Canadian Literature," *Queen's Quarterly* 34 (January–March, April–June 1927), pp. 298–312, 398–419; and Alec Lucas, "Nature Writers and the Animal Story," in Carl F. Klinck, ed., *Literary History of Canada: Canadian Literature in English* (Toronto: University of Toronto Press, 1965), pp. 364–88.

67. Halsey, "Rise of the Nature Writers," p. 570; Ernest Thompson Seton, *Wild Animals I Have Known* (New York: Charles Scribner's Sons, 1898), copyright page of 16th printing (1902).

68. Seton, *Wild Animals*, pp. 46–47, 49.

69. Roberts, *Kindred of the Wild*, pp. 273–84.

70. Seton, *Wild Animals*, p. 12; Thomas R. Dunlap, *Saving America's Wildlife* (Princeton, NJ: Princeton University Press, 1988), pp. 18–33; Roberts, *Kindred of the Wild*, p. 29.

71. James Polk, "Lives of the Hunted," *Canadian Literature* 53 (Summer 1972), pp. 51–59; Roberts, *Kindred of the Wild*, p. 24.

72. Olive Thorne Miller, *Bird-Ways* (Boston: Houghton Mifflin, 1885), p. v.

73. "Holiday Publications," *Dial* 33 (1 December 1902), p. 398; William J. Long, *Ways of Wood Folk* (Boston: Ginn & Co., 1899), pp. 52–53.

74. Jack London, *The Call of the Wild* (Boston: Houghton Mifflin, 1900). For popular accounts of Alaska during the gold rush, see: *Klondike: The Chicago Record's Book for Gold Seekers* (Chicago: Chicago Record Co., 1897); Ernest Ingersoll, *Gold Fields of the Klondike and the Wonders of Alaska* (Edgewood Publishing Co., 1897);

and May Kellogg Sullivan, *A Woman Who Went to Alaska* (Boston: James H. Earle & Co., 1902).

75. John Muir, *Mountains of California* (New York: Century Co., 1894), pp. 226–42, 276–99; John Muir, "An Adventure with a Dog and Glacier," *Century* 54 (September 1897), pp. 769–76; John Muir, *Stickeen* (Boston: Houghton Mifflin, 1909); Clara Barrus, *Life & Letters of John Burroughs*, 2 vols. (Boston: Houghton Mifflin, 1925), 1:360. See also John Muir, *Travels in Alaska* (Boston: Houghton Mifflin, 1915), pp. 246–57; and S. Hall Young, *Alaska Days with John Muir* (New York: Fleming H. Revell, 1915), pp. 163–98.

76. "Wilderness Ways," *Our Animal Friends* 28 (August 1901), p. 285.

Chapter Two. John Burroughs and William J. Long—The Battle Begins

1. John Burroughs, "Real and Sham Natural History," *Atlantic Monthly* 91 (March 1903), p. 298.

2. "Wilderness Ways," *Our Dumb Animals* 28 (August 1901), p. 285; Charles Atwood Kofoid, "The Innings of the Animals," *Dial* 21 (1 December 1901), pp. 439–40; Charles Atwood Kofoid, "Beasts, Birds, and Fishes," *Dial* 33 (16 October 1902), p. 240; Ernest Ingersoll, "Nature Books," *Book Buyer* 25 (December 1902): p. 427.

3. Dallas Lore Sharp to JB, 22 December 1902, Sharp Papers, Boston University Library; Burroughs, "Real and Sham Natural History," pp. 298–309.

   Seven years later, Burroughs's comments about Sharp were used as an endorsement of Sharp's *A Watcher in the Woods* (New York: Century, 1910). In its introduction, C. N. Millard wrote, "No less an authority than John Burroughs, in an article in the *Atlantic Monthly* entitled 'Real and Sham Natural History,' made the statement that 'of all the nature books of recent years, I look upon Mr. Sharp's as the best,' " (pp. vii–viii).

4. Charles G. D. Roberts, *The Kindred of the Wild: A Book of Animal Life* (Boston: L. C. Page & Co., 1902).

5. Ernest Thompson Seton, *Wild Animals I Have Known* (New York: Charles Scribner's Sons, 1898), p. 9.

6. William J. Long, *School of the Woods* (Boston: Ginn & Co., 1902).

7. Clara Barrus, *Life & Letters of John Burroughs*, 2 vols. (Boston: Houghton Mifflin, 1925), 2:48–49; Dallas Lore Sharp to JB, 22 December 1902. A few years later, Sharp convinced one publisher not to publish Gene Stratton Porter's sentimental nature novel *A Girl of the Limberlost* only to see it become a bestseller under another (Waitstill H. Sharp, letter to author, 31 August 1979). Throughout the controversy, apparently, Burroughs also sent drafts of his attacks to William J. Long, but Long burned them (telephone interview with Frances Long Woodbridge, 6 July 1979).

8. JB to Bliss Perry, 27 December [1902], HL; Barrus, *Life and Letters*, 2:49; JB to TR, 10 March 1903, LC.

9. Barrus, *Life and Letters*, 2:48, 1:336; TR to JB, 7 March 1903, LC.

10. JB to TR, 10 March 1903, LC.

11. At first, Roosevelt began his letters with "My dear Mr. Burroughs," but by the end of their Yellowstone adventure he began letters with "Dear Oom John," using a Dutch term for uncle. The president, who did not like being called His Excellency, was delighted with Burroughs's nickname for him, His Transparency, coined because the naturalist believed Roosevelt's motives were transparent (Barrus, *Life and Letters*, 2:67).

12. Charles Prescott Daniels, "Discord in the Forest: John Burroughs versus William J. Long," *Boston Evening Transcript* (7 March 1903), p. 23.

13. Wm J. Long, "Science, Nature and Criticism," *Science* 19 (13 May 1904), p. 762.

14. [Thomas Wentworth Higginson], "The Contributors' Club," *Atlantic Monthly* (March 1880), pp. 417–18. See John Burroughs, *Signs and Seasons*, Riverby ed. (Boston: Houghton Mifflin, 1904), pp. 29–31.

15. William J. Long, "Wm. J. Long in Defense: The Young Naturalist Replies to John Burroughs," *Boston Evening Transcript* (14 March 1903), p. 20; Mark Sullivan, *Our Times: The United States, 1900–1925; Pre-War America* (New York: Charles Scribner's Sons, 1930), p. 154n.

    Nevertheless, decades later Long continued to deny that he had been influenced by Seton. "The facts are that I had written over 30 wildlife studies and had published three books before I ever heard of Seton Thompson, as he was called. Since then I have read about one-half of just one of his books, called 'Wild Animals I Have Known,'" Long wrote. "That half was plenty for me, and the book was never again opened" (William J. Long, "That Woodcock Again," *Sports Afield* 118 [July 1947], p. 34).

16. Ernest Thompson Seton, *Trail of an Artist-Naturalist* (New York: Charles Scribner's Sons, 1940), pp. 367–68; John Henry Wadland, *Ernest Thompson Seton: Man in Nature and the Progressive Era, 1880–1915* (New York: Arno Press, 1978), p. 184; Hamlin Garland, "My Friend John Burroughs," *Century Magazine* 102 (September 1921), pp. 737–38.

17. Andrew Carnegie, *Autobiography of Andrew Carnegie* (Boston: Houghton Mifflin, 1920), pp. 292–93.

18. Garland, "My Friend John Burroughs," p. 738. Garland's memory was not entirely accurate on at least one point: The term *fakers* was not used until more than four years after this event.

19. Seton, *Artist-Naturalist*, pp. 367–71.

20. This wolf discussion is puzzling, since Burroughs's article criticized Seton's fox stories and made only one passing reference to wolves. It may be that Seton's memory was faulty here. Seton finally met Long in May when he visited Seton's home in Cos Cob, Conn. Unfortunately, there is no record of what took place (Journals of Ernest Thompson Seton, Box 13, 6 May [1903], Rare Books Room, American Museum of Natural History, New York).

    More than forty years later, Long recalled things differently. "Before he staged this emotional conversation," Long wrote, "Seton had met me several times, had questioned me about my wilderness trips, and had heard me address one large gathering of sportsmen and another of professional men" [William J. Long, "That Woodcock Again," p. 102]. There is a possibility, however, that Long's memory of the chronology was incorrect.

21. Journals of Ernest Thompson Seton, 28 March [1903]; Elizabeth Burroughs Kelley, *John Burroughs: Naturalist* (New York: Exposition Press, 1959), p. 175. Seton later added a note to his journal entry indicating that this was the "historic" meeting. This note was in a different ink and most likely added many years later, perhaps when Seton was preparing his 1940 autobiography.

22. Frank M. Chapman, *Autobiography of a Bird-Lover* (New York: D. Appleton-Century Co., 1933), pp. 63, 77, 182–83.

23. Lida Rose McCabe, "At Home with Ernest Thompson Seton," *Book Buyer* 25 (August 1902), pp. 21–28; Charles G. D. Roberts, "The Home of a Naturalist," *Country Life in America* 5 (December 1903), p. 152; Seton, *Artist-Naturalist*, p. 371. Seton's detailed account of what he had to show Burroughs was probably

exaggerated. See also Edward F. Bigelow, "'Wyndygoul,' Home of Ernest Thompson Seton," *Guide to Nature* 2 (January 1910), pp. 312–21.

Burroughs, though, did not like Seton's extravagant style of living. "His way of loving nature is not mine," Burroughs wrote after his visit to Wyndygoul, "but doubtless it is just as genuine." He appears to have first visited in 1905 (Clara Barrus, *Life & Letters of John Burroughs*, 2 vols. [Boston: Houghton Mifflin, 1925], 2:87).

24. For the life of Seton, see Seton, *Artist-Naturalist*; Betty Keller, *Black Wolf: The Life of Ernest Thompson Seton* (Vancouver: Douglas & McIntyre, 1984); John Henry Wadland, *Ernest Thompson Seton: Man in Nature and the Progressive Era, 1880–1915* (New York: Arno Press, 1978); and H. Allen Anderson, *The Chief: Ernest Thompson Seton and the Changing West* (College Station: Texas A&M University Press, 1986). "'Nature Fakir' Books Are Used in Public Schools," *Minneapolis Journal* (2 June 1907), p. 2. Wadland, in *Ernest Thompson Seton*, provides a detailed examination of Seton's stories, scientific standing, and position in the controversy (pp. 166–297). For excellent reproductions of Seton's artwork, see John G. Samson, ed., *The Worlds of Ernest Thompson Seton* (New York: Alfred A. Knopf, 1976).

25. Wadland, *Ernest Thompson Seton*, pp. 122–42.

26. Seton, *Artist-Naturalist*, p. 371.

27. John Burroughs, "The Literary Treatment of Nature," *Atlantic Monthly* 94 (July 1904), p. 42; Barrus, *Life and Letters*, 2:88–89. When Burroughs reprinted the *Atlantic* essay the sentence was altered to read, "Mr. Thompson Seton, as an artist and *raconteur*, ranks by far the highest in his field, but in reading his works as natural history, one has to be constantly on guard against his romantic tendencies" (John Burroughs, *Ways of Nature*, Riverby ed. [Boston: Houghton Mifflin, 1905], p. 203).

28. This account of their trip is derived largely from Barrus, *Life and Letters*, 2:59–67. See also John Burroughs, *Camping & Tramping with Roosevelt* (Boston: Houghton Mifflin, 1906).

29. Barrus, *Life and Letters*, 2:62–63.

30. John Burroughs, *Camping & Tramping with President Roosevelt* (Boston: Houghton Mifflin, 1906), pp. 14–15.

31. Hermit, "The Intelligence of the Wild Things: False Natural History," *Forest and Stream* 60 (18 April 1903), pp. 304–5.

32. TR to George Bird Grinnell, 24 April 1903, LC; TR to JB, 19 May 1903, LC; JB to TR, 6 June 1903 LC; TR to JB, 23 December 1903, LC.

33. John R. Spears, "Mr. Spears on John Burroughs's Criticism of Thompson Seton," *New York Times Saturday Review of Books* (25 April 1903), p. 288.

34. Mason A. Walton, *A Hermit's Wild Friends* (Boston: Dana Estes, 1903), pp. v–vi; May Estelle Cook, "Recent Nature Chronicles," *Dial* 35 (16 December 1903), p. 468.

35. [Francis Trevelyan Miller], "Criticism of Connecticut Naturalists by John Burroughs in the *Atlantic Monthly*," *Connecticut Magazine* 8 (1903), pp. 145–47.

36. William J. Long, "'The School of the Woods,'" *Connecticut Magazine* 8 (1903), pp. 148–52.

37. William J. Long, "Nature and Books," *Dial* 34 (1 June 1903), pp. 357–60.

38. There is little biographical information available on Long. Sources include: Charles Prescott Daniels, "Discord in the Forest: John Burroughs versus William J. Long," *Boston Evening Transcript* (7 March 1903), p. 23; Colonel N. G. Osborn, *Men of Mark in Connecticut*, vol. 2 (Hartford, CT: William R. Goodspeed, 1907), pp. 21–22; "William Joseph Long," *Harvard College, Class of 1892: Report XI*

(Norwood, MA: Plimpton Press, 1928), pp. 131–35; "Long, William Joseph," *The National Cyclopaedia of American Biography* (New York: James T. White & Co., 1934), pp. 354–55; "William Joseph Long," *Harvard College, Class of 1892: Report XV* (Norwood, MA: Plimpton Press, 1942), pp. 191–95; Dorothy G. Wayman, "Pastor Irked T. R. on Hunting Ethics," *Boston Sunday Globe* (17 August 1952), pp. 1, 38; "Dr. W. J. Long, 86, Naturalist, Dies," *New York Times* (10 November 1952), p. 29; "Naturalist Dies: Retired Cleric, 86, a Noted Writer of Outdoor Life," *Stamford Advocate* (10 November 1952), p. 1; and Woodbridge Interviews. I am relying on these except where otherwise noted. There is confusion regarding the year of Long's birth. Various biographies list it as either 1866 or 1867. His birth certificate is not on file at either Attleboro or North Attleboro, which divided from Attleboro in 1887. (The historical spelling is Attleborough.) I am accepting 1866, the date given in *Harvard College, Class of 1892* accounts and on his death certificate (Stamford, CT). His daughter reports that Long was never sure how old he was (Woodbridge Interviews).

39. *Who's Who: Seventy-fifth Anniversary, State Normal School, Bridgewater, Mass.* (Bridgewater, MA: Arthur H. Willis, 1915), p. 77; *State Normal School at Bridgewater, Mass.: Catalogue and Circular* (Boston: Wright & Potter, 1883–87); Nantucket School Committee Minutes, 1 September & 6 December 1888, 14 August 1891, Bridgewater Historical Association Research Center Collection 88, Book 37; W. F. M., letter, Nantucket *Inquirer and Mirror*, (11 July 1885); "About Nantucket's First Public Schools," Nantucket *Inquirer and Mirror* (18 August 1917).

40. Margaret E. Law, Harvard University Registrar, letter to author, 12 September 1978; "A Significant Ordination," *Outlook* 63 (25 November 1899), p. 705. "William J. Long," *General Catalogue of the Theological Seminary, Andover, Massachusetts, 1808–1908* (Boston: Thomas Todd, 1908), p. 482. Long's visit to the Vatican Library was likely informal or through the University of Rome; the library has no record of the visit (La Biblioteca Apostolica Vaticana, letter to author, 18 October 1978). Long's Ph.D. thesis was titled "Hume's Doctrine of Ideas and Substance, Compared with Berkeley's and Locke's" ("Ueber Hume's Lehre von den Ideen und der Substanz in ihrem Zusammenhang mit Derjenigen Locke's und Berkeley's") (Inaug. diss., University of Heidelberg, J. Horning, 1897).

41. He preached for a short while in Orange, Mass., before moving to Cambridge.

42. "Unanimous Call Extended," 7 May; "New Cambridge Minister," 6 June; "Dr. Long Withdraws," 25 June; additional clippings in Long's student file, Andover Newton Theological School Archives, Franklin Trask Library, Newton Center, MA. Daniels, "Discord in the Forest"; "A Candidate Rejected," *Outlook* 59 (2 July 1898), p. 490; "The North Cambridge Council," *Outlook* 59 (9 July 1898), pp. 612–14 (quotation); "Letter from Mr. Long," *Outlook* 59 (9 July 1898), p. 644; "Lots of Company, Scores of Clergymen Do Hold His Views," *Boston Globe*, evening ed. (9 July 1898), p. 10; "The Cambridge Council," *Congregationalist* 82 (23 June 1898), p. 906; "The Cambridge Council—A Universalist's Account" (quotation), *Congregationalist* 82 (30 June 1898), p. 963; "The Guidance of the Spirit," *Congregationalist* 83 (7 July 1898), p. 6; "North Avenue Church and Dr. Long" (quotation), *Congregationalist* 83 (7 July 1898), p. 30; "Mr. Long and the Cambridge Council," *Congregationalist* 83 (14 July 1898), pp. 38–39; "Andover and Other Creeds," *Congregationalist* 83 (25 August 1898), p. 266.

43. "Dr. Long Can Preach Again," 30 September 1898; "Dr. Long Installed," 17 November 1899; clippings in Long's student file, Andover Newton Theological School Archives, Franklin Trask Library, Newton Center, MA. "Dr. Long and the Andover Association," *Congregationalist* 83 (6 October 1898), p. 464; quotation

from "Installation at Stamford, CT.," *Congregationalist* 84 (23 November 1899), p. 789; "A Significant Ordination," *Outlook* 63 (25 November 1899), p. 705; *Manual 4*, First Congregational Church, Stamford, CT (1915), p. 17; clipping on marriage, 7 September 1900, in Frances Bancroft file, Phillips Academy Archives, Andover, MA; William J. Long, *The Making of Zimri Bunker: A Story of Nantucket in the Early Days* (Boston: L. C. Page & Co., 1899); William J. Long, *Ways of Wood Folk* (Boston: Ginn & Co., 1899); William J. Long, *Wilderness Ways* (Boston: Ginn & Co., 1900).

44. "Resignations," *Congregationalist* 88 (31 January 1903), p. 171; *Manual 4*, p. 17.

45. "Dr. Long Practically Blind," Stamford *Daily Advocate* (10 December 1904), p. 1; Wayman, "Pastor Irked T. R.," p. 38; Daniels, "Discord in the Forest"; Chapman, *Autobiography*, p. 183; *Manual 4*, pp. 17–18.

My assessment of this aspect of Long's personality is based on my reading of the literature and was confirmed in general terms by his daughter (Woodbridge Interviews). While the Stamford church praised Long for his intellect and spirituality, it praised his successor, Reverend Louis F. Berry, saying, "Never obscure, never aiming for oratorical effect, he had maintained the high standards of the church and developed an era of conspicuous harmony in its affairs," and noted his humor and friendliness. Reverend Berry, who continued with the church until his death in 1916, may have faced a troubled church when he arrived on the heels of William J. Long (*300th Anniversary Booklet*, First Congregational Church, Stamford, CT [1935], p. 11).

46. William J. Long, "The Modern School of Nature-Study and Its Critics," *North American Review* 176 (May 1903), pp. 687–98.

47. This assessment was derived from my reading of Long's character from the literature and was verified by his daughter (Woodbridge Interviews).

48. Wm Harper Davis, "Natural and Unnatural History," *Science* 19 (22 April 1904), p. 668; Wm J. Long, "Science, Nature and Criticism," *Science* 19 (13 May 1904), pp. 765–66; William T. Hornaday to TR, 29 May 1907, LC.

49. John Burroughs, "Birds and Strings," in *Ways of Nature*, Riverby ed. (Boston: Houghton Mifflin, 1905), pp. 246–48; Long, "Nature and Books," LC; JB to TR, 5 May 1903, LC; JB to TR, 15 June 1903, LC; JB to TR, 20 July & 20 September 1903, LC; TR to JB, 12 October 1903, LC; JB to Bliss Perry, 30 June, 10 July & 22 July 1903, HL; John Burroughs, "Current Misconceptions in Natural History," *Century Magazine* 67 (February 1904), p. 510.

50. Barrus, *Life and Letters*, 2:68–71; TR to JB, 6 July 1903, LC; JB to TR, 20 July 1903, LC.

51. "Wood Folk at School," *Journal of Education* 57 (18 June 1903), p. 394; L. A. O., "Of Interest to Teachers," *Ypsilantian* (Michigan) (16 July 1903); William J. Long, *Wood Folk at School* (Boston: Ginn & Co., 1903); JB to TR, 31 December 1903, LC. The Ginn & Co. pamphlet is a thirty-two-page compilation of excerpts, "Typical Letters and Reviews in Reply to Mr. Burroughs' Unwarranted Attack on Mr. Long," in Bowditch I.

52. Robert Lacey, *Ford: The Men and the Machines* (Boston: Little, Brown, 1986), pp. 74–77.

53. TR to JB, 12 October 1903, LC; Caspar Whitney, "The Sportsman's View-Point," *Outing Magazine* 42 (July 1903), pp. 503–5. Whitney had put off responding to the controversy but finally bowed to pressure from readers and friends (Whitney, "The Sportsman's View-Point," *Outing Magazine* 42 [June 1903], p. 380). The president dismissed Whitney as an untrustworthy observer, despite his strengths as a soldier and seasoned outdoorsman, and branded many of *Outing Magazine*'s nature articles

"preposterous." Roosevelt conceded, though, that Whitney's response was better than those of Burroughs's other critics (TR to JB, 11 June & 6 July 1903, LC).

54. John Burroughs, "Current Misconceptions in Natural History," _Century Magazine_ 67 (February 1904), p. 515; JB to TR, 6 June 1903, LC; TR to JB, 6 July 1903, LC; JB to TR, 20 July 1903, LC; TR to JB, 1 August & 12 October 1903, LC. Quotations from 6 July & 1 August letters.

55. TR to JB, 28 November 1903, LC; JB to TR, 3 December 1903, LC; TR to JB, 16 October 1905, LC.

Chapter Three. Telling the Animals from the Wildflowers

1. Ralph Hoffmann, _A Guide to the Birds of New England and Eastern New York_ (Boston: Houghton Mifflin, 1904), p. 3; "We Americans and the Other Animals," _Century Magazine_ 67 (February 1904), p. 626; cartoon, _Century Magazine_ 70 (June 1905), p. 320; Hans Huth, _Nature and the American: Three Centuries of Changing Attitudes_ (1957; reprint ed., Lincoln: University of Nebraska Press, 1972), p. 180.

2. "We Americans," _Century Magazine_; William L. Bowers, _The Country Life Movement in America, 1900–1920_ (New York: Kennikat Press, 1974); Anna Botsford Comstock, _Handbook of Nature-Study_, 24th ed. (Ithaca, NY: Comstock Publishing Associates, 1939), pp. ix–xi.

3. Rena A. Phillips, "The Woman in the Woods," _Outing Magazine_ 46 (July 1905), p. 473; "We Americans," _Century Magazine_.

4. Ernest Thompson Seton, _Trail of an Artist-Naturalist_ (New York: Charles Scribner's Sons, 1940), pp. 376–85; Ernest Thompson Seton, _Two Little Savages: Being the Adventures of Two Boys Who Lived as Indians and What They Learned_ (New York: Doubleday, Page & Co., 1903); Ernest Thompson Seton, _The Book of Woodcraft and Indian Lore_ (London: Constable & Co., 1912), p. 9. See also John Henry Wadland, _Ernest Thompson Seton: Man in Nature and the Progressive Era, 1880–1915_ (New York: Arno Press, 1978), pp. 298–445; and H. Allen Anderson, _The Chief: Ernest Thompson Seton and the Changing West_ (College Station: Texas A&M University Press, 1986), pp. 138–50.

5. Stephen R. Kellert and Miriam O. Westervelt, "Historical Trends in American Animal Use and Perception," in _Transactions of the 47th North American Wildlife and Natural Resources Conference_ (Washington, DC: Wildlife Management Institute, 1982), pp. 649–63; Stephen R. Kellert, "Historical Trends in Perceptions and Uses of Animals in 20th Century America," _Environmental Review_ 9 (Spring 1985), pp. 19–33. In the period 1900–1906, the prevalence of these attitudes was: utilitarian, 52.2 percent; humanistic, 16.2 percent; negativistic, 11.4 percent; scientistic, 10.6 percent. These were only the most common of ten attitudes studied.

6. May Estelle Cook, "Recent Nature Chronicles," _Dial_ 35 (16 December 1903), pp. 469–70.

7. William J. Long, _A Little Brother to the Bear, and Other Animal Stories_ (Boston: Ginn & Co., 1903); _New York Times Review of Books and Art_ (25 July 1903), p. 510.

8. Long, _A Little Brother_, pp. xiv–xv, 109–25; TR to JB, 28 November 1903, LC; JB to TR, 3 December & 31 December 1903, LC; TR to JB, 2 January 1904, LC; JB to TR, 20 September 1903, LC; TR to JB, 22 September & 12 October 1903, LC.

9. "Animal Surgery," in Long, _A Little Brother_, pp. 219–38, originally published in _Outlook_ 75 (12 September 1903), pp. 122–27; TR to JB, 12 October 1903, LC; JB to TR, 9 June 1905, LC; John Burroughs, _Ways of Nature_ (Boston: Houghton Mifflin, 1905), pp. 180–82.

10. Ernest Thompson Seton, _The Biography of a Grizzly_ (New York: Century Co.,

1904), pp. 70–71.

11. Clarence Hawkes, *The Trail to the Woods* (New York: American Book Co., 1907), pp. 29–30; "Afield with a Blind Naturalist," *Outing Magazine* 51 (December 1907), pp. 345–47; Clarence Hawkes, *Hitting the Dark Trail* (New York: Henry Holt & Co., 1915); JB to TR, 30 May [1907], LC.

12. Cook, "Recent Nature Chronicles," p. 468.

13. "A Woodcock Genius," in Long, *A Little Brother*, pp. 101–6.

14. William Morton Wheeler, *Science* 19 (26 February 1904), pp. 347–50.

15. Frank M. Chapman, "The Case of William J. Long," *Science* 19 (4 March 1904), pp. 387–89.

16. E. C. Case, "Nature Study," *Science* 19 (1 April 1904), pp. 550–51; Wm Harper Davis, "Natural and Unnatural History," *Science* 19 (22 April 1904), pp. 667–75.

17. W. F. Ganong, "The Writings of William J. Long," *Science* 19 (15 April 1904), pp. 623–25.

18. Ellen Hayes, letter, *Science* 19 (15 April 1904), pp. 625–26.

19. William J. Long, "Science, Nature and Criticism," *Science* 19 (13 May 1904), pp. 760–67. In a footnote added to the "Woodcock Genius" essay in the school edition of *A Little Brother to the Bear*, Long referred his young readers to this *Science* letter for proof that "this habit of setting a broken leg in a clay cast is more widespread among woodcock and snipe than I had believed possible" ([Boston: Ginn & Co., 1904], p. 63).

20. Frank M. Chapman, *Autobiography of a Bird-Lover* (New York: D. Appleton-Century Co., 1933), p. 183.

21. William T. Hornaday, *The American Natural History* (New York: Charles Scribner's Sons, 1904), p. xxiii.

22. "Bird Surgery," *Oologist* 4 (March–May 1887), p. 75.

23. Ernest Thompson Seton, *Lives of the Hunted* (New York: Charles Scribner's Sons, 1901), pp. 132–33.

24. Harold Bowditch note, 24 August 1907, Bowditch II; William Brewster to Harold Bowditch, 2 September & 23 September 1907, Bowditch II; John Hardy to Harold Bowditch, 2 October 1907, Bowditch II; Harold Bowditch notes, 22 October 1907 & 18 March 1912, Bowditch II; Harold Bowditch to William Brewster, 29 September 1907, library, Museum of Comparative Zoology, Harvard University, Cambridge, MA; Charles Foster Batchelder, *An Account of the Nuttall Ornithological Club, 1873–1919*, memoirs no. 8 (Cambridge, MA: Nuttall Ornithological Club, 1937), pp. 64, 79, 85, 93.

The original x-ray of the pectoral sandpiper has been lost, but the specimen still exists in the collections of the Museum of Comparative Zoology. The lump on the bird's leg is a mass of dark brown material and feathers. Under a microscope the material looks more like plastic than mud. In 1988 the injury was examined by a team of veterinarians at the Tufts University School of Veterinary Medicine. The mass turned out to be a blood clot with feathers and other debris adhering to it. Shorebirds often stand on one leg and the sandpiper certainly favored its good leg, drawing its injured leg up against its body, where its feathers stuck to the bloody injury. X-rays revealed that the leg was not broken; rather, the joint had been injured, creating a bloody swelling. The injury was more than a month old when John Hardy found the bird, because the clot had begun to calcify. The clot and bony calcification probably served as an effective cast and immobilized the injured joint. This cast, though, was the result of chance rather than design. The specimen is in the Museum of Comparative Zoology, Harvard University, Cambridge, Mass., catalog no. 292,135. See Brewster's note in his catalog, no.

(2)48,906 ("Examination of Pectoral Sandpiper," 6 June 1988, Mark A. Pokras, D.V.M., Tufts University School of Veterinary Medicine, letter to author). An x-ray and a copy of the report have been deposited in the Museum of Comparative Zoology with the specimen.

25. The grouse specimen had been sent to Long from Scotland and was, he protested, not a ruffed grouse. "'I Propose to Smoke Roosevelt Out'—Dr. Long," *New York Times* (2 June 1907), pt. 5, p. 2; William J. Long, "Dr. Long Tells More Animal Stories in an Effort to Confute the President," *New York Times* (7 July 1907), pt. 5, p. 11.

    Long, however, continued to hold to his views on this matter. Forty years later, he restated his case in "That Woodcock Again," *Sports Afield* 118 (July 1947), pp. 34, 102.

26. William G. Sheldon, *The Book of the American Woodcock* (Amherst: University of Massachusetts Press, 1967), pp. 149–50.

27. "Kingfisher's Kindergarten," in Long, *A Little Brother*, pp. 179–90.

28. "A School for Little Fishermen," in William J. Long, *School of the Woods* (Boston: Ginn & Co., 1902), pp. 99–114.

29. John Burroughs, "Real and Sham Natural History," *Atlantic Monthly* 91 (March 1903), p. 308; William J. Long, "The Modern School of Nature-Study and Its Critics," *North American Review* 176 (May 1903), p. 695.

30. W. F. Ganong, "New Brunswick Animals and Animal Romancers," *Saint John* (New Brunswick) *Globe* (5 March 1904); W. F. Ganong, "The Writings of William J. Long," *Science* 19 (15 April 1904), p. 224; W. F. Ganong, "New Brunswick Animals and the Animal Romancers," *Bulletin of the Natural History Society of New Brunswick* 5 (1905), pp. 299–304; Harold Bowditch notes, 24 August 1907, Bowditch II; William Brewster to Harold Bowditch, 2 September & 23 September 1907, Bowditch II.

31. William J. Long, "Reply to Prof. Ganong," *Saint John* (New Brunswick) *Globe* (19 March 1904). See also W. F. Ganong, "Prof. Ganong's Rejoinder to Mr. Long," *Saint John* (New Brunswick) *Globe* (29 March 1904).

32. John Burroughs, "Current Misconceptions in Natural History," *Century Magazine* 67 (February 1904), pp. 509–17; John Burroughs, "On Humanizing the Animals," *Century Magazine* 67 (March 1904), pp. 773–80; John Burroughs, "What Do Animals Know?" *Century Magazine* 68 (August 1904), pp. 555–63. Quote in "On Humanizing the Animals," p. 780.

33. Frederick A. Church, "A Lesson in Wisdom," *Century Magazine* 67 (March 1904), p. 772; Ernest Thompson Seton, "Fable & Woodmyth: The Fate of Little Mucky," *Century Magazine* 67 (February 1904), p. 500.

34. John Burroughs, "The Literary Treatment of Nature," *Atlantic Monthly* 94 (July 1904), pp. 38–43; TR to JB, 12 August 1904, LC.

35. "Rev. Dr. Long Goes Blind," *New York Times* (10 December 1904), p. 1; "Dr. Long Practically Blind," *Stamford Daily Advocate* (10 December 1904), p. 1; William J. Long, *Northern Trails: Some Studies of Animal Life in the Far North* (Boston: Ginn & Co., 1905), p. xxi; William J. Long, "Foreword to the New Edition," *Brier-Patch Philosophy, by "Peter Rabbit"* (New York: Harper & Brothers, 1923), pp. xii; Woodbridge Interviews.

36. Clipping, February 1906, Frances Bancroft file, Phillips Academy Archives, Andover, MA; "William Joseph Long," *Harvard College Class of 1892, Report XI, 1892–1928* (Norwood, MA: Plimpton Press, 1928), pp. 132–33.

    Long had a history of poor sight in one eye, but total blindness was something new. He had volunteered for military service in 1898, just two weeks before the beginning of the Spanish-American War, but was rejected because of a problem with his eyesight. Five years later, the problem became severe and contributed to his resignation as church pastor in January 1903. Now, with the passage of two more years, he was blind in both eyes. Although the attending physician attributed the loss of sight in his second eye to a hemorrhage, this may have been little more than a convenient explanation for the unexplained loss of sight. (At the time, very few large hospitals even had the means to examine the interior of the eye and confirm whether there actually was a hemorrhage.)

It is unusual for someone to experience the repeated, temporary loss of sight in both eyes. This is especially true in people who are otherwise in good physical health, and William J. Long was a healthy, vigorous man who lived to the age of eighty-six and continued to fish the streams of New Brunswick into the last years of his life. The symptoms appeared to be a sudden onset of blindness in both eyes, but the report that he rested in a darkened room suggests that his eyes were still sensitive to light. He recovered his sight over a period of weeks, but was required to avoid preaching and public speaking. He was, though, able to continue writing during the blindness.

The most likely explanations of Long's loss of sight lie in the brain rather than in damage to the eyes themselves. The first possibility is migraine. His needs for rest and to avoid lights are consistent with this diagnosis. Migraines, though, are most likely to begin in the late teens and to be accompanied by severe headaches, neither of which seemed to be the case for Long. His problems might have been caused by seizures, but seizures rarely produce these symptoms. A third and more likely explanation is transient ischemic attacks, or episodes of reduced blood flow to the brain, which can be warning signs of a stroke. An actual stroke would likely have impaired his vision for quite a while.

The most interesting and most likely explanation of Long's problem is psychiatric hysteria. Hysterical blindness is difficult to diagnose, but the facts that the problems with his eyesight came during periods of stress and that he was able to continue writing during these periods support this diagnosis. The treatment would have been rest in a darkened room and avoidance of stress. It is clear that he had other problems in addition to his sight. By one account, Long resigned from his church in 1903 because "his eyesight and nerves became so seriously impaired," and another account reported that he suffered a nervous breakdown. Perhaps it was a nervous breakdown and hysterical blindness that struck in December 1904. This may explain the dedication of one of his books to his daughter, who was born in the spring following his blindness: "To Frances, my little daughter of the revolution."

This analysis of the possible cause of Long's blindness is based on conversations with Booker Bush, M.D., of the Harvard Medical School, Cambridge, MA; Booker Bush, M.D., letter to author, 31 August 1988; clipping [May 1898], William J. Long file, Andover Newton Theological School Archives, Franklin Trask Library, Newton Center, MA; Lawrence J. Sweet, Sr. (Long's fishing guide in his later years), letter to author, 17 May 1988; "Dr. Long Practically Blind"; Dorothy G. Wyman, "Pastor Irked T. R. on Hunting Ethics," *Boston Sunday Globe* (17 August 1952), p. 38; and William J. Long, *American Literature* (Boston: Ginn & Co., 1913), p. iii. Long's description of the physiological effects of strychnine, when used as a medication for "wretched nerves," is so vivid that it may be based on personal experience (William J. Long, *Mother Nature: A Study of Animal Life and Death* [New York: Harper & Brothers, 1923], p. 188).

37. William J. Long, *Brier-Patch Philosophy, by "Peter Rabbit"* (Boston: Ginn & Co.,

1906), pp. xi, 1, xvi–xvii.

38. TR to JB, 29 May 1905, LC; JB to TR, 9 June 1905, LC; TR to JB, 12 June 1905, LC.

39. On the other side of the Atlantic, the great British nature writer W. H. Hudson was weary of the debate. One day he received Roberts's *Red Fox* and Burroughs's *Ways of Nature* wrapped together in the same package. "It is," he wrote, "as if your two dear friends, who hate each other with a fierce hatred, should by an unhappy chance drop in upon you at the same moment." He agreed with Burroughs about the importance of scientific accuracy, but he also felt "it is a petty quarrel, amusing to the looker-on, but it does not concern us." The English, he wrote, "are a sober-minded people not at all likely to be carried away by anything this romantic school can send us, and this being so we can receive their books without apprehension and read and enjoy them" (W. H. Hudson, "Truth Plain and Coloured," *Speaker* 13 [9 December 1905], p. 248).

40. Burroughs's column in *Outing Magazine* began in April 1904. Initially published on a monthly basis, it reverted to an irregular feature and lost its character as a column after a few years. John Burroughs, "Do Animals Reason?" *Outing Magazine* 45 (March 1905), pp. 758–59; C. F. Deacon, "Do Animals Reason?" *Outing Magazine* 45 (March 1905), pp. 760–61; John Burroughs, *Ways of Nature* (Boston: Houghton Mifflin, 1905), pp. v–vi; Barrus, *Life and Letters*, 2:87. See also John Burroughs, "Sham Natural History," *Outing Magazine* 46 (April 1905), pp. 118–19.

41. JB to TR, 30 September 1905, LC; William J. Long, "The Question of Animal Reason," *Harper's Monthly Magazine* 111 (September 1905), pp. 588–94. However, Burroughs thought Long's effort to cloud the distinction between instinct and intelligence was not helpful.

42. George H. Locke to TR, 20 September 1905, LC; TR to George Locke, 27 September 1905, LC; Elting E. Morison, ed., *The Letters of Theodore Roosevelt*, 8 vols. (Cambridge: Harvard University Press, 1952), 5:39n. Although it is quite possible that news of Roosevelt's private complaints had made its way to both Long and Ginn & Company, there is no evidence that it had reached Locke.

43. Long, *Northern Trails*, p. xiv; Mabel Osgood Wright, "Nature as a Field for Fiction," *New York Times Review of Books* (9 December 1905), p. 872; Long, *Northern Trails*, p. xv. By "my Indians," Long must have been referring to his guides.

44. "Wayeeses the Strong One," in Long, *Northern Trails*, pp. 1–172.

45. Long, *Northern Trails*, pp. 85–86, 165–66.

46. TR to George Locke, 27 September 1905, LC.

47. TR to George Locke, 27 September 1905, LC; Copeland illustration in Long, *Northern Trails*, p. 163. Although wolves will attack a caribou's flank, more recent research indicates that they tend to concentrate on the front portions (shoulder, neck, side) of caribou. They do focus on the rear portions of other animals (L. David Mech, *The Wolf: The Ecology and Behavior of an Endangered Species* [1970; reprint ed., Minneapolis: University of Minnesota Press, 1981], p. 234).

48. Jack London, *The Call of the Wild* (1900), in *Great Short Works of Jack London* (New York: Harper & Row, Perennial Classic, 1965), pp. 4, 28, 34; Theodore Roosevelt, *Hunting the Grisly and Other Sketches*, Homeward Bound ed. (New York: Review of Reviews Co., 1910), pp. 224, 221, 213–47. See also Valerie M. Fogleman, "American Attitudes towards Wolves: A History of Misperception," *Environmental Review* 13 (Spring 1989), pp. 63–94.

49. Farley Mowat, *Never Cry Wolf* (Boston: Little, Brown & Co., 1963); Barry

Holstun Lopez, *Of Wolves and Men* (New York: Charles Scribner's Sons, 1978); Edward F. Bigelow, "Rev. William J. Long's Homes and Work" (part 2), *The Guide to Nature* 2 (April 1910), p. 383.

50. Betty Keller, *Black Wolf: The Life of Ernest Thompson Seton* (Vancouver: Douglas & McIntyre, 1984), p. 127, ill. following p. 92; Seton, *Artist-Naturalist*, pp. 287–89, 291; John G. Samson, ed., *The Worlds of Ernest Thompson Seton* (New York: Alfred A. Knopf, 1976), pp. 88–89, 168; "Lobo: The King of Currumpaw," in Ernest Thompson Seton, *Wild Animals I Have Known* (New York: Charles Scribner's Sons, 1898), pp. 17–54; "The Homeward Trail," in Charles G. D. Roberts, *The Watchers of the Trails: A Book of Animal Life* (Boston: L. C. Page & Co., 1904), pp. 351–61.

51. TR to JB, 27 September 1905, LC; JB to TR, 30 September 1905, LC; TR to JB, 16 October 1905, LC.

52. Harold Bowditch notes, 22 October 1907, Bowditch II. As the story comes fourth hand (Worcester to a friend to John Hardy to Harold Bowditch), it may not be accurate. However, Long did have a friend named Worcester and some years later their families traveled together to Canada (Woodbridge Interviews); it is likely that the substance of the story is correct.

53. Theodore Roosevelt, *Outdoor Pastimes of an American Hunter* (New York: Charles Scribner's Sons, 1905), p. v; JB to TR, 1 November 1905, LC; Barrus, *Life and Letters*, 2:53–54, 72.

54. May Estelle Cook, "A Group of Holiday Nature-Books," *Dial* 39 (1 December 1905), pp. 372–75.

55. Barrus, *Life and Letters*, 2:87, 88–89, 97; Richard Watson Gilder to JB, 1 June 1906, LC; JB to TR, 2 July 1906, LC; TR to JB, 3 July 1906, LC.

56. John Burroughs, "Real and Sham Natural History," *Atlantic Monthly* 91 (March 1903), p. 299.

57. Charles G. D. Roberts, *The Watchers of the Trails: A Book of Animal Life* (Boston: L. C. Page & Co., 1904), p. ix.

58. For the life of Roberts, see E. M. Pomeroy, *Sir Charles G. D. Roberts: A Biography* (Toronto: Ryerson Press, 1943); and W. J. Keith, *Charles G. D. Roberts* (Copp Clark Publishing Co., 1969).

59. Ganong, "New Brunswick Animals" (1905), p. 302; Roberts, *Watchers of the Trails*, p. ix.

60. Charles G. D. Roberts, *Red Fox* (Boston: L. C. Page & Co., 1905), p. vii; Dallas Lore Sharp, "Out-of-Doors from Labrador to Africa," *Critic* 48 (February 1906), p. 122; Roberts, *Red Fox*, p. viii.

61. John Burroughs, "Mr. Roberts' 'Red Fox,'" *Outing Magazine* 48 (July 1906), pp. 512a–12b.

62. Roberts, *Red Fox*, p. 88.

63. Ibid., p. 289.

64. Ibid., pp. 13–14; Seton, *Wild Animals I Have Known*, p. 212.

65. William J. Long, "The Modern School of Nature-Study and Its Critics," *North American Review* 176 (May 1903), p. 694.

66. Mary Hufford, "The Fox," in Angus K. Gillespie and Jay Mechling, eds., *American Wildlife in Symbol and Story* (Knoxville: University of Tennessee Press, 1987), pp. 163–202; Roberts, *Red Fox*, pp. 83–84, 304; William J. Long, *Beasts of the Fields* (Boston: Ginn & Co., 1901), pp. 300–301; Seton, *Wild Animals I Have Known*, p. 221; William J. Long, "'The School of the Woods,'" *Connecticut Magazine* 8 (1903), p. 150. See also Ernest Thompson Seton, *Lives of Game Animals*, 4 vols. (1925–28; reprint ed., New York: Literary Guild of America, 1937), 1:543–44.

67. May Estelle Cook, "Nature-Books for the Holidays," *Dial* 41 (1 December 1906), p. 390; "Nature-Study," *Nation* 83 (22 November 1906), p. 448.

Chapter Four. Roosevelt's War with the Nature Fakers

1. For a glimpse of the negotiations, see TR to Henry Cabot Lodge, 2 September 1905, in Elting E. Morison, ed., *The Letters of Theodore Roosevelt*, 8 vols. (Cambridge: Harvard University Press, 1951–54), 5:2–10; TR to Kermit Roosevelt, 5 December 1906, *Letters of Theodore Roosevelt*, 5:520–22; and TR to J. Lovland, 10 December 1906, *Letters of Theodore Roosevelt*, 5:524.
2. TR to JB, 12 March 1907, LC; Mark Sullivan, *Our Times; The United States, 1900–1925: III, Pre-War America* (New York: Charles Scribner's Sons, 1930), pp. 146–49.
3. Sullivan, *Our Times*, pp. 146–50; Edward B. Clark to Hermann Hagdorn, 30 December 1921, bound with the original manuscript "Roosevelt on the Nature Fakirs by Edward B. Clark: With corrections and additions by Theodore Roosevelt, 1907," HL; Clark to TR, 6 February 1907, LC; TR to JB, 12 March 1907, LC; Edward B. Clark, "Eighteen Years in the Press Gallery at Washington," *Illustrated World* 36 (February 1922), p. 843. Some pages of the original manuscript showing Roosevelt's changes are reproduced on p. 842.
4. TR to Caspar Whitney, 14 August 1907, LC.
5. "Hobbling Back to Nature," *Nation* 84 (21 March 1907), pp. 259–60.
6. John Burroughs, "Fake Natural History: Gold Bricks for the Editors," *Outing Magazine* 49 (February 1907), pp. 665–68. Harvard ornithologist William Brewster pointed out that the photos were of posed dead and mounted specimens. The writer, Josef Brunner, vehemently defended the legitimacy of his photographs, to no avail. A year later *Country Life in America* published an article by nature study proponent Professor Clifton Hodge that included photographs of a grouse drumming on a log (Josef Brunner, "The Love-making of the Grouse," *Country Life in America* 7 [February 1905], pp. 343–47; William Brewster, "Mr. Brunner's Grouse Pictures," *Country Life in America* 7 [April 1905], pp. 688, 690; Josef Brunner, "Mr. Brunner's Defense of His Grouse Pictures," *Country Life in America* 8 [May 1905], pp. 105–8; C. F. Hodge, "Domesticating the Roughed Grouse," *Country Life in America* 9 [April 1906], pp. 686–90).
7. Harold S. Deming, "Hours with a Crow: A 'Brier–Town' Sketch," *Harper's Monthly* 111 (October 1905), pp. 704–11; Harold S. Deming, "'Briartown' Nature Sketches: The Rubythroat's Nests—A Drawn Fight," *Harper's Monthly* 112 (May 1906), pp. 919–23; Burroughs, "Fake Natural History."
8. "Baseless Charges by Mr. John Burroughs," *Harper's Weekly* 51 (23 March 1907), p. 418; Connecticut, "Mr. John Burroughs and Fake Natural History," *Harper's Weekly* 51 (23 March 1907), p. 421. The different spellings "Briertown," "Briertown," and "Briartown" reflect differences in the authors' usages.
9. Harold S. Deming, "Mr. John Burroughs on Fake Natural History," *Outing Magazine* 50 (April 1907), pp. 124–27.
10. John R. Spears, "Mr. Spears Finds Nature Books Useful," *New York Times Saturday Review of Books* (25 May 1907), p. 338.
11. Clara Barrus, *Life & Letters of John Burroughs*, 2 vols. (Boston: Houghton Mifflin, 1925), 2:107, 110.
12. Frances Long Woodbridge, letter to author, 19 September 1979.
13. Edward B. Clark, "Roosevelt on the Nature Fakirs," *Everybody's Magazine* 16 (June 1907), pp. 770–74.

14. "Roosevelt Only a Gamekiller—Long," *New York Times* (23 May 1907), p. 6; William J. Long to TR, 22 May 1907, LC.

15. "Roosevelt Only a Gamekiller—Long," *New York Times*; Henry Pringle, *Theodore Roosevelt: A Biography* (New York: Harcourt, Brace & Co., 1931), p. 467. See "Heroes Who Hunt Rabbits," in William J. Long, *Brier-Patch Philosophy* (Boston: Ginn & Co., 1906), pp. 159–84, with its page decorations of a hunter (who bears a striking resemblance to Roosevelt) standing with a shotgun in one hand and proudly holding a dead rabbit high in the other.

    The reporter misquoted Long's reference to his book *Wilderness Ways* (Boston: Ginn & Co., 1900), a school reader. It included the essay "Upweekis the Shadow," which Roosevelt described in the *Everybody's Magazine* interview this way: "There are all kinds of absurdities in this lynx 'study.' "

16. Edward B. Clark to TR, 31 May 1907, LC; "Roosevelt Only a Gamekiller—Long," *New York Times*; Clark, "Nature Fakirs," pp. 772–73; TR to George Locke, 27 September 1905, LC.

17. "Long Writes Roosevelt" and "Not a Pretty Quarrel As It Stands," *New York Times* (24 May 1907), pp. 2, 8.

18. "Long Attacks Whitney," *New York Times* (25 May 1907), p. 8.

19. "London Zoologist Upholds Roosevelt," *New York Times* (26 May 1907), pt. 3, p. 1.

20. "He Demands an Apology," *Boston Daily Globe*, morning ed. (29 May 1907), p. 1; "Long Offers Proof," *New York Times* (29 May 1907), p. 6; Dorothy Wyman, "Pastor Irked T. R. on Hunting Ethics," *Boston Sunday Globe* (17 August 1952), pp. 1, 38. Gavin later became an editor of the *Globe* and the student, Henry P. Roberts, became foreman of the composing room.

21. William J. Long to TR, 29 May 1907, LC; affidavit (attached), Stephen Jones, 24 May 1907, LC; George R. Smith to TR, 2 June 1907, LC. Lyman Abbott of the *Outlook* later vouched for Reverend Ryder and reported that Jones was preparing himself as a teacher and missionary ("The Roosevelt–Long Controversy," *Outlook* 86 [8 June 1907], p. 263).

22. R. M. Strong to TR, 29 May 1907, LC; JB to TR, 30 May 1907, LC; William T. Hornaday to TR, 29 May 1907, LC; George Shiras, III to William Loeb, Jr., 30 May 1907, LC; Levant Fred Brown, "Life of the Wild," *New York Times* (26 May 1907), p. 2; "Dog Committed Suicide," *New York Times* (14 June 1907), p. 6.

23. "'Nature Fakir' Books Are Used in Public Schools," *Minneapolis Journal* (2 June 1907), p. 2.

24. Proof sheet and note, William J. Long to TR, placed 2 June 1907, LC; "'I Propose to Smoke Roosevelt Out'—Dr. Long," *New York Times* (2 June 1907), pt. 5, p. 2; "Naturalist to Keep Fighting President," Philadelphia *Public Ledger* (2 June 1907); "No Naturalist, No Sportsman," *Boston Sunday Globe* (2 June 1907), p. 17. The following quotations are from the *New York Times* version.

25. "Roosevelt's Shack," Philadelphia *Public Ledger* (2 June 1907).

26. "The Nature Controversy," *New York Times* (8 June 1907), p. 8; "John Burroughs Supports the President," *New York Times* (9 June 1907), pt. 5, p. 2.

27. "Defends Nature Stories," *New York Times* (14 June 1907), p. 6.

28. "Animals Disprove Both Burroughs and Long," *New York Times* (16 June 1907), pt. 5, p. 2.

29. William J. Long, "Dr. Long Tells More . . . ," *New York Times* (7 July 1907), pt. 5, p. 11; JB to Houghton Mifflin, 20 August 1907, HL.

30. George Shiras to TR, 30 May 1907, LC; JB to TR, 30 May 1907, LC; T. E. Powers, "The Ananias Club," *New York Evening Journal* (24 May 1907), p. 22.

31. F. P. Dunne, "Mr. Dooley on the Call of the Wild," _New York Times_ (2 June 1907), pt. 5, p. 1.

32. Robert Williams Wood, _How to Tell the Birds from the Flowers: A Manual of Flornithology for Beginners_ (San Francisco: Paul Elder & Co., 1907). A sequel followed the next year: Robert Williams Wood, _Animal Analogues_ (San Francisco: Paul Elder & Co., 1908). These were later combined as _How to Tell the Birds from the Flowers and Other Wood-cuts_ (New York: Dodd, Mead & Co., 1917), which went through twenty editions by 1941.

33. Quoted in Barrus, _Life & Letters_, 2:55–56.

34. William J. Long, "Good Fishing," Independent 62 (6 June 1907), pp. 1339–44; John Burroughs, "The Credible and the Incredible in Natural History," _Independent_ 62 (6 June 1907), pp. 1344–47; "Still Fishing," _New York Times_ (9 June 1907), p. 8.

35. "Nature-Writers Scored by the President," _Literary Digest_ 34 (1 June 1907), pp. 882–83; _Canadian Magazine_ 29 (July 1907), p. 278; "'Nature Faking,' " _Current Literature_ 43 (July 1907), pp. 94–97; "Chronicle and Comment: Mr. Roosevelt and the Nature 'Fakirs,' " _Bookman_ 25 (July 1907), pp. 449–54.

36. Edward B. Clark to TR, 5 July 1907, LC; St. Louis _Republican_ (24 May 1907), quoted in Paul Russell Cutright, _Theodore Roosevelt: The Naturalist_ (New York: Harper & Brothers, 1956), p. 136; May Estelle Cook, "Dramas of the Wild," _Dial_ 42 (16 June 1907), p. 370.

37. [Lyman Abbott], "The Roosevelt–Long Controversy" and "Imagination in Natural History," _Outlook_ 86 (8 June 1907), pp. 263–64.

38. JB to TR, 13 June 1907, LC; TR to JB, 15 June 1907, LC; John Burroughs, "Imagination in Natural History," _Outlook_ 86 (29 June 1907), pp. 457–59; TR to JB, 15 June 1907, LC.

39. Lawrence F. Abbott to TR, 6 July 1907, LC; [Lawrence F. Abbott], "Imagination in Natural History" [editor's note], _Outlook_ 86 (29 June 1907), pp. 459–60.

40. JB to TR, 28 June 1907, LC; TR to Editors of _Outlook_, 3 July 1907, in Morison, _Letters of Theodore Roosevelt_, 5:700–4; Theodore Roosevelt, _Presidential Addresses and State Papers_, Homeward Bound ed., 7 vols. (New York: Review of Reviews Co., 1910), 6:1327, 1328.

41. Lawrence F. Abbott to TR, 6 July 1907, LC.

42. TR to Lawrence Fraser Abbott, 8 July 1907, in Morison, _Letters of Theodore Roosevelt_, 5:707–8; Lawrence F. Abbott to TR, 10 July 1907, LC; John Burroughs, "President Roosevelt as a Nature Lover and Observer," _Outlook_ 87 (13 July 1907), pp. 547–53.

43. John Burroughs, _Under the Maples_, Riverby ed. (Boston: Houghton Mifflin, 1921), pp. 102–3; John Burroughs, _Birds and Poets_, Riverby ed. (Boston: Houghton Mifflin, 1904), p. 89; JB to TR, 30 May & 13 June 1907, LC; Paul Russell Cutright, _Theodore Roosevelt: The Making of a Conservationist_ (Urbana: University of Illinois Press, 1985), pp. 245–46.

44. TR to JB, 11 & 19 July 1907, LC.

45. Henry F. Pringle, _Theodore Roosevelt: A Biography_ (New York: Harcourt, Brace & Co., 1931), pp. 398–412.

46. TR to Henry L. Stimson, 14 August 1907, LC; William J. Long, _Fowls of the Air_ (Boston: Ginn & Co., 1901), pp. 147–52, 195–212.

47. William J. Long, _Whose Home Is the Wilderness_ (Boston: Ginn & Co., 1907), pp. xv–xvi, xvi–xvii.

48. JB to TR, 13 June 1907, LC; George Shiras, III, to William Loeb, Jr., 30 May 1907, LC; Edward B. Clark to TR, 31 May 1907, LC; J. O'Hare Cosgrave to William

Loeb, Jr., 27 June 1907, LC; C. Hart Merriam to TR, 4 July 1907, LC.

49. George Shiras, III, to William Loeb, Jr., 30 May 1907, LC; TR to George Shiras, 23 July 1907, LC; J. O'Hare Cosgrave to William Loeb, Jr., 3 August 1907, LC.

50. TR to Edward Nelson, 5 August 1907, LC; J. O'Hare Cosgrave to William Loeb, Jr., 27 June, 16, 20 & 30 July, 3 August 1907, LC; Edward B. Clark to TR, 8 August 1907, LC. Nelson eventually became the third chief of the Biological Survey, serving from 1916–1927 (Keir B. Sterling, "Builders of the U.S. Biological Survey, 1885–1930," *Journal of Forest History* 4 [October 1989], p. 185).

51. Edward B. Clark to TR, 5 July 1907, LC; Draft of TR's "note" on nature fakers, 22 June 1907, LC; J. O'Hare Cosgrave to William Loeb, Jr., 16 & 20 July 1907, LC; William Patten to William Loeb, Jr., 17 & 25 July 1907, LC.

52. Caspar Whitney to TR, 3, 15 & 22 July, 10 & 14 August 1907, LC; TR to Caspar Whitney, 29 June, 4, 15, 22 & 23 July, 14 & 19 August, 7 September 1907, LC.

53. TR to Ernest Hamlin Abbott, 23 August 1907, LC; E. H. Abbott to TR, 27 August 1907, LC.

54. "A Candidate Rejected," *Outlook* 59 (2 July 1898), p. 490; "The North Cambridge Council," *Outlook* 59 (9 July 1898), pp. 612–14; Gerald H. Beard, "Installation at Stamford, CT.," *Congregationalist* 84 (23 November 1899), p. 789; "Dr. Long Installed," 17 November 1899, clipping in William J. Long file, Andover Newton Theological School Archives, Franklin Trask Library, Newton Center, MA; "Abbott, Lyman," The Congregational Year-Book: Statistics for 1922 (Cooperstown, NY: Cooperstown Press, n.d.), p. 457.

55. "Roosevelt Whacks Dr. Long Once More," *New York Times* (21 August 1907), p. 7; Edward B. Clark, "Real Naturalists on Nature Faking," *Everybody's Magazine* 17 (September 1907), pp. 423–27; Theodore Roosevelt, "'Nature Fakers,'" *Everybody's Magazine* 17 (September 1907), pp. 427–30; J. O'Hare Cosgrave to TR, 27 June 1907, LC.

56. Floyd Malvern Murdoch, "For the Birds: Backgrounds of the Anglo–American Bird Treaty of 1916" (Ph.D. diss., American University, 1975), pp. 283–84. See William J. Long, *Northern Trails* (Boston: Ginn & Co., 1905), pp. 6–12.

57. "A Second Shot at Small Game," *New York Times* (21 August 1907), p. 6.

58. Caspar Whitney, "The View-Point," *Outing Magazine* 50 (September 1907), pp. 748–52.

59. JB to TR, 1 September 1907, LC; TR to JB, 3 September 1907, LC; Caspar Whitney to TR, 7 September 1907, LC; TR to Caspar Whitney, 7 September 1907, LC; William Patten to William Loeb, Jr., 9 September 1907, LC; Caspar Whitney to TR, 10 September 1907, LC.

60. "Noted Naturalist Defends Dr. Long," *New York Times* (22 August 1907), p. 1, col. 3.

61. "The War of the Naturalists," *New York Times* (23 August 1907), p. 6; "Nature Myths" (3 letters), *New York Times* (24 August 1907), p. 6.

62. "An Old-Time Hunter Answers the President," *New York Times* (15 September 1907), pt. 5, p. 6.

63. Ernest Thompson Seton, "The Natural History of the Ten Commandments," *Century Magazine* 75 (November 1907), pp. 24–33; John Burroughs, *Time and Change* (Boston: Houghton Mifflin, 1912), p. 256.

64. Jack London, "The Other Animals," *Collier's* 41, no. 24 (5 September 1908), pp. 10–11, 25, 26.

65. TR to Mark Sullivan, 9 September 1908, in Morison, ed., *Letters of Theodore Roosevelt*, 6:1220–23.

66. "Roosevelt Whacks Dr. Long Once More," *New York Times*; "Roosevelt Only

Nature Faker—Long," *New York Times* (8 October 1907), p. 10.

67. "Long Calls Killing She Bear Butchery," *Boston Herald* (23 October 1907), p. 2, col. 7; TR to JB, 13 October 1907, LC.

68. William J. Long, *Northern Trails: Book I* (Boston: Ginn & Co., 1908), p. viii (later published under the title *Wayeeses, the White Wolf: From "Northern Trails"*).

69. William J. Long, *Wayeeses, the White Wolf*, Holiday ed. (Boston: Ginn & Co., 1907). The Library of Congress copy of this book notes that the copyright was entered on June 14, 1907. Long, *Northern Trails, Book I*; William J. Long, *Northern Trails, Book II* (Boston: Ginn & Co., 1908) (later titled *Stories from Northern Trails*); "Drop Dr. Long's Books," *New York Times* (9 December 1908), p. 1.

70. Clarence Hawkes, *The Light That Did Not Fail* (Boston: Chapman & Grimes, 1935), p. 118; Paul Brooks, letter to author, 9 July 1979; Dallas Lore Sharp, *The Fall of the Year* (Boston: Houghton Mifflin, 1911), p. xiii; Frank M. Chapman, *Autobiography of a Bird-Lover* (New York: D. Appleton-Century, 1933), pp. 183–84.

Although standards did improve, this does not mean that Long's views vanished or that all books conformed to the personal standards of Burroughs and Roosevelt. Ten years after the controversy ended, for example, one author repeated William J. Long's tales of animal surgery and told of bears that treated their wounds with spruce resin and clay. The same author also reported that "domestic horses and dogs wear hats in summer, and possibly in the future they will learn the enormous importance of wearing clothes! Trained monkeys already take great delight in dressing up, and dogs like smart suits" (Royal Dixon, *The Human Side of Animals* [New York: Frederick A. Stokes, 1918], pp. 126–28).

The notion that a fox will ride a sheep in order to lose the hounds continues to survive. It is probably renewed as each new generation rediscovers Ernest Thompson Seton. In 1988, it was reported as a "Fun Farm Fact" in a syndicated comic strip (Jim Davis, "U.S. Acres," *Boston Sunday Globe* [3 April 1988]).

Chapter Five. In Search of an Earthly Eden

1. Joseph Conrad, *Lord Jim* (1899; reprint ed., New York: Modern Library, 1931), p. 208; John Burroughs, *Summit of the Years*, Riverby ed. (Boston: Houghton Mifflin, 1913), p. 68.

2. Henry Adams, *The Education of Henry Adams* (1918; reprint ed., New York: Modern Library, 1931), p. 380. See Leo Marx, *The Machine in the Garden* (London: Oxford University Press, 1964), pp. 345–50.

3. Adams, *The Education of Henry Adams*, p. 384.

4. What follows is a very simplified summary of the situation. There is an extensive literature regarding this history. See, for example, Lynn White, Jr., "The Historic Roots of Our Ecologic Crisis," *Science* 155 (10 March 1967), pp. 1203–7; William Leiss, *The Domination of Nature* (Boston: Beacon Press, 1974); Ian G. Barbour, ed., *Western Man and Environmental Ethics: Attitudes toward Nature and Technology* (Reading, MA: Addison-Wesley Publishing Co., 1973); Donald Worster, *Nature's Economy: The Roots of Ecology* (Garden City, NY: Anchor Press, 1979), pp. 26–55; and Carolyn Merchant, *The Death of Nature: Women, Ecology, and the Scientific Revolution* (San Francisco: Harper & Row, 1980). See also Calvin Martin, *Keepers of the Game: Indian-Animal Relationships and the Fur Trade* (Berkeley and Los Angeles: University of California Press, 1978); and J. Donald Hughes, *American Indian Ecology* (El Paso: Texas Western Press, 1983).

This is not to say that the Judeo-Christian tradition is without ecologically sustaining values. See Susan Power Bratton, "The Original Desert Solitaire: Early Christian Monasticism and Wilderness," *Environmental Ethics* 10 (Spring 1988), pp. 31–53; Jeanne Kay, "Concepts of Nature in the Hebrew Bible," *Environmental Ethics* 10 (Winter 1988), pp. 309–27; and Susan Power Bratton, "Oaks, Wolves and Love: Celtic Monks and Northern Forests," *Journal of Forest History* 33 (January 1989), pp. 4–20. For some current explorations of Christian ecology, see the special issues of *Epiphany*: 6, no. 1 (Fall 1985); 8, no. 1 (Fall 1987); and 8, no. 2 (Winter 1988).

5. Charles G. D. Roberts, *The Kindred of the Wild* (Boston: L. C. Page & Co., 1902), pp. 20–21.

6. James Turner, *Reckoning with the Beast: Animals, Pain and Humanity in the Victorian Mind* (Baltimore: Johns Hopkins University Press, 1980), pp. 1–14; Gerald Carson, *Men, Beasts, and Gods* (New York: Charles Scribner's Sons, 1972), pp. 36–42; Merchant, *Death of Nature*, pp. 192–215; René Descartes, "Discourse on the Method of Rightly Conducting the Reason" (1637), in *Great Books of the Western World*, 54 vols. (Chicago: Encyclopaedia Britannica, 1952), 31:60.

7. Burroughs, *Summit of the Years*, pp. 127, 128.

8. For pre-Darwinian scientific views of animal psychology, see Robert J. Richards, *Darwin and the Emergence of Evolutionary Theories of Mind and Behavior* (Chicago: University of Chicago Press, 1987), pp. 20–70.

9. Theodore Roosevelt, *Hunting Trips on the Prairie and in the Mountains*, Homeward Bound ed. (New York: Review of Reviews Co., 1910), pp. 262–63, 269–70.

10. There has been a good deal of critical commentary on the managerial stewardship philosophy. See, for example, Aldo Leopold's famous "The Land Ethic," in his *A Sand County Almanac and Sketches Here and There* (New York: Oxford University Press, 1949), pp. 201–26; Merchant, *Death of Nature*, pp. 246–52; Bill Devall and George Sessions, *Deep Ecology* (Salt Lake City: Gibbs M. Smith, 1985), pp. 52–61.

11. Kenneth E. Boulding, "The Economics of the Coming Spaceship Earth," in Henry Jarrett, ed., *Environmental Quality in a Growing Economy* (Baltimore, MD: Johns Hopkins University Press, 1966), pp. 3–14.

12. Clifton F. Hodge, *Nature Study and Life* (Boston: Ginn & Co., 1902), p. 20.

13. John Burroughs, *Birds and Poets* (New York: Hurd & Houghton, 1877), p. 175.

14. Roberts, *Kindred of the Wild*, pp. 21, 23.

15. Thomas R. Dunlap, "'The Old Kinship of Earth': Science, Man and Nature in the Animal Stories of Charles G. D. Roberts," *Journal of Canadian Studies* 22 (Spring 1987), pp. 104–20.

16. William T. Hornaday, *The American Natural History* (New York: Charles Scribner's Sons, 1904), p. xxiii; Theodore Roosevelt, *The Wilderness Hunter*, Homeward Bound ed. (New York: Review of Reviews, 1910), p. 193. It is very easy to fall into anthropomorphism. For example, when two cats stare at each other at close range, one will eventually look away as a sign of submission or appeasement. If a cat does this when we stare at it, we often interpret this as our pet's display of self-satisfaction or disdain (James Serpell, *In the Company of Animals: A Study of Human-Animal Relationships* [New York: Basil Blackwell, 1986], p. 111).

17. Ernest Thompson Seton, *Wild Animals I Have Known* (New York: Charles Scribner's Sons, 1898), p. 13.

18. Robert H. MacDonald, "The Revolt against Instinct," *Canadian Literature* 84 (Spring 1980), pp. 18–28; Dunlap, "'The Old Kinship'"; Thomas R. Dunlap, *Saving America's Wildlife* (Princeton, NJ: Princeton University Press, 1988), pp. 19–27; Ernest Thompson Seton, "The Natural History of the Ten Commandments," *Century Magazine* 75 (November 1907), p. 24; William J. Long, *Brier-Patch*

Philosophy, by "Peter Rabbit" (Boston: Ginn & Co., 1906), pp. 242, 268.

19. John Henry Wadland, *Ernest Thompson Seton: Man in Nature and the Progressive Era, 1880–1915* (New York: Arno Press, 1978), pp. 198–206, 216–28, 449.

20. Long, *Brier-Patch Philosophy*, p. 192.

21. Joseph Kastner, *A World of Watchers: An Informal History of the American Passion for Birds* (San Francisco: Sierra Club Books, 1986), pp. 97–112, describes changing views regarding the role of collecting in the study of birds. Roger Tory Peterson, *A Field Guide to the Birds*, rev. ed. (Boston: Houghton Mifflin, 1939), p. v.; Ernest Thompson Seton, *Two Little Savages* (New York: Doubleday, Page & Co., 1903), pp. 385–93.

22. J. P. Mowbray, *A Journey to Nature* (New York: Doubleday, Page & Co., 1901), p. 45; Clarence Hawkes, *Tenants of the Trees* (Boston: L. C. Page & Co., 1907), pp. 73–86; William J. Long, *A Little Brother to the Bear* (Boston: Ginn & Co., 1903), p. 229.

23. Wadland, *Ernest Thompson Seton*, pp. 166–80ff., 297, 447–53; Turner, *Reckoning with the Beast*, pp. 122–37; Dunlap, "'The Old Kinship'"; Ernest Thompson Seton, *Animal Heroes* (New York: Charles Scribner's Sons, 1905), p. 320.

24. Long, *Brier-Patch Philosophy*, p. 162; William J. Long, *School of the Woods* (Boston: Ginn & Co., 1902), pp. 309–61, quotations on pp. 328, 330; William J. Long, *Mother Nature: A Study of Animal Life and Death* (New York: Harper & Brothers, 1923).

25. Woodbridge Interviews; Long, *Mother Nature*, pp. 173–76.

26. Long, *Brier-Patch Philosophy*, pp. 159–84, quotations on pp. 176, 179; Woodbridge Interviews.

27. William H. Boardman, *The Lovers of the Woods* (New York: McClure, Phillips, 1901), p. 208.

28. Norman Foerster, "The Nature Cult To-Day," *Nation* 94 (11 April 1912), p. 358; Henry Childs Merwin, "Books about Nature," *Scribner's Magazine* 33 (April 1903), p. 437.

29. William A. Quayle, *In God's Out-of-Doors* (New York: Abingdon Press, 1902), pp. 19.

30. At mid-century, Rachel Carson made one of the great statements of this theme in *The Sense of Wonder* (New York: Harper & Row, 1965). The text originally appeared as a *Woman's Home Companion* article in 1956.

31. Hamilton Wright Mabie, *Under the Trees* (New York: Dodd, Mead, 1902), pp. 18, 164.

32. John Muir, *A Thousand-Mile Walk to the Gulf* (Boston: Houghton Mifflin, 1916), p. 212; Bradford quoted in Roderick Nash, *Wilderness and the American Mind*, 3rd ed. (New Haven, CT: Yale University Press, 1982), pp. 23–24. For an examination of Muir's religious experience of nature, see Michael P. Cohen, *The Pathless Way: John Muir and American Wilderness* (Madison: University of Wisconsin Press, 1984). Stephen Fox places Muir's religious views within the wider context of the religions of environmentalists in *John Muir and His Legacy: The American Conservation Movement* (Boston: Little, Brown, 1981), pp. 359–74.

33. Ralph Waldo Emerson, "Nature," in Brooks Atkinson, ed., *The Selected Writings of Ralph Waldo Emerson* (New York: Modern Library, 1950), p. 6; John Muir, *Our National Parks* (Boston: Houghton Mifflin, 1901), pp. 131–36.

34. Clara Barrus, ed., *The Heart of Burroughs's Journals* (Boston: Houghton Mifflin, 1928), p. 88; Charles J. Pelfry, "Elements of Mysticism in the Writings of John Burroughs and John Muir" (Ph.D. diss., University of Kentucky, 1958), p. 213; John Burroughs, *The Light of Day* (Boston: Houghton Mifflin, 1900), pp. 171, viii.

See Clifford Hazeldine Osborne, *The Religion of John Burroughs* (Boston: Houghton Mifflin, 1930); and Perry D. Westbrook, *John Burroughs* (New York: Twayne, 1974), pp. 100–26.

35. David Grayson [Ray Stannard Baker], *Adventures in Contentment* (New York: Doubleday, Page, 1907), p. 38.

36. Fox, *John Muir and His Legacy*, pp. 350–51; Richard F. Fleck, *Henry Thoreau and John Muir among the Indians* (Hamden, CT: Archon Books, 1985).

37. Ernest Thompson Seton, *Trail of an Artist Naturalist* (New York: Charles Scribner's Sons, 1940), pp. 261–65, 355–56, 374–76, quotation on p. 375; Wadland, *Ernest Thompson Seton*, pp. 307–34, 451–52; H. Allen Anderson, *The Chief: Ernest Thompson Seton and the Changing West* (College Station: Texas A&M University Press, 1986), pp. x, 129–31, 200–202, 222.

38. Long, *Brier-Patch Philosophy*, p. 216; Edward F. Bigelow, "Rev. William J. Long's Homes and Work," *Guide to Nature* 2 (April 1910), p. 377; Frances Long Woodbridge, letter to author, n.d. [Fall 1979]. Long's daughter, Frances, did not recall his speaking of pantheism, but felt it would have appealed to him (Woodbridge Interviews).

    Long's pantheistic views may have been shaped during his student days in Europe. He studied with Kuno Fisher, a prominent philosopher and historian, who had been dismissed from the University of Heidelberg early in his career as a result of his pantheistic views. Years later, however, Fisher returned to the university, where he taught for three decades (Woodbridge Interviews; Paul Edwards, ed., *The Encyclopaedia of Philosophy*, 8 vols. [1967; reprint ed., New York: Macmillan, 1972], 3:203).

39. Long, *Brier-Patch Philosophy*, p. 105.

40. Richards, *Darwin and Emergence of Evolutionary Theories*, pp. 176–84.

41. Roberts, *Kindred of the Wild*, pp. 22, 28.

42. Long, *Brier-Patch Philosophy*, pp. 208, 213–33, 292–94. See also pp. 207–36 and pp. 273–96 for Long's religious views regarding animals.

43. Long, *Brier-Patch Philosophy*, pp. 295–96.

44. John Burroughs, *Accepting the Universe*, Riverby ed. (Boston: Houghton Mifflin, 1920), p. 252.

45. "Human Nature in Animals Says Long," *Boston Herald* (20 February 1908), p. 2.

46. Although these terms are best used in an analysis of cultures, I will also apply them to the differences between individual authors. See Robert Redfield, *The Primitive World and Its Transformations* (Ithaca, NY: Cornell University Press, 1953), pp. 85–86; and Clifford Geertz, "World-View and the Analysis of Sacred Symbols," *Antioch Review* 17 (1957), pp. 421–22.

47. Clara Barrus, *Life & Letters of John Burroughs*, 2 vols. (Boston: Houghton Mifflin, 1925), 2:301–5; Norman Foerster, *Nature in American Literature* (1923; reprint ed., New York: Russell & Russell, 1958), p. 303; Osborne, *Religion of John Burroughs*, pp. 44–53.

48. John Burroughs, *Birds and Poets*, Riverby ed. (Boston: Houghton Mifflin, 1904), p. 51.

49. Seton, *Wild Animals I Have Known*, p. 12.

50. Charles G. D. Roberts, *The Watchers of the Trails: A Book of Animal Life* (Boston: L. C. Page & Co., 1904), pp. 94–95, 188.

51. Jack London, "The Law of Life," in Earle Labor, ed., *Great Short Works of Jack London* (New York: Harper & Row, Perennial Classic, 1965), pp. 321–22.

52. Ernest Thompson Seton, *The Biography of a Grizzly* (New York: Century Co., 1904), pp. 162, 164.

53. Joseph Gold, "The Precious Speck of Life," *Canadian Literature* 26 (Autumn 1965), pp. 22–32; Joseph Gold, Introduction to Charles G. D. Roberts, *King of Beasts and Other Stories* (Toronto: Ryerson Press, 1967), pp. ix–xx; Roberts, *Watchers of the Trails*, p. 152.

54. Barrus, *Life and Letters*, 1:259.

55. Petr Kropotkin, *Mutual Aid: A Factor of Evolution* (1902; reprint ed., Boston: Porter Sargent, Extending Horizons Books, n.d.), p. 5; Marston Bates, *The Nature of Natural History* (New York: Charles Scribner's Sons, 1950), p. 108; Jerram L. Brown, *The Evolution of Behavior* (New York: W. W. Norton, 1975), pp. 186–213.

56. Long, "How the Animals Die," in *School of the Woods*, pp. 345–61. He elaborated upon his views regarding animal suffering and death in nature in his later book *Mother Nature*.

57. Charles Darwin, *The Origin of Species*, 6th ed., 2 vols. (1872; reprint ed., New York: D. Appleton, 1889), 1:96.

58. Roberts, *Watchers of the Trails*, p. 204; Dallas Lore Sharp, *The Fall of the Year* (Boston: Houghton Mifflin, 1911), p. xiv; Louis W. Pettis, "Recent Approaches to Nature: Viewpoints of Selected American Non-Fiction Nature Writers, 1945–1964" (Ph.D. diss., George Peabody College for Teachers, 1965), pp. 156–61.

59. Long, *School of the Woods*, p. 342; William J. Long, "Nature Books," *Dial* 34 (1 June 1903), pp. 358–59.

60. This and other conflicts led to the demise of the nature study movement. See Richard R. Olmsted, "The Nature-Study Movement in American Education" (Ed.D. diss., Indiana University, 1967), pp. 130–57, also pp. 64–129; and Ralph H. Lutts, "Nature Fakers: Conflicting Perspectives of Nature," in Robert C. Schultz and J. Donald Hughes, eds., *Ecological Consciousness: Essays from the Earthday X Colloquium* (Washington, DC: University Press of America, 1981), pp. 201–2. This conflict is being repeated in today's environmental education movement.

61. "The Record of Admissions: Class 101 Admitted 7 Feb 1883, Long, Wm. Joseph," handwritten record book in Special Collections/Archives, Clement C. Maxwell Library, Bridgewater State College, MA; S. Mabel Bates, Maxwell Library, letter to author, 11 May 1988. The amount of science that prospective teachers were required to study during this period makes science educators envious a century later, when science plays a much greater role in American society yet most teachers are poorly prepared to teach it.

62. Long, *Brier-Patch Philosophy*, p. 288.

63. William J. Long, "The Modern School of Nature-Study and Its Critics," *North American Review* 176 (May 1903), p. 888; Long, *Brier-Patch Philosophy*, p. 189; Long, "Modern School," p. 689.

64. Hornaday, *American Natural History*, p. xxiv.

65. John Burroughs, *The Summit of the Years*, Riverby ed. (Boston: Houghton Mifflin, 1913), pp. 197–99; Roger Lewin, "Do Animals Read Minds, Tell Lies?" *Science* 238 (4 December 1987), pp. 1350–51; M. E. Betterman, "Creative Deception," *Science* 239 (December 1987), p. 1360; David Faust and Jay Ziskin, "The Expert Witness in Psychology and Psychiatry," *Science* 241 (1 July 1988), pp. 31–35. See also R. J. Hoage and Larry Goldman, eds., *Animal Intelligence: Insights into the Animal Mind* (Washington, DC: Smithsonian Institution Press, 1986); Donald R. Griffin, *The Question of Animal Awareness: Evolutionary Continuity and Mental Experience*, rev. ed. (New York: Rockefeller University Press, 1981); Donald R. Griffin, *Animal Thinking* (Cambridge: Harvard University Press, 1984); and James L. Gould and

Peter Marler, "Learning by Instinct," *Scientific American* 256, no. 1 (January 1987), pp. 74–85.

66. Herbert H. Beck, "The Occult Senses in Birds," *Auk* 37, no. 1 (January 1920), reprinted from *Smithsonian Report for 1920* (Washington, DC: Government Printing Office, 1922), pp. 439–42. Migratory birds were later found able to sense the earth's magnetic field, but vultures still rely on familiar senses to find a meal and some insects have been discovered to give off odors, pheromones, that attract mates.

67. W. F. Ganong, "Writings of William J. Long," *Science* 19 (15 April 1904), pp. 624–25, 623.

68. Richard Harding Davis, "The Nature Faker," *Collier's Weekly* 46 (10 December 1910), pp. 17–19, 34–35.

69. See Charles G. D. Roberts's description of Seton's home, which I quoted in chapter two, p. 48.

70. Lutts, "Nature Fakers," pp. 183–208; John Burroughs, "On Humanizing the Animals," *Century Magazine* 67 (March 1904), p. 780.

71. Sharp, *The Fall of the Year*, p. xiii; Norman Foerster, "The Nature Cult To-Day," *Nation* 94 (11 April 1912), pp. 357–59.

72. The following discussion is based on Ernst Mayr, "The Nature of the Darwinian Revolution," *Science* 176 (1972), pp. 981–89. See also Ernst Mayr, *The Growth of Biological Thought: Diversity, Evolution, and Inheritance* (Cambridge, MA: Belknap Press, 1982), pp. 501–34; and Loren Eiseley, *Darwin's Century: Evolution and the Men Who Discovered It* (New York: Doubleday, 1958).

Chapter Six. Their Paths Diverge

1. W. J. Keith, *Charles G. D. Roberts* (Copp Clark, 1969), pp. 18-21.

2. Carlton Jackson, *Zane Grey* (New York: Twayne, 1973), p. 138; Ernest Thompson Seton to JB, 18 November 1907, Collection of Elizabeth Burroughs Kelley, West Park, NY; Ernest Thompson Seton, *Life Histories of Northern Animals*, 2 vols. (New York: Charles Scribner's Sons, 1909); Ernest Thompson Seton, *Lives of Game Animals*, 4 vols. (Garden City, NY: Doubleday, Page, 1925–28).

3. This scouting section is based on John Henry Wadland, *Ernest Thompson Seton: Man in Nature and the Progressive Era 1880-1915* (New York: Arno Press, 1978), pp. 298–445; and H. Allen Anderson, *The Chief: Ernest Thompson Seton and the Changing West* (College Station: Texas A&M University Press, 1986), pp. 151–75. See also David Irving MacLeod, "Good Boys Made Better: The Boy Scouts of America, Boys' Bregades, and YMCA Boys' Work, 1880–1920" (Ph.D. diss., University of Wisconsin, 1973).

4. TR to James Edward West, 30 November 1915, in Elting E. Morison, ed., *The Letters of Theodore Roosevelt*, 8 vols. (Cambridge: Harvard University Press, 1951-54), 8:992–93.

5. Anderson, *The Chief*, pp. 214–50.

6. Paul Russell Cutright, *Theodore Roosevelt: The Naturalist* (New York: Harper & Brothers, 1956), pp. 241-55.

7. Clara Barrus, ed., *The Heart of Burroughs's Journals* (Boston: Houghton Mifflin, 1928), pp. 320-21; *Theodore Roosevelt: Memorial Addresses Delivered before the Century Association, February 9, 1919* (New York: Century Association, 1919), p. 60. See also Clara Barrus, *The Life & Letters of John Burroughs*, 2 vols. (Boston: Houghton Mifflin, 1925), 2:363–65.

8. John Burroughs, *Under the Maples*, Riverby ed. (Boston: Houghton Mifflin, 1921),

pp. 109–26; Barrus, *Life & Letters*, 2:185–87, 195; Clifton Johnson, *John Burroughs Talks* (Boston: Houghton Mifflin, 1922), pp. 325–37; Robert Lacey, *Ford: The Men and the Machine* (Boston: Little, Brown, 1986), pp. 110–13, 203–4.

9. Helen Mahoney, Ginn & Co., letter to author, 11 October 1978; Janet D. McCarthy, Silver Burdett & Ginn, letter to author, 12 May 1988. The dates that Long's works went out of print, where known, are listed in the bibliography at the end of this book.

10. William J. Long, "Stories from the Trail," *Independent* 64 (4 June 1908), pp. 1273–80; William J. Long, "The Sociology of a Wolf Pack," *Independent* 66 (3 June 1909), pp. 1179–85, buck killed on p. 1181; William J. Long, "On the Trail of the Loup Garou," *Independent* 68 (2 June 1910), pp. 1218–27. Information about Long's work for the Canadian government is sketchy. Long reported that he conducted a winter study of wolves (probably in 1907/08) to recommend ways to spare the deer herd from predation (William J. Long to Clarence Hawkes, 25 December 1908, Hawkes Collection, Forbes Library, Northampton, MA). An obituary, "Dr. W. J. Long Passes Away," in an unknown Canadian newspaper mentioned that Long conducted "a study of wild life" for the government (clipping provided by Frances Long Woodbridge, in author's file). One of Long's fishing guides recalls that Long once told of conducting a year-long wolf study for Quebec (Lawrence J. Sweet, Sr., letter to author, 17 May 1988).

11. It appears, though, that Long's change in literary careers did not originate with Theodore Roosevelt's attacks. A biographical sketch published in 1907 announced, somewhat prematurely, that Long had published *English Life and Literature* that year. This was probably a working title for his *English Literature*. If so, Long surely began work on the book before the *Everybody's Magazine* articles about nature faking (Colonel N. G. Osborn, ed., *Men of Mark in Connecticut* [Hartford, CT: William R. Goodspeed, 1907], p. 22).

12. William J. Long, *English Literature: Its History and Its Significance for the Life of the English-Speaking World* (Boston: Ginn & Co., 1909); "English Literature," *Catholic World* 90 (December 1909), p. 398; "Educational Books of the Year," *Independent* 69 (28 July 1910), p. 239; William J. Long, *American Literature: A Study of the Men and the Books That in the Earlier and Later Times Reflect the American Spirit* (Boston: Ginn & Co., 1913); Lewis Carroll, *Alice's Adventures in Wonderland*, ed. by William J. Long (Boston: Ginn & Co., 1917). Long's *Alice* annotations received some criticism: "Alice in Wonderland," *New York Times Book Review* (31 March 1918), p. 138. A bibliography of Long's other books appears at the end of this volume.

13. Terence L. Connolly, *An Introduction to Chaucer and Langland* (A Corrective of *Long's History of English Literature*) (New York: Fordham University Press, 1925), p. 7; William J. Long, *English Literature: Its History and Its Significance for the Life of the English-Speaking World*, Enlarged ed. (Boston: Ginn & Co., 1945); Mahoney to author. (Connolly refers to the book as *History of English Literature*. Perhaps this title was used in an overseas edition.)

14. Woodbridge Interviews; Frances Long Woodbridge, letter to author, 19 September 1919. The cow was probably the one in Long's tale "Two Ends of a Bear Story," in *Wood-Folk Comedies* (New York: Harper & Brothers, 1920), pp. 176–83.

15. Woodbridge Interviews; Edward F. Bigelow, "Rev. William J. Long's Homes and Work," *Guide to Nature* 2 (February–March 1910), pp. 345–46.

16. William J. Long, "The Bull Moose as a Political Totem," *Independent* 73 (4 July 1912), pp. 85–90.

    Clarence Hawkes raised the same issue four years earlier and achieved his own modest revenge against Roosevelt. Hawkes was never an object of Roosevelt's or Burroughs's public criticism, but the debate had shaken him. In 1908, while researching a new book, the blind naturalist came across Roosevelt's description of a galloping moose. Hawkes was sure a moose could not gallop and wrote the president to challenge him on the point. At first, Roosevelt said he could not recall the matter and asked whether he had actually written of elk. After Hawkes pressed him on the issue, though, the president wrote back that he was "upset" by the matter. "That book was written many years ago," he wrote, "and I have since been a middling busy man in many other directions, so it is out of the question for me to say exactly what it was upon which I based my statement." Roosevelt did not want to be quoted as an authority on galloping moose (Clarence Hawkes, *The Light That Did Not Fail* [Boston: Chapman & Grimes, 1935], p. 119; TR to Clarence Hawkes, 14 & 27 November 1908, LC).

17. William J. Long, *How Animals Talk, and Other Pleasant Studies of Birds and Beasts* (New York: Harper & Brothers, 1919); William J. Long, *Wood-Folk Comedies: The Play of Wild-Animal Life on a Natural Stage* (New York: Harper & Brothers, 1920); William J. Long, *Mother Nature: A Study of Animal Life and Death* (New York: Harper & Brothers, 1923); William J. Long, *Brier-Patch Philosophy, by "Peter Rabbit"* (1906; reprint ed., New York: Harper & Brothers, n.d.); "How Animals Talk," *New York Times Book Review* (14 September 1919), p. 462.

18. *Harvard College Class of 1892, Report XI, 1892–1928* (Norwood, MA: Plimpton Press, 1928), p. 133; Long, *Mother Nature*, p. 21.

19. William J. Long, "Timber Wolves and Men," *New York Times* (28 January 1923), pt. 8, p. 2.

20. "Stir in Connecticut over Marriage Ruling Barring Ceremonies by Retired Clergymen," *New York Times* (20 August 1927), p. 5; Frances Long Woodbridge, letter to author, 19 September 1979.

21. "Long, William Joseph," *National Cyclopaedia of American Biography* (New York: James T. White, 1934), p. 355; *Harvard College Class of 1892, Report XV* (Norwood, MA: Plimpton Press, 1942), p. 192; Glenn W. Moon, *Story of Our Land and People* (New York: H. Holt, 1938); Irene Meuvelt, Harcourt Brace Jovanovich, letter to author, 3 May 1988 (Holt, Rinehart & Winston is now a unit within Harcourt Brace Jovanovich); interview with Glenn W. Moon, 6 May 1988.

   At one point in their collaboration, Long made a revealing statement. "Moon," he said, "the more stubborn you are, the more likely you are to be right." Moon later became the principal of Dolan Junior High School.

22. Clippings on wife's death in Frances Bancroft file, Phillips Academy Archives, Andover, MA; Woodbridge Interviews; undated obituary, "Dr. W. J. Long Passes Away," provided by Frances Long Woodbridge; Lawrence J. Sweet, Sr., letter to author, 17 May 1988; "Dr. W. J. Long, 86, Naturalist, Dies," *New York Times* (10 November 1952), p. 29; "Retired Cleric, 86, a Noted Writer on Outdoor Life," *Stamford Advocate* (10 November 1952), pp. 1, 16; death certificate, William J. Long, 9 December 1952, Stamford, CT.

23. Dorothy G. Wyman, "Pastor Irked T. R. on Hunting Ethics," *Boston Sunday Globe* (7 August 1952), pp. 1, 38.

24. Robert Page Lincoln, "The Incomparable Mr. Seton," *Sports Afield* 117 (April–June 1947); William J. Long, "That Woodcock, Again," *Sports Afield* 118 (July 1947), pp. 34, 102; Bill Torporcer, "Seton vs. Long," *Sports Afield* 118 (December 1947), p. 6; William J. Long, "Learning from the Deer," *Sports Afield* 122 (October 1949), pp. 42–43, 89–94; William J. Long, "Learning from the Moose," *Sports Afield* 123 (February 1950), pp. 27–28, 62–66; William J. Long, "Learning from the Caribou,"

Sports Afield 123 (April 1950), pp. 26–27, 92–99; William J. Long, "Learning from the Salmon," _Sports Afield_ 124 (December 1950), pp. 27–28, 79, 83, 88–89; William J. Long, "Learning from the Pheasants," _Sports Afield_ 127 (January 1952), pp. 42–43, 60–62; William J. Long, "Learning from the Mountain Lion," _Sports Afield_ 127 (March 1952), pp. 30–31, 63–68; William J. Long, "Learning from the Fox," _Sports Afield_ 128 (August 1952), pp. 30–33, 91–95; William J. Long, "Learning from the Woodcock," _Sports Afield_ 129 (June 1953), pp. 30–33; William J. Long, "Wintering with Beavers," _Nature Magazine_ 44 (February 1951), pp. 71–74; Wayne Hanley, "Peculiar Bill, Eyes Show Woodcock Worm Specialist," _Boston Sunday Herald_ (6 March 1955). See also William J. Long, "Bre'r Rabbit Frolic," _Reader's Digest_ 37, no. 221 (September 1940), pp. 23–24.

25. William J. Long [Lois Long Fox, ed.], _The Spirit of the Wild_ (New York: Doubleday, 1956), pp. 5–6; William J. Long, "Learning from the Fox," _Sports Illustrated_ 3, no. 25 (19 December 1955), pp. 32–34, 63, quote on p. 32; William J. Long, "The Muskrat: Rogue of the Marshes," _Sports Illustrated_ 4, no. 4 (23 January 1956), pp. 33–37 (see p. 34 re: _Sports Afield_); William J. Long, "Can the Porcupine Throw Its Quills?" _Sports Illustrated_ 4, no. 16 (16 April 1956), pp. 50–52; William J. Long, "Safe in the Wild," _Sports Illustrated_ 4, no. 22 (28 May 1956): 62–67; William J. Long [Lois Long Fox, ed.], _Wings of the Forest_ (New York: Doubleday, 1957).

The "Learning from the Fox" article, though, actually had been published earlier in _Sports Afield_, whose editor, Ted Kesting, was not happy to see it published in _Sports Illustrated_ without permission. Kesting praised Long, writing that, "I personally feel that there has never been better natural-history stuff written than that of Dr. Long's." "Learning from the Fox," _Sports Illustrated_ 4, no. 4 (23 January 1956), p. 34.

26. Alan Devoe, "Mr. Mother Nature," _Saturday Review of Literature_ 37 (6 March 1954), pp. 20–21; Anderson, _The Chief_, p. 244; Alan Devoe to Brian Long, 16 November 1952, copy provided by Frances Long Woodbridge; Alan Devoe, _This Fascinating Animal World_ (New York: McGraw–Hill, 1951), pp. 40, 36–47, 109–10.

27. J. Donald Adams, "Speaking of Books," _New York Times Book Review_ (8 July 1956), p. 2.

28. "Celeb Lit. 101," _Boston Globe_ (31 March 1987), p. 2; Shirley Katzander, for Reading Is Fundamental (RIF), letter to author, 7 April 1987, with RIF press release giving RIF survey results (n.d., ca. March 1987); Ronald Reagan to Mrs. Elliot Richardson and Ruth Graves, 27 October 1986, copy provided by Shirley Katzander.

29. Burroughs, _Summit of Years_, p. vi.

Afterword: The Fakers Today

1. Rudy Schafer, letter to author, 30 October 1988; Kathleen Harris Regnier, with Michael Gross and Ron Zimmerman, eds., _The Nature Fakir's Handbook: Presentation Skills for the Interpretive Naturalist_ (Stevens Point, WI: UW–SP Foundation Press, 1988), inside front cover. See, for example, S. F. Aaron, "Nature Faking," _Scientific American_ 134 (1926), pp. 122–23; William J. Maddox, "Insect Stories and Nature Fakes," _Hygeia_ 4 (December 1926), pp. 689–91; "Wildlife Misinformation," _Nature Magazine_ 24 (December 1934), p. 245; and S. F. Aaron, "Nature Faking Again," _Scientific American_ (October 1935), pp. 186–87.

Other derogatory terms used to taunt ranger–naturalists included "posy pickers," "tree huggers," and "butterfly chasers." In the mid-1930s, the National

Park Service established a practice, which continued into the 1960s, of not hiring women as rangers, despite their important contributions in earlier years. In part, this was an effort by male rangers to increase their credibility as they tried to professionalize the position of ranger–naturalist. Nevertheless, traditional rangers still viewed the naturalists' work as insufficiently masculine and expressed this view through derogatory humor. Polly Welts Kaufman, "Challenging Traditions: Pioneer Women Naturalists in the National Park Service," *Forest & Conservation History* 34 (January 1990), pp. 4–16.

The original meaning of "nature faker" was not completely lost. A 1965 letter to the Los Angeles *Times*, for example, labeled Walt Disney "a shameless nature faker in his fictionalized animal stories," despite his fine nature films (Frances Clarke Sayers, Los Angeles *Times* [25 April 1965], quoted in Richard Schickel, *The Disney Version* [New York: Simon & Schuster, 1968], p. 350).

2. "An Imposter," *Nature–Study Review* 3 (October 1907), p. 190; Joseph Knowles, *Alone in the Wilderness* (Boston: Small, Maynard, 1913); Roderick Nash, *Wilderness and the American Mind*, 3rd ed. (New Haven, CT: Yale University Press), pp. 141–43.

3. Questions do continue to rise. Farley Mowat, for example, was criticized for fictionalizing his supposedly true encounters with wolves. In general, though, his natural history held up under examination (see L. David Mech, *The Wolf: The Ecology and Behavior of an Endangered Species* [Minneapolis: University of Minnesota Press, 1970], p. 340; and Thomas R. Dunlap, *Saving America's Wildlife* [Princeton, NJ: Princeton University Press, 1988], pp. 107–8, 202).

4. Peter Benesh, "Books of 'Medicine Woman' Called Fake," *Boston Globe* (18 December 1988), p. 106.

5. John F. Baker, "Questionable Publishing Judgments," *Publishers Weekly* 232, no. 7 (14 August 1987), p. 12; Edward Beecher Claflin, "When Is a True Story True?" *Publishers Weekly* 232, no. 7 (14 August 1987), pp. 23–26; Martin Gardner, "The Obligation to Disclose Fraud," *Skeptical Inquirer* 12 (Spring 1988), pp. 240–43. On the psychological basis for alien abduction fantasies, see Robert A. Baker, "The Aliens among Us: Hypnotic Regression Revisited," *Skeptical Inquirer* 12 (Winter 1987–88), pp. 147–62; and Bill Ellis, "The Varieties of Alien Experiences," *Skeptical Inquirer* 12 (Spring 1988), pp. 263–69.

6. Christopher D. Stone, *Should Trees Have Standing?: Toward Legal Rights for Natural Objects* (Los Altos, CA: William Kaufmann, 1974).

7. Maynard Shipley, "Growth of the Anti–Evolution Movement," *Current History* (N. Y. Times) 32 (May 1930), pp. 330–32; Robert W. Hanson, ed., *Science and Creation: Geological, Theological, and Educational Perspectives* (New York: Macmillan, 1986), p. 190. The second volume provides a useful history of the issue and includes appendices with the full text of the Arkansas law and the legal opinion that overturned it.

8. "The Upanishads," in Lin Yutang, ed., *The Wisdom of China and India* (New York: Modern Library, 1942), pp. 34–35.

9. Robert MacKenzie, "The Life and Times of Grizzly Adams," *TV Guide* (28 May 1977), p. 34.

10. Peter Steinhart, "Electronic Intimacies," *Audubon* 90, no. 6 (November 1988), pp. 10–13; M. R. Montgomery, "TV's Nature Lessons," *Boston Globe* (31 October 1988), p. 17; Boyce Rensberger, *The Cult of the Wild* (New York: Anchor Press/Doubleday, 1977), p. 217. See Rensberger's iconoclastic book for a broad treatment of these and related issues.

11. Mortality is only one of a number of factors that can determine whether an

individual will be successful in producing young and passing its genetic heritage on to future generations.

12. Annie Dillard, *Pilgrim at Tinker Creek* (New York: Harper's Magazine Press, 1974), p. 233; George C. Williams, "Huxley's Evolution and Ethics in Sociobiological Perspective," *Zygon* 23 (December 1988), pp. 283–407. This entire issue of *Zygon* is devoted to the theme "Evolutionary Biology and the Problem of Evil."

13. Bradford Torrey, *A Rambler's Lease* (Boston: Houghton Mifflin, 1889), pp. 103–5.

14. Ibid., p. 71.

15. In most cases the "orphans" are fledgling birds that have left the nest before they are able to fly. This is a normal part of growing up for many birds and they remain under the care of their parents while their wings continue to grow and strengthen. People who pick up these "orphans" mean well, but they are actually kidnapping the young. Such actions result from the combination of a concern for the welfare of the birds, ignorance of natural history, and a belief that it is wrong to let nature take its course if the young bird is in harm's way.

16. Robert W. Loftin, "The Medical Treatment of Wild Animals," *Environmental Ethics* 7 (Fall 1985), pp. 231–39. See also Roland C. Clement, "Beyond the Medical Treatment of Wild Animals," *Environmental Ethics* 8 (Spring 1986), pp. 95–96; Carl A. Strang, "The Ethics of Wildlife Rehabilitation," *Environmental Ethics* 8 (Summer 1986), pp. 183–85; and R. Wills Flowers, "Ethics and the Hypermodern Species," *Environmental Ethics* 8 (Summer 1986), pp. 185–88.

17. Foreword to Felix Salten, *Bambi* (1928; reprint ed., New York: Grosset & Dunlap, n.d.).

18. Thomas R. Dunlap, "That Kaibab Myth," *Journal of Forest History* 32 (April 1988), pp. 60–68. See also Thomas R. Dunlap, *Saving America's Wildlife* (Princeton, NJ: Princeton University Press, 1988); and Susan L. Flader, *Thinking Like a Mountain: Aldo Leopold and the Evolution of an Ecological Attitude toward Deer, Wolves and Forests* (Columbia: University of Missouri Press, 1974).

19. This account of the problems on Angel Island is based on reports in the San Francisco Society for the Prevention of Cruelty to Animals's journal, *Our Animals*: 70, no. 6 (Winter 1976), pp. 4–6; 75, no. 2 (Summer 1981), pp. 3–4, 16–17; 75, no. 3 (Fall 1981), pp. 5, 16–17; 75, no. 4 (Winter 1981), pp. 5, 8, 12, 16–17; 76, no. 3 (Winter 1982), pp. 3–5; 78, no. 1 (Spring 1984), pp. 5–7; and 78, no. 4 (Winter 1984), pp. 6–8. It is also based on Mary K. O'Bryan and Dale R. McCullough, "Survival of Black-Tailed Deer Following Relocation in California," *Journal of Wildlife Management* 49 (1985), pp. 115–19; Fred L. Botti, "Chemosterilants as a Management Option for Deer on Angel Island: Lessons Learned," *Cal–Neva Wildlife Transactions* (1985), pp. 61–65; and Dale McCullough, "North American Deer Ecology: Fifty Years Later," in Thomas Tanner, ed., *Aldo Leopold: The Man and His Legacy* (Ankeny, IA: Soil Conservation Society of America, 1987), pp. 115–22.

20. This account is based on "Who Pays the Bill for Hunting?" *Humane Society News* (Spring 1981); Betsy A. Lehman, "Last-ditch Try to Halt Deer Killing," *Boston Globe* (27 November 1983), pp. 29, 35; Charles A. Radin, "Debate Rages as Reservation Deer Starve," *Boston Globe* (2 April 1984), pp. 17, 19; "Dear Friend" letter by William C. Clendaniel, Trustees of Reservations, and attached "Deer Management Program," 10 January 1985, author's file; Roger Warner, "Ticks and Deer Team Up to Cause Trouble for Man," *Smithsonian* 17, no. 1 (April 1986), pp. 131–46; Jeremiah V. Murphy, "Deer Hunt Is Canceled in Ipswich," *Boston Globe* (28 November 1983), p. 17; Marvin Pave, "Reservation's Problem: How to Deal with Hungry Deer," *Boston Globe* (9 December 1984), p. 42; David Arnold, "State

Panel OK's Killing of Deer in Ipswich Reservation," *Boston Globe* (11 January 1985), pp. 15, 21; David Arnold, "Judge Denies Request of Animal Advocates to Halt Crane Deer Shoot," *Boston Globe* (9 March 1985), p. 23; and "Rise of Lyme Disease Tied to Infested Deer," *Boston Globe* (19 January 1989), p. 26.

21. Advertisement in *Boston Globe* (22 October 1989), p. 91; Sean O'Gara, "The Bear," *Animal's Agenda* 9, no. 11 (December 1989), pp. 50–51; Pauline Kael, "Current Cinema," *New Yorker* (13 November 1989), pp. 121–23.

22. William H. Magee, "The Animal Story: A Challenge in Technique," *Dalhousie Review* 44 (Summer 1964), pp. 156–64.

23. William Gould Vinal, *Nature Guiding* (Ithaca, NY: Comstock, 1926), pp. 303–4.

24. They sometimes do express concern for the welfare of lobsters, particularly in the context of rescuing them from the dinner table. See, for example, Lisa M. Hamm, "Boiling Mad, Animal Activists Liberate Lobsters," *Boston Globe* (10 December 1988), p. 7.

25. It is encouraging to see that David Patrice Greanville, editor-at-large of the *Animal's Agenda* and an advocate of animal rights, has proposed a "tactical alliance between environmentalists and animal liberationists" to achieve the goals they share in common (Greanville, "Environmentalists and Animal Rightists—The New Odd Couple?" *Animal's Agenda* 9, no. 8 [October 1989], pp. 22–24; see the letters in response to Greanville's article in *Animal's Agenda* 10, no. 1 [January/February 1990], pp. 3–4).

INDEX

Nature Fakers

Designed by Richard Firmage
Composed in ITC Goudy by Jay Staten
Typeset by LaserWriting, Inc.
Englewood, Colorado, on a Linotronic 300
Books printed and bound by
R.R. Donnelley and Sons, Harrisonburg, Virginia
Printed on Sebago Antique, acid free paper